Bad Things in the Night

Bad Things in the Night

BETH ELLIS

Edited by
Cherry Potter

EBURY
PRESS

1 3 5 7 9 10 8 6 4 2

Published in 2010 by Ebury Press, an imprint of Ebury Publishing
A Random House Group Company

The Random House Group Limited Reg. No. 954009

Addresses for companies within the Random House Group
can be found at www.randomhouse.co.uk

A CIP catalogue record for this book
is available from the British Library

The Random House Group Limited supports The Forest Stewardship
Council (FSC®), the leading international forest certification organisation.
Our books carrying the FSC label are printed on FSC® certified paper. FSC is
the only forest certification scheme endorsed by the leading environmental
organisations, including Greenpeace. Our paper procurement policy can be
found at www.randomhouse.co.uk/environment

MIX
Paper from
responsible sources
FSC® C016897

Printed and bound by CPI Group (UK) Ltd, Croydon, CR0 4YY

ISBN 9780091946746

To buy books by your favourite authors and register for offers visit
www.randomhouse.co.uk

For Ella, Natalie and Stuart

Making the Statement

In December 2005 I finally made the statement to the
police. I'd put it off as long as I could but now I had to do
it because I was going abroad for Christmas and I thought
that would make it easier, make it feel safer. The night before
had been dreadful. I'd been alone in my flat, feeling the
insanity rise within me. What I was about to do was impossible, dangerous and far, far beyond my capabilities. I could
of course change my mind. And then again, I could not.

At around 9 p.m. that evening I ran from the house.
Wine would save me. Wine would distract me and make me
laugh at the terror and finally knock me out. Running from
the shop with a bottle of marvellous medicine, I rounded
the corner to find a recent ex on my doorstep. He'd broken
with me a month earlier and I'd later found out that he'd
been cheating on me all along. My first thought was that
he'd come to apologise and I waited a short time for those
words to come. But from the grin on his face I saw that he
didn't know that I knew about the cheating. My mind made
a feeble and short-lived attempt to straddle these two
universes: the volcano of panic coursing through me, and
the cold smiling calmness on the doorstep. I couldn't think
of a way to deal with this Bridget Jones-type situation while
my life was so much more Stephen King, so I just entered
the house, closed the door on the creepy ex and ran up the

stairs to take my medicine. I drank the whole bottle in less than an hour and I willed and begged my mind to focus on the TV. I tried to distract myself by going back in time to the doorstep and constructing put-downs so witty and razor-sharp that they fully restored my dignity while cutting the ex down to a sobbing, tattered wreck. But it was no use; the worry enveloped the whole of me. If the feeling had taken physical form it would have been a thousand lacerations a second, all evening and much of the night, for hours and hours and hours. And nothing could make me forget what I was about to do.

I must have passed out around 4 a.m. Three hours later my alarm screeched, and immediately the feeling was on me again. I get that anyway sometimes – though not usually so intensely – and it's the worst. To wake up with fear and panic and dread and with a whole day stretched ahead, a whole day to fill up searching (consciously or unconsciously) for the thing, the thing, the thing, that will make it better, please God let there be a thing – an event, a book, some words, a smile, a connection of some kind, any kind – to take me away from the dread and the fear and the panic, please.

I considered wearing tweed trousers, but they made me itch and so I thought better of it. I wore the next smartest outfit I owned; a pinstripe-shirt dress over jeans, so the police would take me seriously and at a glance know that I was not a mad case but someone perfectly capable of ironing and therefore reliable, truthful and good.

Outside the police station I shakily lit a cigarette. I could

2

still change my mind. And yet again I could not. I walked inside and, confronted by the bullet-proof glass that separated me from the desk-sergeant, I felt a wave of relief because from now on decisions would be made for me. I'd survived the night, I'd got myself there and part of me must have realised that the hardest bit was over. I'd left insanity and entered reality. I was now a citizen reporting a crime and today there were rules and procedures and official reports, where yesterday there had been only falling.

The detective who was to take my statement was already waiting at the desk for me. I was greeted and ushered through the opens-only-from-inside door and an interview room was found for us. It smelled pretty bad in there, a chemically, covering-up type smell and the room was stuffy and hot. I was left alone while the detective made tea and collected pens and paper, for it was to be a written statement, rather than a recorded or videoed one, which is why it took six hours. I had to explain to her that even though I refer to my abuser by a variety of nouns, calling him either my father, my step-father or by his name, Karl, I was always talking about the same wretched person. There were long gaps between my sentences while she struggled to write down all that I said. I spent a lot of time watching her write and thinking about what her life might be like and what possible motivations she might have to devote so much time listening to women and men talk about how their fathers, step-fathers, teachers, uncles, scout-leaders, church-leaders and so on used to touch them. She didn't look much older than me, but then she was in better shape. She was possessed of the kind of healthy figure that can only be maintained through regular exercise. She had kind of a regular face, not pretty, not plain, and her hair that she swept into a thick pony-tail was shiny and thick and just the right side of mousy; she reminded me of a girl I knew who used to ride horses.

I told her about rapes and about beatings. I told her everything I remembered. I left nothing out though I squirmed to be away from there and the sheer physical discomfort of the plastic straight-back chair and the smell and stuffy heat and I am proud of that. I broke down only once. I did not cry, but describing one particularly humiliating event, I said to her, 'I feel so ashamed'. She replied, without looking up from her writing, that my reaction was 'very common'. There was no comfort, sympathy or empathy to be had from her in that room and for me. Her job was a piece of administration; there was no room for me to cry, and so I didn't. For the last few pages she had to stop many times and massage her hand, which was red where the pen dug in. When it was over, I was dying to leave but she had forgotten to number the pages as she went along, or to keep them in any kind of order, and so I had to wait as she shuffled and read and numbered and passed them to me to be signed.

When I left it was like being let out of school. I had done my bit, I had done my difficult thing and now the statement was to be sent to the CID in Wales and I had only to sit back and wait to hear from them.

My best friend Stuart was waiting for me on the doorstep when I got home. We let ourselves in and he cooked me

4

some dinner and I talked to him about what I had just been through at the police station. I felt elated, and I didn't feel mad and terrified and I wasn't expecting that. I talked excitedly and I was proud of myself, as if I'd just aced an exam, but of course, more important than that, an exam upon which my life depended.

Golden Needles

I hope one day all these things will fall away, like the tears I've shed now for years and years – but I don't know what will be left without them.

Angels carried me from my childhood – I have no doubt about that. I do not doubt the existence of angels – I have my very own angels. But I must carry myself the rest of the way – through life – learning even the most basic skills while fending off the demons. I know that my life has only got better the further I have got from Karl and that if the trajectory were to continue I would roll down the hillside, collecting soft needles of gold which, with each tumble, would coat me thickly and each press of my flesh against the earth would work the sharper needles into my skin, so that the mellow light would be within me as well as covering me.

Perfect

When I am really little Mum sits me on the kitchen counter and we make a cake together. I hold the sieve and she pours in puffs of white flour. I have to be very careful not to drop the sieve and to hold it right over the bowl so that it doesn't go on my legs. Some of the white does get on my dress. Mum says it doesn't matter. She says all the things out loud before she does them, 'I'm going to need three eggs. I better find them. And one teaspoon of vanilla flavour; Beth can you hold the spoon? That's right, hold it tight. Now pour in the batter, that's right. Good, now do you want to crack an egg? Here you go, I'll help you. One, two, three. Okay, it doesn't matter, I can fish those bits out…Let's see, what's next…'

My legs dangle in mid air. I am utterly enchanted. I watch my mother's curly hair brush against her skin, her face moving as she talks, I am so busy watching that sometimes I forget to listen and she has to tell me things twice. Her steady hands fold in butter and sugar. The electric whisk is too heavy for me and so we hold it together and push the mixture round the bowl. It makes a loud noise and when Mum switches it off for a few moments the world goes quiet, like when I put my head underwater in the bath. She pours the yellow goo into two round tins and lets me smooth it down. She ignores the fact that I don't make it smooth and beams at me, 'Perfect!'

7

Childhood

When the breaks came that was worst. Breaks in school like Christmas. Then it happened worse because he didn't work nine to five like other daddies. He could be home at any time because sometimes he worked nights. So on breaks from school you'd never know where you'd find him or when he'd come through the door. Sometimes we'd be doing something that only Mum lets us do, like sliding down the stairs on blankets, our favourite game. We'd pile up lots of duvets and blankets at the bottom of the stairs then my brother and I would race each other. Our baby sister Katie would sit on our laps. Sometimes we'd hit the front door because it was so close to the foot of the stairs. Dad didn't like it; he was angry when we had fun. He didn't know how to have fun so he would spoil it for everybody else. If I'm honest I felt that he was an idiot. But he was a very powerful idiot – like a bad-tempered ogre from a storybook because he could do what he liked. He was way bigger than us and he didn't mind hitting; there was nobody to stop him.

Living with him is very hard. The house becomes cold when he enters. The air changes and we all have to think about everything we do, every little thing. I hate Christmas day because everyone else is having a nice time and we aren't. We aren't allowed to have presents and I feel embarrassed about it – I don't like being a Jehovah's Witness. I don't like it because it means I'm different and also sometimes people make jokes about it or I hear jokes on the telly. Also it's boring – so boring. I hate the meetings – they seem five years long. We have to sit very still or Dad hits us – sometimes he hits us anyway and if you say, 'I haven't done anything wrong,' then you get hit again because that is the wrong thing to say because he is in charge of everything and mustn't be challenged. It's normal to hit children in the Kingdom Hall so he can do it and not worry – he is the big man.

But it is interesting to see him around 'worldly' people (that's what people who are not Jehovah's Witnesses are called), like teachers at school or the neighbours or people in shops, because then he pretends that he is nice and nudges me jokingly or even puts his arm around me, pretending love. Even though he is so mean, I really want him to love me for real – I imagine being able to cuddle into his chest and have him look after me when I am sad.

But he isn't like that, usually he gets angry if I am sad and he hits me or raises his hand to hit me. I try to stop crying but it is very very hard to do this. He says, 'Stop crying,' and he raises his hand and counts slowly to three and if I haven't stopped in that time then he brings his hand down on me. Lots of times I have promised myself that I will never cry again, that that was the last time. I want to lose my feelings but I can't lose them. I feel like if he makes me cry then I am not brave and he has won. Like I should be able to withstand everything without feelings. There aren't really any rules. He just hits us when he wants to. He never has to explain himself to us. He sometimes says, 'This hurts me more than it hurts you,' but I think that's bull crap. The angriest I get with my brother Isaac is if he tells on me or tries to get me into trouble. But, in the end he gets hit too, because that's what happens in our house.

What is the worst is waiting to be hit. If you've done something he doesn't like – accidentally breaking a bowl or saying something 'worldly' or singing a pop song he doesn't approve of – and if he is busy or in the middle of something he says, 'You're going to get smacked for that later.' Then you have to live the rest of the day waiting for when he'll do it, feeling scared and upset and wanting to talk him out of it. Sometimes we try but that just makes it worse. He makes us lie across his lap, one at a time, the other two watching and waiting for their turn, and he pulls down our pants and trousers or pulls up a skirt so that our bottoms are bare and then he hits us, either with his hand or a slipper or with a wooden spoon. It stings for ages. One time when he is hitting me I catch my brother's eye – my brother is watching from the top bunk and he and I burst out laughing. It is a cheeky laugh because we know that what's happening is perverse and sexual and the embarrassment and titillation of that knowledge, and also the utter absurdness of this grim pervert that we are forced to put up with, is just too much to take seriously all of the time. Of course nothing angers Dad more than the sound of laughter – especially at that moment – so then we both get it even worse.

When I see him with other adults who are not in the family and not Jehovah's Witnesses then I see what he's really like and how he really feels. He's often nervous and shy. Especially with my neighbour from next door who is a big man. I can tell he doesn't like Dad. Dad says 'howdy' and 'cheerio' but he says them nervously even though they are friendly words. I get the impression that he is quite stupid and that people don't like him very much.

He is thin with very hairy legs. He has a big nose and is unattractive. He always has a pile of dandruff sitting on the shoulders of his suits, even though he uses dandruff shampoo. His penis is big, or at least it seems big to me. When I was little, not much more than a baby, he would put it in my mouth and hold me by the neck so that my feet were off the floor and he would pull me back and forth, masturbating with me. This would be so frightening that I would have no feelings at all. I would leave my body completely and when I remember these things it's as if I were a doll.

He used to make fun of me because of how much I loved my teddies and he would throw them around, throw them out of windows. I don't like it when Dad is around living things. I like it best when he is driving a car because then his hands are busy. Even then he turns around in his seat and slaps us if we make him angry but at least he doesn't poke us and do the other stuff. He is a completely selfish person. He never thinks that anyone else has feelings. It is worse when he says he loves me because then I have to say it back. I don't love him and I don't like to say lies.

School is much nicer than being at home. There are lots of toys and things to play with and I am very clever at reading and doing my letters and numbers. The teachers are nice most of the time but I get very scared if I am in trouble. I try to be good and mostly that is quite easy. I love having a story at home time but I don't like going home. I like my mum but I hate my dad, even though I am supposed to love him. Sometimes when we walk home from school we go to the woodsy park. There are two parks near my house. One is the normal park at the end of my street. The other park is in the woods – 'the woodsy park'. Neither of them is better really but the woodsy park is more of a treat because it is further from our house so we don't go there so often. Mum asks, 'Do you want to go to the woodsy park?' and we say, 'YEAH!' and cheer because it will be fun and also it will be longer before we go home. I don't like Dad to be around and I would be happy if my mum could be there all the time – just her.

At the weekends Dad is in the garage working on a car. He wears his old suit trousers, which have dirt and oil on the knees and a jumper with oil in a big patch over his chest. He smells of oil and has oil under his fingernails and in the creases of his hands. I like him best now because he is pre-occupied and I can imagine that he is a normal dad who loves me and carries me around and protects me. I want that a lot.

I daydream of a better life. Usually in the daydreams there is no Dad but I am rich, like I am a little girl but I have inherited money and have the nicest bedroom with a TV in it and in the kitchen there isn't water in the taps: in one tap there is cola and in the other there is lemonade. In my dream I have a butler who looks after me and everybody thinks I'm really pretty but really nice as well and sometimes other children at school are jealous because I have so much stuff but I'm quite noble about it.

I'd like the opportunity to look down on people, even though I wouldn't use it. But in my real life there isn't anyone who I could look down on. Except maybe Joanna at school who smells of wee and wears really old dresses, like ones only old women wear. But I don't look down on her. She has terrible eczema all over her face and body and she is stick-thin with dirty blonde hair. I feel sorry for her but also feel akin to her – she looks how I feel. Sometimes the boys are really mean about her but she doesn't even look like it hurts her – she just looks tired – weary – like it was a blow she was expecting, so she isn't a very good target. There is little reason to bully me – I look nice, Mum sees to that, and I don't smell. In fact I like taking baths.

Mum bathes the three of us all at once and we play tidal waves – all going in one direction and then the other so that the water splashes over the tub and on to the floor. We shout 'Tidal wave!' and laugh. Mum pretends to be annoyed but she isn't really – she loves it when we have fun. It breaks my heart now to think of her – kneeling on the bathroom floor – holding towels ready to pick us out of the bath one by one. She'd only have been 22 or 23 years old then. Though of course I didn't think of all that, I just thought she was a grown-up with choices; I didn't know that she had no choices. She is a goddess to me, in the same way that Karl is God, he takes up the world, blocks out the light. Except that I love my goddess. I worship her daily; bring to her what offerings I find. Fistfuls of bluebells, grubby little daisy chains, mud-pies, pictures drawn at school. I run to her, clutching these pictures, run through the school gates and into her knees, desperate to show her as quick as I can, 'I made this for you.' 'I made this for you'; 'I picked these for you'; 'I baked this for you, try it'. I love you I love you I love you.

Realisation

It's no coincidence that I only realised that I had been sexually abused when I was 18. It was 1997 and I was in my first year of university in London. I say *realised* rather than remembered because there were instances that I'd always remembered, it's just that I'd never identified them as abuse. In my memory-store marked 'childhood' lay a shelf of jars containing toxic substances and all of them had been sweetly pasted over with labels that read: 'Jam' or 'Honey'.

There were two triggers to my realisation. The first was the physical distance that lay between me and Karl and the places and the people that had surrounded the abuse. The second trigger came from a girl I knew.

Jo lived in the same building as me at university and we were friends for a while, though not close. She was a scrap of a girl, probably weighed about the same as one of my legs. She had black hair and was beautiful in a Hammer Horror sort of way.

One night I was getting ready for bed when I heard a tap on the door, I opened it to find Jo standing there in an over-sized T-shirt, her skinny little corned-beef legs bare from mid-thigh down; she was shaking and her eyes were sore with tears. She wanted me to go to her room so, of course, I did. When we were there she got under her duvet and I sat on the end of her bed. She told me that when she was ten her step-father had raped her. She kept crying. I felt a surge of rage towards her step-father. Jo looked so tiny and helpless at 18; it wasn't much of a leap to imagine her as a little girl. I made us cups of tea and tried to conjure the right words to comfort her.

When Jo was all cried out and starting to fall asleep I went back to my room. I felt restless; I couldn't for the life of me get to sleep. I sat up in bed, fidgeting with the remote control for my hi-fi. I played a song over and over – 'Travelling Light' by the Tindersticks. It's about this guy who says he's fine and has no problems and no baggage but really he does. And a scene from my childhood came to me.

I'm about seven or eight years old, in the cold, damp bathroom of my family home. I'm lying face-down on a wicker wash basket. I'm naked. Karl is standing directly behind me and in the corner, near the toilet, his friend, Adrian, is coldly staring at my body. This scene plays over and over as I lay in bed and I can't figure out why those pictures are there and why so insistent. The old label around this memory-jar used to read: *There's a huge insect stuck to my back and Karl and Adrian are trying to remove it.* The insect wasn't something I was told about; it was something that I made up, to protect them so they wouldn't have to be monsters, and to protect myself so I wouldn't have to be monster food. In all the intervening years I'd never questioned why it would take two grown men to remove a beetle from a little girl's back, why I would have to be completely naked or why I was told to stay so quiet. Why would I question it? You're told the world is square – why would the world not be square? Hours and hours of this scene dance in front of my eyes and all I wanted to do was get some sleep so that for once I might not miss my 9 p.m. lecture.

And then the strangest thing happens. The world stops turning. I get out of bed and I realise that I was abused. A split-second later the world starts up again, but it's a different shape now, and so am I.

I take a look round the new world and fuck, there's toxic waste all over the place. All the times Karl squeezed washing-up liquid into my anus: *He was helping me because I was always constipated* (of course I was always constipated, I was terrified of being in the bathroom for more than three seconds at a time). The time he marched into the kitchen, picked me up by the collar of my dressing gown and slammed me, over and over, into the wall: *I did something really bad*. And bless me, even at 18 I'm thinking, well, I must have done something bad to provoke him to do that. And the times that he made me share his bed and I would scrunch up, as close to the wall as possible, trying to evade the grabbing arm that would always get me in the end (actually, I didn't have a label for that one).

I was reeling, my brain buzzed with a thousand messages. So many things finally made sense: why I'd cried so much all my life (I didn't have an adolescence, I had a flood); why I'd never pursued contact with Karl after I'd left his house; why I felt so different from everyone else; why when I was a child I honestly believed that I was an alien. At the same time as I was honouring how important this discovery was another piece of knowledge rose in me even more strongly: that I must never tell anyone.

Today I Cannot Go Outside

Some days I cannot go outside. Today is one of those days. And it's fine to spend a day indoors, sometimes it is a joyous thing to be cut off from the world, but not if you have no choice in the matter. My flat, with its view of the Pavilion and its yellow roses and its (thankfully) stocked fridge, is a prison – beautiful, but a prison nonetheless. And I'm panicking about the things I cannot do and I try to tell myself that it is only today, it is not forever, but it does not help. I wonder what the fuck would help? The medication I keep being offered, though I refuse it? Why do I refuse it? Because I have an idea that this is a process that I need to go through: these feelings, this panic, this pain, is part of my recovery. To fully recover I must fully feel the pain. I'm so fucking frustrated. I want to have something else, something other than this roaring whirlwind in my chest. I want to feel free to go for a walk, maybe strike up a conversation with a stranger, and I want to feel entitled to those things, not like I'm stealing them. I want them to be mine; authentically mine. Why can't this be so? I guess he did a pretty good job on me, right? And I'm crying now and pitying myself. I hate it. I hate a world that can offer so much but deny it to me.

I feel an intense amount of body-hatred today. So there is the first prison. I hate my clumsy, too-heavy, hideous body and I avoided looking at it earlier, when I was in the bath. And it hurts too: my back and my shoulders, with the tension.

My life is so seriously impaired by what are, essentially, emotional responses. It is quite incredible that this should be so. Angers and upsets and fears from so long ago swamp me so entirely that I am surprised when I look up and see the bookshelves and the roses that belong to my Brighton life. I am so completely in my father's house, in every single sense, except, that is, materially.

The Meetings

The defining mood of my childhood, apart from terror and shame, is boredom. As one might explore the Antarctic, I fully chart and map vast expanses of boredom. On Sunday mornings and Tuesday and Thursday evenings we go to meetings. On Sundays and Thursdays the meetings are in the big Kingdom Hall and there are lots of people there, including Nana and Grandad. Dad's parents are Jehovah's Witnesses too, but they go to a different Kingdom Hall that's nearer their house.

On Tuesdays we have Bible study in small groups sat in the living room of one of the Elders. At Bible study there aren't enough chairs and I sit on the floor and pick at the carpet. I think about my body, the thickness of my thighs, my bitten nails, the dry bits of skin that callous my lips; I pick at myself. Before Bible study and the meetings at the Kingdom Hall we sit down and learn what questions will be asked by the speaker that week. The questions are in the *Watchtower* magazine that Dad buys on Thursday nights from the counter at the back of the Kingdom Hall. He likes us to be able to answer a question every week, or at least put our hands up to answer even if we don't get picked. I feel shy and I don't like the way my voice sounds when I have to talk in front of all those people but Dad nudges me to put my hand up. The talks are always about the signs of the coming Armageddon, signs like wars, famines, AIDS and delinquent youths.

Mum sits like a statue in the meetings, there is no expression on her face. They try to sit so that there is an adult between each of us so that we don't act up and start hitting each other. Sometimes we get the giggles though; we can't help it. My brother's face is so funny when he makes his eyes crazy and besides, we stopped listening ages ago because the talk is so boring. We both laugh out loud and Dad hits us both at the same time – his big hands coming down again and again. Even then it takes a while for us to stop laughing because laughing is like magic and you can't just make it go away. Sometimes in my head I think, what if we never stopped? What would happen then? Maybe we would be carried away like loonies and spend our days in a white hospital room making funny eyes at each other and laughing.

But we do stop. It helps not to look at each other. And now we aren't friends anymore, now the plea-bargaining begins. 'It wasn't my fault, Isaac was looking at me. He made me laugh.'

Karl spit-whispers through bared teeth, 'You're the eldest, you should know better.' He punctuates each word by poking me hard in the chest. 'You (poke) are (poke) both (poke) going to be (poke) in trouble (poke) when (poke) we (poke) get (poke) home (poke).' As he says all this his mouth is curved into the shape of a smile, for the benefit of anyone who might be looking. The whole time my mother sits perfectly still. She doesn't even turn her head.

Karl faces forward again and Isaac and I sneak a look at

each other. I kind of hate him but I also want to laugh. I do laugh, just a little bit, oh no! I quickly turn it into a hacking cough. Isaac starts coughing too. Karl doesn't turn to look at us, he just raises his hand.

Cherry

In the spring of 2004 I receive a letter from my university. Three years ago I left university because I was having a breakdown but I'd agreed to return when I felt better and complete the course. The letter says that the law department is willing to award me a bare pass on the basis of the work I have already done and that I must either accept the pass or come back in September and complete the course; I can defer no more. My ego won't allow me accept a pass and so, although I have no idea whether I will really be able to cope, I write back and promise to enrol in the autumn term.

I re-arrange my life to fit the new circumstances. I move into a flat with my friend Nancy. In the new flat I am close to the train station, ready for the commute to university. I don't even consider moving back to London. I buy warm clothes for travelling and make budget plans. I research grants and loans and crises funds. I tell Ella, my therapist, that I am going to put counselling on hold while I finish the degree and I give her a turquoise stone, one of a pair, the other stone I keep because I want us to stay connected somehow. My plan is to put all my problems to one side and concentrate on learning. It is a good plan, though fundamentally flawed. I bargain desperately with the crying child inside of me: *Please, please, let me finish my degree, and then, then I'll report him to the police, I promise.* If I finish college it will mean all those years studying were worth something after all and it will prove that I am not a total loser.

In autumn it begins. Lectures, tutorials, trains and packed lunches. I get into a groove with the commute. I appreciate the learning in a way that I didn't when I was here before, my brain is working better now. I find it difficult though to make friends and I spend a lot of time alone, in the library, which at least helps keep my grades up.

The first term passes away and the bad feelings break out of their box. Ella is not surprised to hear from me and she welcomes me back and we carry on with our work, whatever that is. I grow more tired and less confident as the academic year progresses and I am something of a wreck by the time exam term creeps up. But I know that I could do well, exams suit me, I don't panic, I write fast and I am not stupid, and so I push through.

I sit in my final exam, waiting, in silence, for the po-faced invigilators to collect up all the exam papers. I look around at the glossy-beautiful Asian girls with their thick ebony hair and long shiny fingernails; the boys with short clipped hair, wire-rim glasses and long hands they've yet to grow into. I look from them to my own mottled bitten hands, the tiny, almost empty bottle of Rescue Remedy, well used, resting beside the thick, inky booklet of dates and case names that I am already beginning to forget. And I wonder to myself, what on earth am I doing here? I try to think back down the years. When I was 18 and chose this subject I had fantasies of becoming a human rights lawyer – defending the weak, making a difference.

A couple of months after the exams I pick up the phone and call the law department for my results. 'Congratulations,' the secretary says brightly. 'You achieved a 2.1.' From those cheerily spoken words, which make not one jot of difference to my crippled self-esteem, I learn the most important lesson of my life – finishing the degree doesn't mean anything, *nothing* will ever mean anything until I face my past. The one place I don't want to go – I have to go back there and reclaim what was stolen from me.

That same day – results day – I start a new cleaning job. Cleaning's the only cash-in-hand work I know of that's easy to come by and cash in hand is important because you're not supposed to work and be on benefits – but benefit money is barely enough to live on, let alone having enough left over to pay for therapy. I fish around in my handbag for the address, written on a torn piece of brown envelope. It says Cherry and Brian, a phone number and an address. I have it written here that they both work from home – damn – I prefer key jobs – more opportunity to skive and smoke cigarettes. But the job is just round the corner and besides, I can't afford to be choosy. The student grants have long run out. I need money to pay for my therapy.

Newly overqualified for the task in hand I walk out into the world and in the direction of this scrap-paper job.

Cherry and Brian are both there to greet me. They present a united front of friendliness. They smile widely and offer tea. Cherry is petite, with a beautiful face, round brown eyes and high cheekbones. She is slim which makes her look young but the expression on her face is serious, resolute.

*

Brian is older, with a white beard but somehow boy-like, he wears his heart in his eyes. They are kind. I can tell immediately they will not mind about cigarette breaks. We make small talk; Cherry tells me she is a writer and a psychotherapist, Brian a playwright and screenwriter. They instruct me to do whatever I think needs doing and they retire to their separate offices. I explore their house with relish, duster in hand.

In the conservatory sit piles of newspaper supplements, pot-plants brighten windowsills, the doors open on to a small courtyard where roses climb a trellis, a metal table stands with two chairs leaning against it and black and purple pansies sit smugly in their beds. In the living room there is one long wall of floor-to-ceiling bookshelves, two pink battered sofas sit at right angles to one another, cats escape from under them at the sound of the hoover. Brian's office is smoky and jumbled; his latest play plotted out in green marker pen and tacked to the wall. More books in the bedroom and on the landing and in Cherry's office – novels, books on filmmaking, a small library of feminist writing. Her office is set up too for her psychotherapy practice, with two comfy chairs turned to face each other, a box of tissues placed discreetly to one side.

A few weeks after starting there I grandly announce to Cherry, 'I am not really a cleaner you know. I'm a writer!'

Unlike everyone else Cherry does not say, 'That's nice,' and move on. She stops and cocks her head; I have her full attention. 'What do you write?' she asks.

26

'Urr…well, I'm *going* to write novels.'

'And will you write genre or literary fiction?'

It's a tough question to answer because I don't actually write anything, I just daydream about it. Besides, I'm not absolutely sure what either term means. I search my brain while Cherry waits. Genre, I think, means thriller or romance, and literary, I think, means really good, like Virginia Woolf or Toni Morrison. 'I'm going to write literary novels,' I decide. Cherry, satisfied, returns to her office.

I have two cleaning jobs now but this one is by far my favourite, it is true that Cherry and Brian are less straightforward and more messy than my other clients, but they are not dull and I garner hope from the way they live. One day when I am hoovering the stairs Brian rushes from his office in a state of excitement. I switch off the hoover so that I can hear him speak. 'Do you know anything about corporate takeovers?' he asks, breathlessly. 'Urr,' I shrug and gesture towards the hoover as if to say – Brian, I am a cleaner. If I knew anything about the world of corporate finance I'd probably be earning more than six pounds an hour. He stands waiting for a reply so I say, 'No Brian, I'm afraid I don't know anything about the world of big business.' Brian throws up his hands and rushes back into his office mumbling that he will phone some friend or other and ask them. Here is a man, caught up in the frenzy of his own story, a writer – it is possible to live like that, here is proof.

Another week, while taking a tea break, Cherry says, 'You must show me some of your writing.'

I have to confess to her that I hardly do any writing at all. 'I'm too scared. I'm scared it won't be any good.'

'Iris Murdoch once said, "The most important quality a writer must possess is courage."' Cherry disappears upstairs then and when she returns it is with a copy of her own book – on screenwriting. She hands it to me. 'This is for you. Most of it is about film and screenwriting but the chapter on free-writing might be useful to you. It might help get you started.'

When she is gone I open up the book. On the inside cover is written. *To Beth, be brave, love Cherry.*

At home I start doing the free-writing exercises she describes, which means setting my alarm clock an hour before I usually wake, grabbing pen and paper and writing, without stopping, for a whole hour. I do this most mornings for months until I have two notebooks full of writing. Most of it is me complaining about being awake, about cramp in my hand, about feeling tired. There are a few stories though, threads of colour amongst the mundane.

One of the stories is about abuse and I use it for the basis of an article, which I submit to the Survivors' Network newsletter. They like the piece and promise to print it in their spring edition. Next I take it to Cherry. I mean to ask her permission to name check her book and also, in a way, I have written it for her; I have written it to have something to show her. Cherry wants to read it while I am still at her home. This scenario had never occurred to me, I had planned to leave it on the kitchen table when I left. There's a slight tussle, 'I have time to read it now,' she says and I grudgingly surrender it into her hands.

Cherry sits on the edge of the bath reading my piece while nervously I hoover her study. It's not just the writing I worry about, this is the first she will hear of my having been abused, not something I usually tell employers – not something I usually tell anyone. The carpet is sucked spotless and I hear the bathroom door creak open so I lift myself to my full height and prepare for the worst. Cherry looks up at me, 'I responded to the article in two ways. First, as a psychotherapist I feel very concerned about what you have been through. But as a writer I think it's a very good piece. I'm famously nitpicky about people's writing but really I thought it was very good. A very good start.' I listen only to the second part. Cherry can keep her concern. I am fine – I can write. I've been told!

My Mother

With long legs I stalk through the grass looking for odd shapes, bright colours. I am 'it' and the others are hiding. My brother and Alex and Davy from the estate are hiding in here somewhere. The grass is so high that the tallest bits tickle my chin. I take long strides, trampling down big patches of grass like a giant. I catch a glimpse of Alex's T-shirt, then a skinny piece of arm. I pounce, 'Ah-ha!' I say and I jump on him and hold him to the ground. 'You're it, you're it.'

I spring to my feet and run as fast as I can. Alex turns to face the ground and starts counting, 'One…Two…Three… Four…Five.'

I run as fast as my legs will carry me. I find a pristine patch of grass and take a big leap into it so there's no obvious path leading to me. My heart beats – boom boom – in my ears and my mouth is dry. I can hear the sound of crickets and above them Alex counting: 'Eight, Nine, Ten. Ready or not here I come.'

I giggle and have to cover my mouth. I always giggle in hiding games, I get so excited. I keep my head down and listen for sounds of tramping grass but Alex is being quiet, he's good at catching people unawares. An orange and brown butterfly lands near my nose, I hold my breath so as not to scare it away. I want to look at it, but I'm still tired from running and holding my breath is making me dizzy and so noisily I let the air out and the butterfly floats away.

I cock my head, listening for Alex; I don't dare take a peek in case he sees me. I lie back and watch the tall grass moving against the blue sky. There is a pulse today that spreads everywhere: the whole world, the sky and grass and insects, the heart of everything beating all together. I pat the earth to check it's really there. I feel like I'm falling, gently, like a feather. The sun is shining directly over my circle of trampled grass and it hurts my eyes so I cover them with my forearm. I keep on falling, into the centre of everything.

A fist punches me hard in the stomach, I suck in air. Startled and blind, tears roll down my cheeks, I don't know where I am. Jumbled spots of yellow light jostle for position. A shadow-person stands over me, and now another and another. One of the shadows sucks in air, 'Aaaauuummmm,' it says. That's my brother, that's my brother's noise for when someone's done bad.

Winded, crying and damp from the heat I try to get to my feet but I can't keep my balance and I roll back on to the ground, 'aaauuummmm'. Grass tickles my bare legs, the sun has moved away and I shiver in the shadow of the three boys. They wait to see what I will do. Will I go tell and spoil their fun? Will I get them in trouble? I have all the power in this moment; all eyes are on me. I opt to leave them guessing. I haul myself on to pins-and-needles legs and shuffle-stamp my way home.

I go to the back of the house. No car, no Dad? You can never be sure, sometimes he parks around the fron' depends how long he's staying. I take the path tha' from the street to my house; not that it's so much a path as a break in the brambles where they've been trampled down. I shiver as I walk past the rusty roofed shed, full of my father's tools and bits of engine, the floor stained with oil patches. Down the centre of the lawn a long line of laundry hangs still in the hot sun. I push my face into a bedsheet, it's damp and smells of pine. I pretend to be a ghost, making noises, 'Wooooooooo wooooo wooooooo,' raising the sheet up and down with my arms. But there is no one in the garden to scare. The dampness makes the sheet stick to my face and that frightens me so I tear it away and take a deep breath.

I walk up the steps to the grey concrete which encircles the back of the house. Underneath the kitchen window a small piece of coal has escaped the coalbunker and I crush it into the ground and try to write my name with the heel of my shoe but it just becomes one big smudge. I hear Katie laughing. Three sharp taps on the kitchen window. I look up. My sister's big smile and shiny naked body fill my view and Mum behind her, smiling and waving with a hand that holds a scrunched yellow flannel; she is bathing Katie in the kitchen sink. I stand and wave and smile because Katie likes to play that game, she laughs at me, and I wave some more. I turn away and open the back door. I lean on the wall just inside the door and bend up one leg at a time so I can see the treads of my trainers, black with coal-dust. I kick off my shoes and leave them at the back door. 'Muuuummmm,' I say, 'I'm thirsty.'

'Wait till I've finished washing your sister and I'll make you a drink.'

I curl into a wooden dining chair and I watch Mum rinse soap suds down my sister's chubby body with a plastic beaker. Katie's eyes are like blue diamonds and when she smiles everyone else feels like smiling too. She is super-good and super-lovely. Mum wraps her in a towel and gives her a kiss. 'Will you hold her while I get you a drink?' Mum asks.

I sit up straight and hold out my arms. Mum almost gives her to me then changes her mind. 'Come into the living room,' she says, 'it'll be easier for you if you sit on a comfy chair.' So I follow her into the living-room, my feet sinking into the woolly brown carpet, the sun streams in so brightly that Mum draws one curtain. Half the room is now bright and dancing with specks of dust. The other half, my half, is in shadow. I jump into a comfy chair, sitting deep into it, so that my feet are a long way from the ground, I sit still and calm like Mum has told me to and hold my breath as Mum drops Katie into my lap.

She stands watching for a few moments then leaves the room. 'Do you want orange or blackcurrant?' she calls back.

'Haven't we got any lemonade?'

'Only squash,' she says.

'Blackcurrant,' I say. 'Pleeeeeeeease.'

I look down at the bundle. She is so soft. Her eyes are still shining and laughing, she smells like flowers. My heart beats fast because I'm afraid of doing something wrong. 'Hello,' I say, 'hello, hello,' and I tickle her under the chin. She giggles. Mum comes in holding a glass of blackcurrant. She gives it to me, and knowing that I can't move to put the glass down, she stands waiting for me to finish. I drink it down in one go, my throat gulp, gulp, gulping. Mum takes the glass from my hand and stands now watching us. 'Will you be okay if I run upstairs and grab some clean clothes?'

I nod and Mum disappears up the stairs, I hear her stopping on the way to pick up piles of toys and clothes. I am sitting in shadow, looking at sunlight; my heart opening to the miracle that sits on my lap.

The Group

After I made the statement to the police I was terribly vulnerable – more vulnerable than I'd ever felt before in my adult life. One of the things that came out of this was that it forced me to ask for help. Not a skill I'd ever acquired – not a skill that was encouraged in my earlier life. In great shame I shuffled along to a drop-in I knew about, one that the Survivors' Network ran. I'd been there a few times when I first started counselling in 2001 but I hated it. I felt too naked there because it's a service exclusively for women who were abused in childhood, so everyone *knows* why you're there. The fact that everyone is there for the same reason doesn't make it better. I didn't want belong to that particular gang – who would?

My whole life, before I made the statement, I was obsessed with fitting in, appearing normal, even though I didn't feel it. But after the statement I have no energy to spare for putting on masks and thus I find myself at a Survivors' Network drop-in session, blubbing my heart out while the other women surround me and hold my hands and tell me about a closed support group that's starting soon. They tell me how useful the last group had been for them and encourage me to put my name down, so I do. I'm assessed by the group facilitators, two women, Angela and Janette, they're kind of like good-cop, bad-cop, except they're both good. But while Angela is a soft maternal type, Janette, with her curly hennaed hair and fiery eyes, makes me feel very glad that she's on *my* side – I wouldn't like to cross her. They tell me that I am perfect for the group; they'd love to have me in it.

Perfect for something at last. I cannot work to support myself, I am incapable of making small talk or functioning socially and maintaining basic hygiene is something of a challenge, but I am perfect for this – it's something.

The group runs for ten weeks from mid-February 2006. Eight women sitting in a circle take turns to speak about their abuse and how it affects their lives. It is absolutely terrifying. Going along to this group has a debilitating effect on the rest of my life. For the first four weeks I don't speak within it except to say how much I hate being there (to which the facilitators reply with caustic levels of compassion – caustic because it is alien to me). I lose the ability to function socially. I am exhausted all of the time. Mostly I spend my days cut off from the rest of the world, reading Harry Potter in my grubby desert island bed.

I don't know how to make that leap, from being alone with my suffering to sharing it. I have never identified myself as part of a group before and now I'm being asked to do that. While I take a dustpan and brush to her fireplace I tell Cherry that I am thinking of quitting the group. She says, 'I know from running psychotherapy groups that everyone wants to quit after the first few weeks,' and she cocks her head and smiles. 'That's precisely when you should stick with it.'

'But I don't have a life,' I say.

And it's true. I'm losing my ability to act normal and fit

in. I go out with old friends and I can no longer put the abuse stuff to one side, it's monolithic. People notice – 'Hey, you're not your usual sparkly self' – No, indeed! At parties I spend half my time in the bathroom having muscle spasms and trying to control the panic. When I try a different tack and tell some of my friends the truth I'm mostly met with silence, literally silence, which leaves me wondering – didn't I just say something? I'm sure I just told you I was abused. Oh you're leaving. Okay then, bye.

So, the old bonds start to loosen and with that my focus changes. I stop worrying about how I seem on the outside and try to speak from an authentic place. I've done this with Ella, but I've never done it with others. Week five and it floods out. How I felt having to listen to my brother being abused, how I hate my body, how I feel shame in the bad choices I've made in relationships and the ways in which I am unable to take care of myself. How fucking angry I am with my mum. How I hate all of you, all you abuse victims because I don't want to fucking be one. And thus, kicking and swearing, I re-enter the world of people.

For nearly all of us group participants this is the first time making connections of this kind. The first time that when talking about abuse it's a reciprocal conversation instead of us just burdening someone else (or feeling that we are). I've always protected my friends from the details because they're so horrible. But here it's okay to say them. Some of the things that are said trigger desperate panic in me and I feel as if the whole room might tilt up and tip us off the edge of the world.

After week five the change in me is both visible and deep. I take my seat. I know more of who I am now because I've taken a look around the hall of mirrors. The women here are hard-working, smart, funny and generous. Yet they believe themselves to be bad, ugly and over-complicated; all the same things that I believe about myself. There is a subtle change, like gold being sifted on to my heart, which is born from witnessing the great disparity between these women's self-images and what is so evidently true. It opens up the vista of *my* life; it means that *I* am not necessarily bad, nor bound forever to badness.

By the last session a real bond has grown between us and I feel high on the warmth of it. I swear to keep in touch with everyone, and I really mean it while I am saying it. But over time those bonds also loosen and then I am left with just one – Katharine.

Katharine and I make friends slowly, and (on my part) hesitantly. She is the quietest in the group and I know her the least. Some weeks we walk the same way and she invites me to come with her to a pub, or a poetry night. She is always going somewhere, and I always pass. If I were to be in the normal world after therapy and someone were to be in the least bit mean or abrupt then I would crumble to dust. But in the weeks after the group ends we do hook up – we meet and drink tea and gently learn each other's lives.

Katharine and I are very different people; all we really have in common is our horrific childhoods and the sense of being stuck in them, like flies in treacle. She's impossible to make plans with, everything is 'perhaps', 'maybe', 'we'll see', and she's always late. I, on the other hand, have to know exactly what is going to happen ages in advance. Katharine is ineffably cool. The only thing that is not cool about her is her goofy laugh – 'Ha…ha…ha' which, when it comes, rises involuntarily, from deep in her stomach – deep under the layers. I am not cool, except in that narrow way that not being cool is cool. Katharine talks in wisecracks, like Dorothy Parker – if Parker had been abused and ended up living in a bedsit in a seaside town, drawing the dole and going to Goth nights. If I ever say something funny then I usually repeat it and laugh at it for ages (not cool). She hordes where I throw out – I am forever having to re-purchase useful things that I've chucked away, whereas Katherine has about ten bin bags of old clothes. Occasionally she has a half-hearted sort out and I go round and try to squeeze my way into her cast-offs. One day she gives me a great old dress, one that she used to wear when she was a fat teenager in the 1980s. It's apron-shaped and covered in tiny pink flowers – it fast becomes my favourite item of clothing.

She is beautiful too. Not cute or pretty but timelessly beautiful. She would have been beautiful when the pyramids were being built, beautiful when they strung Christ up and she is beautiful now. That's what she carries with her, a sense of lineage. Katharine's legs are thin, she totters on them, and for my part I am continually surprised that they hold her up at all. The rest of her is slim and shapely. She has china-blue eyes set into an oval face of pale white skin, all of it framed by cascading hennaed hair. The hardest thing about being her friend is the jealousy I feel at the attention she gets. When we go out together there's always loads of men chatting her up – it's not that she takes the attention away from me – I never get that much attention – it's just that while one after another comes over and talks to her I sit there like an idiot, thinking, 'So what am I exactly? Chopped liver?' (Apparently so.)

We discover that we both love to go out dancing. We like 1950s nights best because the crowds are so random and not too cool: greasy old rockers, drunken office parties and art students with asymmetrical haircuts. The rockabilly music is especially suited to twirling and I do love to twirl. I drink beer from squidgey plastic glasses and she drinks cider. As the night wears on, Katharine, with sparkling inevitability, appears clutching amber shots of whisky, the later it gets the more whisky she ascertains is needed, and there is no refusing her. Sooner or later a record gets played that we just have to dance to. By the end of the night we dance to anything. We are always the last to leave.

The Distancing

Mum organises parties for us. The parties have themes. The themes have nothing to do with Christmas or Easter or birthdays because that is not allowed.

One Saturday she organises a hat party; all of the children wear hats. Mum makes my hat out of an old straw one, which she covers with brightly coloured lace and then glues hundreds of boiled sweets to it, an edible hat – everyone says it's the best one. Isaac wears a cowboy hat and Katie wears a plastic policeman's helmet. At the party there is cake and musical chairs and Grandad – Mum's dad – sings 'The Laughing Policeman'. All the children sit on the floor by his feet and we watch his face grow red as he sings and laughs: 'Ha-Ha-Ha-Ha-Ha-Ha-Ha...Ha-Ha-Ha-Ha-Ha'. On a long table there is a glass bowl of trifle, coloured ruby-red, then yellow then white, with crumbled chocolate on top. There is a golden sponge cake with a line of red jam through the middle and a hedgehog chocolate cake with chocolate button spikes and a cherry nose. We play pass-the-parcel. Layers and layers of newspaper come off and I find a sweetie necklace. When we have been playing a long time I get tired and I sit on my grandad's knee and doze, enjoying his belly heat. Children are asking him to do the Laughing Policeman again but he says, 'Now now...I'll do it for you next time. Shoo now.' That's what he says to other people's children, 'shoo now', like they are naughty puppies. He doesn't say that to us though, because we belong to him. That's why I can climb onto his lap and fall asleep with my head against his soft beating heart.

Sleepy, we are carried to Dad's car and dropped gently in, like porcelain packages. It is cold inside the car. My cheeks glow with the last embers of Grandad. Here we are, a tangle of twitching arms and legs, bellies full of puddings, grouchy from so much fun. Silence now. Mum and Dad in the front seat. The noise of the indictor light softly tick...tick...ticks us home. Dad drives with ease. Mum is deflated. At home she picks my sister and brother out of the car. 'You're too big to be carried,' she says. I cry a little but she doesn't pay any attention. 'Oh, stay out here if you want to.'

One by one the house lights come on and stretch across the scrubby lawn, as though to meet me. I turn around and take a last look at the moon. Turning back towards the house I duck my head and trundle up the path and pass by Dad who stands, teeth bared, holding open the door. I hear the door click shut and I run upstairs and get into bed.

I knew my mother was out of her depth but what could I do? I also knew that I was meant to play – and so I did play. I played and had fun and when she was gone I felt very bad about that, I felt bad that I didn't help her. She would confide in me. Even when I was in a buggy she would tell me things. One day she was pushing me along the road – busy traffic on one side and rolling green fields on the other – and my mother who was barely out of her teens told me that she didn't believe in the Jehovah's Witness religion. 'I don't believe in Jehovah, Beth,' she said to me. And I, no matter that I was so little, felt very nervous for us and sad with the burden of it and sad that my mother was so alone, telling me secrets on main roads.

Other days I would be just like a child – but bossy. I was the one who decided what games to play. My brother and sister deferred to me like an adult and I liked that, I liked being the boss. I would organise playing on the bunk beds; we would drape the lower bunk with blankets and play pirate ships. Like all children's games it was more about the acting than actual rules, the most important thing was that we got to be different people. Sometimes we would rope Mum in. For example if we played Dancing in the Dark she would stand at the light-switch and when the light was off we'd dance around like banshees and when she switched it on we'd have to be still like statues.

The older I got the heavier my heart became. The thing I was most afraid of was that Dad would kill Mum. They would have huge screaming fights. I remember one where they were fighting in the kitchen and I heard plates being smashed against the wall. I stood at the kitchen door listening, my body encased in an electric force field, every hair standing on end. More than anything I didn't want him to hurt Mum and I knew that he could do it because he was so strong and mean.

On the day after these horrible fights Mum would be distant and I would try not to bother her. I would just watch her sometimes. She'd be standing stock-still in the kitchen. Her body like normal, all the torment in her eyes fixed on some far distant place that she couldn't figure out a way to get to. She'd stand there for 15 minutes or an hour, frozen, and I would try to keep the littler ones away from her till she came back to us.

It was hard because as time passed my mother became more and more two-dimensional. She looked the same – except for the far-away eyes.

Wayne Cleaver

11 May 2006

I made the statement in December last year and now, finally,
I'm going to meet the detective who'll be investigating my
case. I've spoken to him on the phone, Detective Constable
Wayne Cleaver. He sounds nice, compassionate and as if he
understands how big a deal this is for me. He says he's bringing a colleague, not a woman like I expected, apparently
there are no female detectives in his department. I'm really,
really scared. I have no idea what he might ask me. I haven't
slept properly for days; fear itches me like wool against my
skin. I'm afraid that these policemen won't believe me, or
that I'll seem mad – but underneath that, the real fear (the
forever fear) – what if the other two men come instead?
What if Karl and Adrian Price turn up at my door, force their
way into the flat and rape me?

I wake exceedingly early and just walk around town, walking
on my nerves, muttering to myself. I'm at Dr Clarke's
surgery as it opens and secure the first available appointment
and sit in her office amid ear torches and boxes of tissues
and I cry molten tears. 'You must have something,' I say,
'just to take the edge off.' She knows of my aversion to
medication. But right now I'd take anything. She prescribes

Diazepam, 2mg to take in the daytime and 5mg at night, to help me sleep. I run off to the chemist. Everything is happening full speed and too bright, like an exam day. I shuffle my feet while the pharmacist fills my prescription. I watch them judging me and inside I scream – *you could do this without medication, could you?*

At home I examine the brown glass bottle of pills. The label says my name and the drug's name. There we are, side by side. I never wanted to do this. I never wanted to be this helpless. I tip the little yellow pills into my hand; they make a tiny, ridged pyramid. I put one in my mouth and gulp it down with water and pour the rest back into the bottle.

Stuart arrives. He gives me a hug, then, with his usual cat-like demeanour, curls into the corner of an armchair and sets about completing the *Guardian* crossword. He watches but does not get involved in my flittering around the room. His quiet observation is slowly soothing; it means so much, doesn't it, to be seen?

By the time the doorbell goes something has worked, either the drugs or the mundane crossword catnip. I am now, as they say in old-fashioned novels, mistress of myself again. I open the front door and there they are. Men! Not the geeky, university-educated boys of my acquaintance. These are manly men, huge, they tower over me.

They introduce themselves, DC Wayne Cleaver and Sergeant Dai Roberts. I ask to see their IDs before admitting them to my flat. They remind me so much of the boys I went to school with, but grown up. If I had stayed at home I would have married a man like these. I feel like I know them before we've even shaken hands. I imagine they take baths rather than showers, there were no showers in the houses they grew up in, a shower never feels quite clean enough. They drink instant coffee and for lunch they buy a pie or pasty and eat it in their car, parked up outside of the baker's. On Sundays they bend to kiss their mothers, in front of whom they are resolutely cheerful. They get very very drunk on Friday nights and they always will do, forever, until finally the doctor insists that they stop.

The detectives wear their half-day political correctness training like ill-fitting shoes; I sense them reminding themselves not to call me 'love'. I don't mind. I live in a town and a life and an age-bracket where we are ironically sexist and ironically racist as a way to beat it but mostly as a way to have fun and that is just as silly a game. I catch them double-taking that I'm from the same town as them. Here I sound normal, but to them I sound posh – perhaps they think I'm putting on airs. Thousands of pounds of student loans may not have bought me a career but it did buy me a middle-class accent and an opinion of Rousseau, and right now, standing face-to-face with my stay-at-home alternatives, nine thousand pounds seems like a bargain.

No offence intended, I do like them, Wayne Cleaver and Dai Roberts. Dai, six foot six, all length and no girth, is absurd-looking, wearing a navy T-shirt with black pin-stripe suit trousers and shiny dress shoes, his face gawky, buck-toothed, jug-eared, his head too small. Some people confuse his gawkiness with stupidity and I can see how he uses this to his advantage. He sits on the sagging sofa, legs stretching halfway across the room, his face a mask of dumb unworldliness, but I catch him, just once or twice, the pinpricks of his pupils sucking me in, seeing, calculating, knowing. Wayne is a different story, Wayne is so heterosexual he is almost camp, with a twinkle in his eye and the clothes of a used car-sales man: black and white checked sports jacket, plain black trousers, top buttons of his shirt undone, no tie; I keep looking for the medallion. His hair short at the sides but luscious on top and silvering, like a club-singer, a ladies' man. He makes me laugh.

I introduce them to Stuart and then Stuart leaves us, as arranged, and waits with his crossword in my bedroom. I am trying to save his ears from the more horrible things that might be said... Wayne describes the contents of my statement as, 'Horrific, it's just horrific', and he shakes his head, as though trying to free it of the horror (I know the feeling). He says he was particularly struck by my description of saying 'Thank you' to Karl after being raped, by which I take it that he's struck by the horror of it but also the authenticity it lends; who would make that up?

In the main Dai stays quiet, it seems he is there mainly in a supervisory role. I expected Wayne to ask me questions about the statement but he doesn't. Instead he asks things like, 'Most of the rape you describe is anal; do you think Karl is homosexual?' It makes me angry because it's a stupid question and how the fuck would I know? But there's also this unexpected relief: I am talking about anal rape with a man who's in a position to do something about it and he is looking me in the eye and I am looking right back: I am a million billion miles from where I have been.

Wayne tells me that he's tracked my brother Isaac down and taken a statement from him. He says Isaac claims to be surprised by these allegations, he says he had a 'happy childhood'. I wasn't expecting him to support my statement, but Jesus, a 'happy childhood'! It doesn't make me angry, just very very sad. Wayne says it's a sore point though, a real problem for the case. He says he really needs Katie to come on board. I tell him that I've spoken to her. That she's willing to talk about physical violence but not sexual abuse. 'She's just not secure enough in her memories.' Wayne hopes she will change her mind. I tell him about what Karl did to Mum. 'If Mum made a statement wouldn't that make a difference to the case?'

'Do you think she'd be prepared to do that?' he asks.

'I don't know, I think so.'

We talk about people I've told over the years and most importantly my counsellor Ella, who can provide him with notes going back nearly five years. I tell him about diaries that I've kept, with details of memories and flashbacks. He doesn't seem to think these are very important.

I ask them philosophical questions – How, in their experience, are people able to do these things? They tell me that they've usually been abused themselves and that it's about power rather than sex. They tell me what they would really like to do to child abusers, if they could get away with it. And Dai leaves me with some advice, 'It's not the cards you're dealt, it's the way you play 'em.' His nonsense leads me to safely conclude that his particular hand contained far fewer brutal rapes than mine.

Junk wisdom aside, I'm pleased with my detectives. They seem like good guys and most importantly they seem to be on my side. They spend some time admiring the flat with its view of the Pavilion Palace and its extensive range of DVDs and fancy *objets d'art*. I explain that most everything belongs to my flatmate but still it's nice that they're impressed. They leave after an hour or so and Stuart reappears and cooks me an omelette and he gets stoned and we watch TV.

When My Mother Left Us

One June morning when I am nine years old I wake before my brother and sister and rush from my bed. I go to my mother's bedroom to wake her and ask her to make me breakfast. She's not there. I run downstairs. The living room is empty. I pass through the living room and into the kitchen, thinking I might see her at the stove. She isn't there. I cross the kitchen, past the chilly back door, and stick my head into the damp bathroom. She isn't there.

Back in the living room my brother now stands, rubbing sleep from his eyes. He joins in the search. We open the front door and poke our heads outside and look up and down the street. We go to the back of the house and look down the long garden. She's not there. We decide that she has gone to the shop. Time passes. Our mother does not return. We start to panic. We check the house again. Every room, four, five, six times. We look for her under beds and in cupboards and drawers and small spaces where no grown person could fit. Then we go back to the living room where we huddle together on the sofa and start to cry and hold on to each other for support. One feeling builds on another as the bottom falls out of our world. It is unthinkable that she's not here, and yet we cannot see her anywhere.

Then I spy the note. It's tucked behind the carriage clock on the mantelpiece. It's her handwriting. My heart leaps.

She has not disappeared, she is back with me again, I did not just imagine my mother, she is a real person, she belongs to me and here is the proof. It is a long note, double-sided, and I sink into panic because it's too long to be telling us merely that she's at the shop. I read the note. My eyes get stuck on the words: *I can no longer cope with the children. They will be better off without me.* She can't mean that – she can't mean it. I read it again, out loud, to my brother as best I can through choking sobs. My mother is absent and in her place is a piece of paper and I fall into the chasm that lies between her and it; between what I need and what I have. Something leaves me then and it never comes back. I don't know the word for it – trust or love or hope – I'm not sure what it is but it's the thing that makes you want to get up in the morning. That was the last time I ever rushed out of bed.

I hear my sister wake and her little body thumping its way downstairs. She is only five, bless her, I cannot bear to tell her the truth. Instead, I tell her that Mum has gone to the shop to buy sweets. This gives me and Isaac a focus as we try to stay calm for Katie's sake. But we can't quite stop ourselves from crying and so the three of us huddle together, soggy and bewildered, and wait for the other grown-up to come home.

The Book

Inspired by my experience of the Survivor's group I write a second article for their newsletter. In it I recount the rollercoaster emotions I went through during the group and also the light that I found within it. It is printed in their 2006 summer edition. Shortly afterwards, in a fit of anxiety, I make my way to a Survivor's drop-in group. Outside it I feel terrified as a woman I vaguely recognise approaches me. 'I wanted to thank you,' she says. 'I came here tonight because of you, because of your article. It reminded me that there are people in the world who understand what it's like for me.' The woman's words encourage me – I am more than just a victim – I can help sometimes too.

I take the article to Cherry who reads it in her study while I clean her bathroom. I'm wiping the sink when she comes and stands inside the doorway. 'It's very good,' she says, 'extremely moving and clear. I'm sure it will help people. I think it should be read by a wider audience. If you'd like I can try and help you get it published. It's the kind of piece the *Guardian* might print.'

I beam at the praise but shake my head, worried about exposing myself in that way. 'I'm not sure about that. But I have been thinking about writing a book about this process

I am going through, the police investigation and eventually when I go to court.'

Cherry cocks her head to indicate that she is listening. I continue, 'You know, before I made the statement I wanted to read a personal account of someone who had gone to court. I looked on the Internet, asked around but there was nothing, the book I needed doesn't exist.' I look past my reflection in the bathroom mirror to the doorway where Cherry stands resolute, petite and solid at the same time.

'I have to warn you, most writers work hard for years and never make any money. It's not an easy way of life. On the other hand, books do get published and the book you have in mind would be of help to a great many people. Perhaps I can help you to write it,' she says. 'Why don't we both get our diaries and make a date to meet and talk about it.'

In June 2006 I have my first writing tutorial with Cherry. I show her a piece of writing, the one about making the statement that opens this book. She likes it, 'It's very good,' she says. We sit together, facing each other, in her study. Outside the bay window seagulls call out, their voices rising and dipping with the air currents.

'Don't put too much pressure on yourself to find a structure yet. Just write pieces as they come to you. We can make a date to meet every three weeks or so and take it from there.'

Butterscotch light filters through the blinds.

'Okay,' I say. I can't believe my luck.

The Waking Nightmare

With Mum gone I become a negative of a person. My life is defined by the things that I do not do. I have stopped going out to play. I feel tired all the time and try to stay as still as possible. I watch television, watch it really closely, I would like to climb inside it and live those other lives. I eat as much as I can, whatever I can get my hands on: fish fingers and oven chips, neopolitan ice cream, rich tea biscuits spread with butter and jam. I like the feeling of food in my mouth and when it is not there I just live in fantasies. Fantasies of being pretty and popular, fantasies that I am the slave girl of an evil prince, fantasies about power and powerlessness. When I am roused from these daydreams by anything in the present I feel angry. I hate being in my life.

I have changed physically, become fat, and I'm too afraid to look anyone in the eye, so my shoulders are hunched from looking at the floor. One day, when we're knocking on people's doors, I hear another Jehovah's Witness girl ask her mother, 'Why does she stand like that?' I feel mortified.

My life is a waking nightmare. The days are bad, they seem to stretch forever, but the nights are even worse. I cry myself to sleep, trying not to wake my brother and sister. I pray for God to bring my mother back. Over and over into my sodden pillow, 'I just want my mum, I just want my mum, I just want my mum.' And then there are the nights when Dad tells me to sleep in his bed and I lie as far away from him as possible, just waiting and hating myself, thinking that somehow my waiting and expecting are causing him to do those things. One morning, after getting up from the crumpled double bed where some nights he rapes me, the father-monster shouts at me because the skirt I've put on for school is too short. He calls me a slut. I almost go mad with the hurt and the confusion.

With my mother gone there is no hope of escape, I am utterly trapped. One by one, like they are light-switches, I turn off my needs. It is unacceptable for me to be vulnerable and so I become responsible, a mini-downtrodden housewife. It makes Dad angry that I have feelings and so I keep them for the nighttime and my pillow. I vow to myself that I will be brave and he will never again make me cry, but always I fail. As he hits me with a leather belt I have to listen to him tell me that what he is doing hurts him more than it hurts me. I live in a world of dualities, where nothing is true. I am taught to believe in a God who I am told is loving but who does not love me as I am, a person with a feeling body. I am learning to distrust my own intuition because it so often contradicts the rest of my whole world. There is always something happening and, underneath that, something else.

Meditations on a Saturday Night

I'm invited to a party, which is nice, except that I cannot go because my back feels like Hades has taken up residence inside it and I keep bursting into tears and I'm really angry. I'm angry because this is my Saturday night and I'm so tired of feeling like shit. The pain in my back is old and recurrent and I know that it needs heat so I pour myself a bath. I light tea-lights and place them on every bare bit of porcelain.

In the bath I'm still angry and I have imagined fights with real people. The pain in my back sharpens and sharpens until it's screaming. I remember a shiatsu massage where the woman encouraged me to visualise the pain, so I picture it as a swarming mass of gooey scorpions and maggots and I imagine them flushing out of my body and through a hole in my back. Then I remember the shiatsu woman told me to make sure the stuff had somewhere to go: somewhere deep in the ground ('They like living in the ground,' she said), or way into space, somewhere far away from me, anyway. And so I imagine a hole in the bath but it has to be one that sucks away the icky stuff but doesn't let out the bathwater and so it's all a bit complicated.

Then the convulsions start and I fucking hate them and I have to remember that they're a good thing because they mean I'm relaxing but I hate them because they still shock me and they hurt. I say to myself, 'It's okay, you're okay, you're safe.' This goes on for ten minutes at least: the jerking and the comforting and I'm fucking sick of it. I'm sick of being brave and being strong and I start crying and I say, 'I want my mummy, I want my mummy, I want my mummy, I want my mummy.' And the voice which says 'I want my mummy' is so sad and so plaintive that my sobs get deeper with each saying.

Out of the bath I rub my body down, hating it for being ugly, then feeling guilty for my harshness I try to be kind to myself ('Oh, it's okay, you're okay'). I feel dizzy and heavy – I'm having trouble standing up. After a while the dizziness passes and I put myself in pyjamas and gather together provisions (two ginger biscuits and three drinks: a tall glass of water; a mug of hot chocolate; a large glass of red wine), my diary and a pen, should they be needed, and my laptop, and I deposit them on and around my bed. In bed I drink the hot chocolate, which is delicious, and the wine, which is effective, and on the laptop I write these words. And this is my Saturday night.

The other day someone described me as a survivor and I was thinking about that earlier. I don't call myself a 'survivor'. 'Victim' used to be an important word for me – because victim is the opposite of everything being your fault. I don't call myself anything – this is my whole world, why would I call it anything. I call the others a name; I call them 'civilians' – the non-abused people. It used to be a private joke; something I just said in my head until the group and now Katherine says it too and it feels delicious and exclusive. There's no corresponding word for us – we're not warriors or soldiers – but we're defiantly not civilians.

I have another friend who hates the word 'survivor', indignantly he says, 'I don't survive, I live!' I won't be making such a grand claim for myself, not tonight at any rate. But is it important? Do I need a word? Do I have to have a definition or a label? Maybe I still hate what I am and what's happened to me (they so often feel like the same thing). I know that I hate telling the Samaritans that I've been abused – every time I call them I'm reluctant to say it. But you have to, firstly, because they ask you ('Have you been feeling like this for a long time, Beth, or is it just today?' – 'Does anything usually trigger these panic attacks?' etc). And secondly because if I didn't tell them it would be like dialling the emergency services but not actually telling them that your house is on fire – just dropping hints and hoping they'll work it out. 'Hello, operator, where I am it's uncomfortably hot, orangey-red shapes are flickering around my feet and my breathing is a little more laboured than usual – can you help?'

A Bag of Spanners

I never really told my mum about the abuse, not as such. Instead, one day when I was 18 and it was the summer between my first and second years of university – a sticky, turbulent summer – I just kept talking one afternoon of how much I wanted to kill Karl. My mother finally looked at me, right into my face, and asked in a soft voice, 'He didn't ever touch you, did he, Beth?'

Volcanoes always erupt some time – this was mine. I cried and cried and cried. I wanted so much for her to take me into her arms and look after me like a baby, which was how I felt, tiny in the face of the remembrances. I wanted her to unpack me like a parcel bound tight with ribbon. I wanted her to open me up and take out the bad bits, take out the bad bits, take out the bad bits…

She doesn't speak for ages, just sits across from me while I cry. I know without looking that her face is soft and caring – her fucking face. Then her voice, soft, like music, 'He did the same thing to me, after your sister was born, just after I brought her home from the hospital, he raped me anally.'

This revelation makes me angry to a degree I could never feel just on my own behalf – and it also scares me and shames me. The words weigh me down and I limp back to college overloaded. I revert to my first instinct: *Never tell anyone.*

*

At college I get drunk all the time, just like everyone else. I couldn't tell you how much I stood out as troubled. I wasn't a good student, but there were others like me, turning up at tutorials sweating with alcohol poisoning, guessing the answers. I can't tell you the number of times I heard the words, 'No, Miss Ellis, that is entirely incorrect. Can anyone else give me the right answer?' I was stressed all the time about assignments, but none of them were compulsory or counted towards my final grade so in the end I just wouldn't do them. My attendance was probably similar to how it had been at secondary school, just above the point where people start nosing around. I smoked constantly, I smoked through colds and chest infections, some days I'd alternate between taking swigs from a bottle of cough medicine and drags on a cigarette. It was around this time that one of the teeth in the side of my mouth rotted and began to crumble away. Most of it just came away one day when I bit into a sandwich. The pain was excruciating, throbbing and raw. I tried to go the dentist but I was terrified. Since that time I've read books about abuse and I know that it's common for persons who've been orally abused to be phobic of dental treatments, terrified of opening their mouths wide. Back then I didn't know anything and time and again I'd make dental appointments, sit in the surgery, wait, then as soon as my name was called I'd run away, back on to the street, into the thin London rain and home. I coped with the pain by taking dental painkillers and swigs of whisky, all through the night sometimes, till finally the nerve died and the broken tooth didn't hurt anymore.

*

To say that my mum handled things badly at this time is an understatement. I mean, it could have been worse: I've met people whose mothers have called them liars and disowned them. She didn't cut me off. What she did though is every time I went back to Wales to visit her and sometimes when she'd phone, she'd pressure me to go to the police. 'What about the other children,' she'd say, 'don't you care that he could be abusing other little children?'

At least if it was a phone-call I could hang up and that's what I would do. But if I was home then I was fucked. By now she had re-married and started another family in a little cottage right in the middle of nowhere so I'd literally be trapped. One time she started up and not wanting to fight with her I simply left the room and went into another, she followed me, followed me right round the house, 'What about the other children!' she screamed. 'Don't you care?'

The thing I never said but always wanted to was, 'Why don't *you* fucking go to the fucking police. Why don't *you* report your rape and protect the fucking children?' But I didn't say that because I knew that even though she was being out of order, a person's rape is a sacred precious thing, like a dead child, and it's up to them if they talk about it or not.

The rest of my family was about as much use to me as a bag of spanners. Katie had taken the earliest opportunity to leave home and set herself up with a job and a boyfriend and a flat. When I tried to talk to her she'd drift off to some far-away place and lock down tight. She hates me talking about

62

it, as though talking about it is the problem, not the fact that it happened.

Isaac still lived with Karl at this time but he had a job and Mum visited him at work. He doesn't say he doesn't believe me, he doesn't say I'm a liar, he says, 'If you put my dad in prison you will never see me again.' He never sees us again anyway.

Grandad – mum's dad – sends me a letter enclosing a cheque and a stern warning that he hopes I am *taking this matter up with the correct authorities* (ur, no Grandad, I'm trying to remember to breathe). And that was it. That was my family.

There was a time that I felt like giving them up altogether, and I didn't go back to Wales for three years. But, although Mum's new marriage hadn't worked out, the product of it was two beautiful babies, Jasmine and Tim, who are such shining stars in the world. I felt, why should I miss out on knowing them? My mother and I came to a careful unspoken truce for years whereby I didn't bother her with my pain and we just talked about the kids.

I Was Raped

By the exam term of my second year of university even heavy drinking doesn't keep the badness away. I pace the corridor of the pastel-walled second floor of the law department trying to pluck up the courage to knock on the door to the Head of Year, Professor Melville. I need to talk to him. I need to tell him about the word blindness. I need to tell him that every time I open a textbook the only words I can see are: I was raped.

As soon as I take a chair opposite him I know I won't be able to say it. Professor Melville is old – he looks more like Mr Burns from *The Simpsons* than any live-action person has the right to. There are other things I can do in this world, perhaps many other things, but one thing I can't do is tell this dusty old professor that my father used to fuck me in the arse and that I'm going insane and can't possibly take these exams and please can I take them next year instead? I've barely even touched the seat before I rise up again, 'I can't,' I say and I run from his office in tears

Outside the law department I push past students and along the greasy main road and towards the dirty canal and I follow it all the way till it opens into Victoria Park, grand and beautiful with its animals, ducks, geese, squirrels and rats, weirdly intimidating, in some weird food-chain role reversal – I swear the squirrels here would mug you as soon as look at you. I take a path that follows the edge of the park, walk way out, further than I've been before, stopping every now and then to let out the tears. The only thing I can think to do is die. I decide to visit a bunch of corner shops and stock up on paracetamol and find a quiet spot and just die. Next door to the first shop stands a payphone. Half the glass has been smashed out and it glitters on the concrete floor. I find myself in there instead of in the shop and I find myself dialling the number of my friend Natalie. The phone doesn't even ring one whole ring, 'Where are you? Professor Melville has been to your house, your housemates are worried about you. Where are you?'

Within minutes she's scooped me into a taxi and carried me home and we are sat facing each other in my bedroom, drinking tea, and I'm crying. Natalie, bless her, is soft-bodied, soft-faced, soft-hearted.

'I can't read,' I say. 'I can't sit my exams.' The sentences come out when they can, in the spaces between heaving sobs. 'I went to see Professor Melville today...I went because I needed to ask him...I need to not sit my exams right now...I needed to ask if I could retake the entire year...I've missed so much.'

To Natalie's soft face I say, 'I was abused. I was raped and abused. By my father. By Karl.'

I look down at the floor, my spine crumbling under the

shame. When I next look up her eyes aren't so soft anymore. 'Can we kill him?' she says. 'Can we kill him?'

Natalie is very gentle with me but she does insist I see a college counsellor and she sits outside while I enter the office of a person who, unfortunately for me, has all the compassion of a lump of concrete. The woman, blonde, plump and hard-faced, sits as expressionless as if I were reading out a shopping list while I spit out embers of buried lava. I walk out of the appointment more burdened than before. 'I am *never* doing that again,' I say.

Natalie urges me to make a complaint about her but I can't so she drops the subject and instead goes on my behalf to Professor Melville and gets him to agree that I can repeat the year.

Given the Circumstances

It's a beautiful bright day and I feel good, comfortable in my skin. I'm about to leave the flat when the phone rings. It's my mother and she's sobbing. It takes her a long time to calm down enough to tell me what is wrong. Between long, trembling breaths she tells me that Wayne Cleaver was meant to visit her two hours ago and has not turned up. It was supposed to be a meeting where they discussed her giving a statement. She tells me that she has got so worked up about this visit, worried about it for days, and now this. She cries and cries. I tell her not to worry; I'll call him.

I feel like I'm walking a tight-rope because I'm really angry with Wayne and can't believe he has done this, but at the same time I don't want Mum to lose faith in him and this process. I leave Mum in tears and call the police station. I ask for Wayne but I'm told he is out. I ask to speak to his superior and I'm put on hold. Dai Roberts comes on the line and he tries to reassure me that it must be a mistake or misunderstanding. I demand to speak to someone higher up and the next officer I speak to I threaten to make a complaint to the Independent Police Complaints Commission but he laughs me off 'for something this small,' he says. Furious, humiliated and impotent, I get him to at least promise that Wayne will phone me at the earliest opportunity.

I leave the flat in a huff and walk in the direction of the fruit market. The sun glints off every pane of glass and the tall trees glory in it. I hear my mobile phone go off. I answer and struggle to hear Wayne Cleaver over the whooshing traffic. I duck down an alley and find myself in the courtyard of a wood recycling centre, stood amongst window-boxes and bird-tables, I struggle to make myself understood. I tell him that Mum has just phoned me in tears, he tuts in sympathy with me; he thinks that I am complaining about *her*.

'She's in tears because you didn't turn up for your appointment,' I say, exasperated.

'Something came up,' he says in his thick Welsh accent. 'I told her that if something came up I might not make it.'

'You didn't think to call her?'

'We're very busy today.'

I take an extra deep breath, 'My mother is crying because she's been worrying for days about meeting with you and you didn't bother turning up or even calling her. I don't feel that you're taking my case seriously.' I look around – blue sky, greasy pigeons and chunky railway-sleeper coffee-tables – I can feel the world spinning beneath me, like when I stand in the sea.

'I'm really offended that you would say that, Beth. We've always had a good relationship. I'm very offended.'

'What do you expect me to think when you don't even phone, or ask someone to phone on your behalf, you just leave my mum sitting there, expecting you any minute.'

'Really, Beth, I'm very offended that you would say that I don't take you seriously. I do take this very seriously.'

I worry about alienating him, so I backtrack as far as I can while still maintaining some pride. 'Well, I'm sure you'll understand my saying it, given the circumstances. Now, will you please phone my mum and arrange another time to see her?'

'Really, Beth, to say I'm not taking the case seriously, I can't tell you how much you've hurt my feelings.'

How did his feelings become the centre of this conversation? 'Okay, I've hurt your feelings but I'm sure you can understand, given the circumstances, why I said it. I have to go now, I have things to do so I'm going to hang up now.' I say ultra loud and clear, like I'm dealing with a crazy person. 'Can you please just phone my mum, okay? Bye.'

I hang up the phone and just stare at it dumbfounded for a few moments before I recollect who I am, where I am, where the fuck I am going and why. I make my way back to the traffic-congested main drag then I think to dial Mum's number and check on her. Good, her number's engaged, he's phoning her at least.

After My Mother

My mother has disappeared. I am nine years old. Our house is cold and has a dark quality to it. Even the garden, which is big and full of nettles as well as a long lawn and some fruit bushes and trees, seems to me to be evil. Evil soil, who knows what's underneath. What might creep out and grab me, drag me under. I am scared of slugs, more than anything else. When it's autumn and they drip and drag themselves everywhere it's hard for me to get around. If the car is parked at the back of the house then I walk all the way down to the end of the street, past Mrs Jones who keeps her big dog chained up so he barks day and night; past the corner house with pretty Lisa and Sara with their violin lessons and nodding yellow sunflowers. I follow the road alongside their long, bountiful garden, round to the back of the houses where my broken family sits waiting for me in the car. We drive to school in silence. Fallen leaves coat the schoolyard and they coat my life. Wet and slippery, they make things difficult for me. What is the bump underneath them? Is it another leaf folded up or is it a slug? It's getting so I can't really go anywhere. It takes me so long to step around the slugs and the suspicious leaves. I try not to go out. People don't call for me so often anymore. Once you say no a few times then they stop trying. I feel embarrassed after they leave, like maybe I should have gone. Maybe I've ruined my whole life by not going to play today, maybe no one will ask me to do anything again. I chew my nails and worry.

Inside the house, unless you sit directly in front of the fire, it is always cold. I sit under blankets. I'm dressed in clothes but sit under blankets. I'm slow to move when it's time to go to a meeting. I hope that Dad will forget and that we can stay at home and watch TV. I don't like seeing people, I don't like them looking at me. Between my legs is hot and sore. The rest of me is cold. I take a long time moving. I am heavy. Dad shouts and raises his hand. I put my shoes on the wrong feet and have to change over. He rubs cold spit on to my face with his finger to take off some dirt. I keep very still; I don't like him being so close, his face right up to mine.

Isaac and Katie clomp down the stairs. Isaac is wearing a navy blue suit, like a mini-man. Katie is wearing a pink flow-ery dress, she is pretty because of her bright blue eyes and she is a good girl. I am wearing a lace-collared dress, navy and printed with dark purple flowers, it has long sleeves and the hem reaches my knees. On my legs the dreaded white knee-length socks, which end in black shoes, almost worn out, the leather cracked and missing from the toes.

In the car we are very quiet. I ride in the passenger seat because I am the oldest and so I'm allowed to. Outside the Kingdom Hall Dad parks the car and we get out. The sky is plain white. The road is wide. The Kingdom Hall is newly-made of brick, plain except for the lettering advertising itself: *Kingdom Hall of Jehovah's Witnesses*; into the foyer with the men's and women's toilets and the wooden collection box; through into the long hall with its rows of grey plastic chairs, their surface satisfyingly rough and bumpy to the touch; the wooden platform with its lectern and vases of flowers; the bookshop at the back of the hall, selling Bibles and song-books and *Watchtower* and *Awake* magazines.

We take seats near the front. I work hard now trying to leave this place, to conjure a daydream big enough to absorb all the boredom. A grey-haired Elder takes to the stage and opens his mouth and boring stuff comes out. I have to leave here soon or my heart will stop. I stare straight ahead and flick through a portfolio of mental images. Me as a film star, as a pop star, the prettiest girl in school, a rich orphan. But I can't make it there. My heart is raw and it weighs three tons and I just want my mum. Tears roll down my face. I cry out the heartbroken tears that I usually save for my pillow, when no one can hear me. Dad looks over, but he doesn't raise his hand, just looks disappointed in me and turns to face the front again. I can't stop, I cry and cry, my face grows bright pink and striped white with hot rivers of tears.

When the talk is over Dad gets up and wanders off, Katie trundles after him and hangs on to the hem of his jacket. 'Get off,' he says to her and brushes her away. Isaac goes off and talks to a group of boys. Everyone can see me now, I am sitting alone and still I cannot stop crying. It is as though my heart has opened and will never again close. Ashamed, I look down at the floor and I wish I could be beamed away from here to a place where I could be by myself. Another wave of tears washes my eyes blind.

When my sight clears I see, in the periphery of my vision, a pair of navy legs. I will them to go away from me but instead they come closer and the man clears his throat to catch my attention. I look up at the rest of the body: white shirt, paisley tie, navy arms, grey hair, angry red face, an Elder of the Kingdom Hall. He glares at me, 'How dare you cry in the house of God,' he says, and he abruptly turns and walks away in disgust. Karl looks over from where he is stood with men in dark suits and women in modest, flowered dresses, he catches my eye and wags his finger to say, 'See, I warned you. Now you've been told off and you deserve it.'

I just sit there wishing I was dead.

I don't die, it's worse than that. Dad roughly calls out to me, 'Come on, it's time to go.' Shaking and ashamed, I rise from my seat and make my way past groups of people to the exit. I want to go right now but Dad takes his time trading unfunny jokes with Adrian Price, the man who was in the bathroom, watching what Dad did to me. If I could not exist it would be better. If only I could not exist.

At last we walk to the car. No one talks to me. Isaac and Katie don't even look at me. Dad is very angry, I can tell by the way he slams the car door shut. I am just relieved to be away from all those people. We're nearly home now, there I can hide. I'm still crying but softly now, the worst of the storm is over; I am exhausted. Dad tuts and I try to stop crying altogether but tightening around the sadness just makes it grow in my chest.

'Your mother is a slut!' he says.

I gasp. Fear claws at my heart. What does he know of her? What has he done to her? But that is all the information he provides. That is all I get of my mother these past two months.

No Angels in this Barren Landscape

Written late on 14 August 2006, the night before a visit to Wales

Engines drone and I fall down down down – into a huge pit, like a lake drained of water, stony, barren and with no sparkle. Angels do not catch me this time and my bones shatter against the rock-dusted earth. I cry out in pain – I scream myself alive. I bash a rock against my skull – the only part of me that is not smashed – I try to smash it. It does not work – I manage only to knock myself out. When I wake I am crying and for a split-second I am completely numb, except for the feel of water against my cheeks – I wonder why I am crying – and then I know why and then I am in pain again – fucking conscious-ness. I try again. Smashing the stone hard against my skull – this time the powder-grey landscape disappears into spots of yellow light – stars of light that crowd me – fly close to me as if wishing to impart something to me. I follow one particular spark – it seems to be insisting that I follow and it also seems to have a personality, both mischievous and trustworthy – I swim through the air after it. I follow it from one end of a rainbow to the other – there is no pot of gold, but there is – blessed water – oh no! It is only my tears again. I pick up a bigger rock.

They're Arresting Him Today

I'm already shot to pieces before the police arrive. I'm halfway through the final day of my visit to Wales. I haven't slept much this past week and I am tired and irritable and itching to get home to Brighton. I feel stuffed full of food and the things I have not been able to say. My mother and I have waited in all day. Her statement detailing her rape has now been taken, but we don't talk about it, we can't, we don't know how. Detective Wayne Cleaver has telephoned twice, to apologise for being delayed, he says it can't be helped, says he's dealing with illegal immigrants. I laugh sarcastically, 'Ha, and I couldn't wait to get out of here.'

I am perched on a hill, perched on a chair, outside my mother's house, the tree-filled valley lies open to my gaze. 'This should be beautiful,' I whisper to myself. Cars pass and I straighten up, then I see that they contain the wrong people and I slump back again. And then they are here. They breeze up to the house in a silver saloon-car. Wayne springs out of the car and strides towards me; Dai Roberts waits in the car. Wayne looks confident and healthy and happy, why shouldn't he be happy? I don't know but it doesn't feel right, it's too sharp a contrast with my own feelings. He pulls up a chair. I feel lumpy and teenaged, sitting between him and my mother.

After nine months of nothing much happening, it comes as a shock when Wayne says, 'We're arresting him on Thursday.' It's my body that reacts to the news. Every muscle in my back and neck tightens and my heart folds in on itself. I feel the urge to take my own life. Another voice, a softer voice inside me, asks, 'Why? Why would you want to do that?' It's the fear I guess. I remember Karl whispering into my ear that if I ever told anyone he would find me and kill me. I remember wanting to get away from him then and his breath and malice but he'd keep hold of my arm ever so tight until finally I'd nod in agreement. That was the pact; as long as I never told I got to live. I've broken the pact.

As Wayne gets up to leave I want to shout out to him, 'Be careful, he's a monster. You don't know him. He's not like other men.' I want to advise him to take a harpoon or some other monster catcher. But he's not afraid like I am.

In the build-up to the arrest I get very little sleep. I'm strung out and edgy. I manage to go about my Brighton life, go to my voluntary work, meet friends for drinks, but I take no pleasure in it. I'm no longer living in real time. I experience things after the event. I enter a room but have no memory of getting there. In this way the world has become shocking.

The day of the arrest comes and I walk around with my heart in my mouth. Mum keeps calling, to see if I've heard anything. I wish she wouldn't. At 2.30 p.m. Wayne calls and he tells me they didn't arrest him, something else came up. He doesn't say what. I'm angry that he left it so late in the day to call me but I don't say anything for worry of causing offence, and I'm also relieved that it didn't happen. That night I sleep soundly for the first time in weeks.

A week later there's a message on my voicemail. It's Wayne. He says they're arresting Karl tomorrow at 6 a.m. There's no disclaimer this time – he doesn't say, 'Of course if something else comes up then it'll have to be next week.' I feel pretty confident that it's going to happen. I sit down and cry. I'm so tired, I feel numb and drugged. I'm definitely depressed. I hate doing things; I hate moving. People are driving me crazy. I just want to be left alone with my bitter wounds. Now that things are changing I find that I don't want them to change. I want to stay here with my soft lemon daydream of rescue. I'm not sure I want to take responsibility for my own life; I'm not sure I want the world to be that real.

Autumn 2000

In the autumn of 2000 I returned to London for what should have been the final year of my degree. Most of my friends had already graduated and left London and so I was forced to look for accommodation with strangers. It had to be cheap because I was broke, and so I answered an ad written on a scrap of paper in the student union, for a room with a very charming address – The Cottages. I get there to find that the cottages are in fact a long row of semi-detached ex-council houses with weed-and-concrete gardens and a view through the front window of a depressing brown high-rise. But the rent is cheap (relatively) and it is clean (relatively) and although I feel intimidated by the other tenants who are all men, classes have started and I am getting desperate. Noting that the bedroom door is fitted with a lock, I move in.

The room is large and furnished for student living. The walls painted the mandatory magnolia and the floor covered in the ubiquitous, hard-wearing denim-blue carpet. There is a fireplace that cannot be used and above it a magnolia-painted plain wooden mantelpiece and above that a large, frameless mirror bolted to the wall. Two brown armchairs sit side by side. There isn't enough room to position the chairs any other way so that if I have a friend round we have to sit next to each other like two people on a bus. Opposite the armchairs crouches a large, ugly but practical (rarely used) desk and above it a few shelves on which I house some books but mainly I use them as a place to store my hi-fi and CDs. A single bed completes the room, the bed, pushed up against a wide radiator, and above the bed a rectangular window, the view from it: rotting mattresses balanced on the rubbish-strewn balconies and boarded-up windows of the high-rise opposite.

It is a horrible place – grimy with a poverty that is hard to look at. I gradually get used to my housemates, two Jordanian students. They speak to each other in Arabic, at a volume and emotional pitch that leads me to assume that they hate each other. But as I get to know them I realise that that's just how they speak: all along they were just asking if the other needed anything from the shop or fancied sharing a pizza.

Throughout the first term my college attendance gradually worsens until I am barely going at all. It isn't that I don't want to go. Every morning I wake up in time for class. I meticulously dress and apply make-up and style my hair, put on my coat (hooded, floor-length, wine-red, I love it) and walk to my bedroom door. And that is it. I cannot leave. I stand at the door for a few minutes but I cannot leave. I settle into my favourite of the armchairs and stay there, staring into space, for the rest of the day. Numb is probably the best way to describe my state. I know that I feel very uncomfortable when I am outside my room but I don't consciously acknowledge that that is why I'm not going outside. It gets so days pass where I don't eat because I can't get to a shop. I don't mind. I don't feel hungry. I don't feel anything.

*

One of the few old friends to come back to uni is Stuart. I got to know him last year when we both worked in the student bar. He would come back to the big, rowdy house I lived in then and just melt into a corner, so quiet and gentle that it was easy to forget he was there. This year though he's different, he has a certain something about him. By the time my sluggish heart figures out that the 'something' is that I fancy him, it's too late and he's been snapped up by another girl.

Months pass and I live in my small way, my bedroom/sitting room like a miry pond, I leap from my lily-pad bed to my lily-pad armchair. I sometimes work at the student bar; I never go to college.

In the spring term Stuart and the brash girl break up and I take him for a drink to help him commiserate. That night he misses the last bus home. I tell him he shouldn't walk home this late at night, it could be dangerous. I invite him to stay at mine. 'The floor is really uncomfortable,' I say. 'Why don't you sleep in the bed with me'. He lies in bed facing the wall, I've never slept with anyone who takes up so little room. I kiss and lick the back of his neck. Like a frog, sticking out its tongue and catching passing prey, I stick out my tongue and pull Stuart into the gloop of my life. He doesn't seem to mind, I don't know that he has a life of his own, or one that he likes anyway. We spend all our time together now: getting stoned, listening to the radio, having sex on the single bed.

I don't tell Stuart about the days when I can't go outside, I wonder if he knows anyway. Luckily for me he tends to express his affection in gifts of food rather than words, and I, ravenous from being unable to get to the shops, gratefully devour these offerings.

It is easier (though not easy) to go out if Stuart is with me. We trundle around together, holding hands; our corduroy flares soaking up filmy East London puddles. We look for what beauty there is: pink daisies poking through cracked tarmac; twisty metal fire escapes; sunset. I like to walk around listening to Scott Walker singing Jacques Brel – the lush orchestral arrangements crashing against, and so colouring, the washed-out concrete poverty.

Home

I used to visit Brighton, before I moved here. I thought it a magical place. I remember my delight at the first sight of the Pavilion Palace, with its domes and minarets, up-lit at night, an incongruous building, transported perhaps by magic from some Arabesque pleasure land. The sea as well offered such relief after London, and clean, fat rain filtered, I guess, through less pollution, and the cream-coloured Regency houses which petticoat the town.

When I moved here Stuart moved with me. I was a fucking mess and I didn't know anything except that I was home. I used to love the sound of seagulls in the morning (at first), like being on holiday every day. We lived in a cramped, cheap houseshare and slowly I unravelled or, I should say, fell apart.

Like I say, back then I didn't know anything, so when I registered with a GP and turned up at my first appointment on a beautiful summer's day in 2001, ready to announce that I had been abused and that I wanted help, I expected a swat team of psychiatrists and therapists to rush in. As it turned out I'd barely finished my sentence before the GP started writing a prescription.

'What's that?' I ask.

'I'm writing you a script for anti-depressants,' she says without looking up.

'But I don't want to take anti-depressants, there's nothing wrong with *me*. I want counselling, I want to deal with this.'

She looks at me warily; I can tell she just wants to get me out of her office. 'I can put you on the waiting list for counselling on the NHS,' she says, 'but the average waiting time is two years.'

I open and close my mouth like a goldfish.

'If you want counselling then I suggest you pay for it privately,' she says and she hands me a card. 'This woman is supposed to be very good.' I take the card, it's light as a feather. She still wants me to get the fuck out of her office and I guess there's nothing left to say. I rise in shock, clinging to the card, it's so tiny I feel sure I'll lose it, drop it. She holds out the green prescription paper. I walk past her and out the door without taking it.

I liked Ella from the first moment I heard her voice. I was waitressing in a pub and in between ferrying plates of food I heard my phone ring. I couldn't answer it right away, but a little later, when the lunch crowd moved on, I took the phone and a cigarette out to the fire escape.

You have one new message. First message, received today, at one fifteen p.m.....beep... 'Hi this is Ella, thanks for your message. I'm sorry I didn't get back to you before but I ran out of credit on my phone. If you'd like to try me again then maybe we can arrange an appointment.'

I don't know why I liked her so immediately, perhaps it was the quality of her voice or the fact that she'd run out of credit for her phone, just like I did all the time. Anyway, I did go and meet her, in a cosy little room behind a record shop.

I don't remember being very afraid that first time. Things were going okay in my life, better than they had been in London. I told her all the worst bits of the abuse. I guess I was justifying my presence there and also testing her – watching for her reaction. She wasn't impassive, like the college counsellor had been, her face moved, she was angry and concerned, just the right mixture of fire and water. My history is a little complicated. Karl was not my real father – my real father was a married man who got my mum pregnant with me when she was only 16. So Ella asks me to draw my family tree. When I'm finished she looks at it for a minute or two. 'There's someone missing,' she says. 'You're not on here'.

We talk money. She offers me a reduced rate. It's not reduced enough but I take it anyway. The next day I look around for better paid work.

I take a job in a call centre, taking incoming calls rather than sales so it's not so bad. I'm still smoking copious amounts of weed, as does everyone in my house and indeed in my life. I even smoke on breaks at work, the security guard and I, we step outside and share a cheeky one-skin. Stuart and I share a room but that's all we share. I don't respect him and mostly I treat him like shit. He's really passive and I run rings around him. He makes his end of the rent doing bar work at a nightclub a couple of days a week and spends the rest of his time smoking weed, watching cricket, putting up with my shit.

Counselling is a trial; even walking there is hard, everything about it is hard. Ella says, 'This is the hardest thing you'll ever have to do.'

'When will I feel better?' I ask.

'It might take some time,' she says, her eyes both steely and sad for me.

'How long?'

'I can't say exactly but it might take some time.'

'Fuck.'

Walking to counselling I feel like I'm on fire, I feel like everyone can see inside of me. In the end Stuart walks me there, and perhaps inspired by Pavlov he waits for me at the end of each session holding a treat, a milkshake or a chocolate muffin, and we trundle off together, me holding my treat.

Life gets really hard now and I experience physical flashbacks, the sensations of rape – sharp pain in my anus. Unaccompanied by any visual or emotional memories, they make me feel insane. I try talking to Stuart and he does listen but there's nothing that he can do. Every now and again I get involuntary movements too – jerking muscle spasms. I name them 'convulsions' and I feel very embarrassed when they happen at work.

I break up with Stuart and tell him he has to move out. Then I get scared and ask him to come back. Then I break up with him again. He's gutted. 'You don't love me anymore,' he says. 'But whatever has happened between us I want you to call me if you need me, day or night; I feel like I'm a part of this too.'

I don't feel anything, except this pain in my anus and sometimes in my vagina now too. I virtually crawl to counselling – one time I turn up drunk. 'How do you feel now that you've come to counselling drunk?' Ella asks disarmingly non-judgementally.

'Urr...Like I'm probably wasting my money.'

*

It's January 2002 and, apart from counselling, everything I do is self-destructive. I go out drinking every night after work. I have a string of sexual encounters that run the gauntlet all the way from tawdry to downright damaging. I'm just chasing my tail, running away from problems that inevitably catch me and bite me on the arse.

By the summer my houseshare is dissolving and I have no money and no plan. I move in with a guy that I've known for a week. I'd say now that my feelings about him are ambivalent because he really took care of me at first and if he hadn't I probably would have ended up in hospital but in the end he was cruel to me and further dented my self-esteem.

Work by now is impossible. My convulsions are really bad and more frequent so I spend half my shift hiding in the toilet. I quit smoking weed, or rather it quits me – the slightest drag on a spliff brings on crippling anxiety.

I have a flashback to being orally abused when I'm a toddler, I see it happening in front of me, as clear as I see this computer screen now: Karl, holding me at the base of my neck and top of my shoulders, my feet dangling a long way clear of the floor. We are in a bathroom; I am wearing green pyjamas with a picture of a cartoon dragon on the chest. There are no physical sensations or emotions to go along with this flashback (thank God); I guess I must have left my body. I know that this is a memory – a real event that happened to me, though I lack the language to convey fully to you *how* I know. The convulsions come on strong now, for hours at a time, my whole body jerking, or sometimes just one leg or one arm. My new boyfriend spends his time arranging cushions around me so that I don't hit the wall. The convulsions are so bad that I often strain muscles. I don't leave his flat for days at a time. I am fired from work.

With no money I have to quit seeing Ella and for months I struggle on, alone in the dark, with no home, no income and a quickly deteriorating relationship. I keep in touch with Stuart; we tentatively try out friendship and meet for games of pool and beers. He makes it very clear that he's still around for the bad stuff if I need him to be.

It's like living in treacle; this time in my life, every movement is a struggle and I feel so disconnected from other beings. Ella calls one day out of the blue and says that she's talked to her boss at the youth centre where she works part time and because I'm under 25 they've okayed it for me to have a few months of free counselling there.

I get there; it's beautiful actually, a low attic room and Ella and I pick up where we left off. Ella encourages me to write about my feelings. I have no money even to buy a notebook so she gives me one – it is yellow with a butterfly pattern.

The Young Persons' Centre also does free food and advice and Ella hooks me up with someone who talks to me about housing. With no deposit money they tell me that my best bet is temporary accommodation and they refer me to a hostel for young persons. It's fucking awful but I take it. I have my own room at least. It comes just in time, catches me as the now quite opposite of caring boyfriend lets me go. I hate it there. I'm allowed one guest at a time in my room but I'm too embarrassed to let anyone except Stuart see that I live there. The staff are functionally helpful in terms of sorting me out with benefits but compassionate they are not – all young people are the enemy as far as they are concerned.

I receive £56 a week income support as I am deemed unfit to work. I spend that money quickly on junk food (the kitchen is too awful to cook in) and on going out occasionally. I meet friends in the pub now and then, try to maintain a front, and when I go home I cry and panic all night. I quickly realise that no one else is going to dig me out of this hole so I take on cash-in-hand cleaning jobs and slowly save up the money for a deposit on a room in a shared house. I've been living in the hostel for eight months and I'm well short of the money when the perfect room comes up. I call Natalie – 'The money will be in your bank account tomorrow,' she says. And so I dig myself out of the deep hole (with a little help) and over the next two years I settle down in a friendly flatshare. In counselling I chip away at the fear factory and Ella becomes the first person since Mum left that I trust. Her office becomes my first home – home being a place you are listened to and respected.

The Waiting Game

I had a dream last night:

I'm running very fast through fields. I am following a rangy old wolf. The wolf reaches a rusted gate and jumps over it. I open the gate and follow him into a field of corn that glows gold and feels like silk against my skin. I can't see the wolf anywhere. When I next catch sight of him he is tearing chunks of meat from what I assume to be an animal. Then I see that it is not an animal – it's Karl. Karl is grey and stands motionless while the wolf rips flesh from his body. Finally, when Karl's skeleton has been picked clean, except for the face, which has been left intact, the wolf knocks the bones down so that Karl's face is resting on the ground and I lean close to it and speak into his ear:

'You shouldn't have done those things, you really hurt me. I hate you and I miss you and I love you. Sometimes it's easier to be a prisoner. I've lived with you so long I don't know how to go along on my own. It's time for me to bury you now.'

And I dig a deep grave with my hands. I drag him by his skeleton feet over to the grave but I'm reluctant to drop him in. Finally I do and I throw handfuls of earth that cover his feet then legs then body then face. I cry huge tears into the grave so that Karl's face becomes muddy. The wolf cries too and I say, 'I couldn't make him love me.' And I cry for what could have been and what should have been and for wasted love and a

*wasted life (his). The grave becomes a river and Karl is washed
along the landscape and out of sight.*

My waking life is like this: A week ago Wayne promised me
they'd be arresting him today and now I'm stuck playing the
waiting game again. I'm waiting for the police to call and
tell me what happened. They were planning to arrest him at
6 a.m., to shake him up and catch him off guard. It's now
three minutes past 2 p.m.. My heart feels frozen. My skull is
filled with glass and it jangles and jars with every movement.
I am clumsy when I move, as though I am wearing clown
shoes. I am embarrassed when people see me, as I am sure
that what they see resembles no other human. And I'm just
waiting; everything else I do is pretence. I pretend to buy
bread and I pretend to eat it. I pretend to talk on the phone
and I pretend to write this. I pretend to be calm. If the police
phone and tell me it didn't happen today I shall scream; I
cannot go through this again.

At 3.30 Wayne calls, and I exhale. They went to Karl's home
at 7.30 this morning. Karl had already left the house so they
went to his place of work and arrested him there. On arrival
at the station he would have been checked in by the custody
sergeant; they would have questioned Karl about his physical and mental health in case he was in need of regular
medication or was a suicide risk. He would have been read
his rights and offered free legal advice. I am told that he
requested a solicitor. It would have taken some time for the
solicitor to arrive and further time for the solicitor to read
through the statements of accusation. Karl would have been

alone in a cell all this time. Not the nicest place in the world. It must have been lonely in there. Surely he spent some time panicking. He would have been taken from his cell and into a room where he could be de-briefed by his solicitor. There he would have been informed of the charges against him and given legal advice.

The interview lasted just over two hours. Karl denied everything of course but was shaky when questioned; Wayne says he gave away a lot with his body language. As Wayne was speaking to me on the phone he casually mentioned that Karl was still at the station waiting to be processed for release (that felt strange and weird and good). He's been charged and bailed for two months and now it's up to the Crown Prosecution Service (CPS) to decide whether there is sufficient evidence to prosecute.

For this they employ two basic tests. Firstly, they consider whether it is in the public interest to prosecute. An allegation of rape or sexual abuse will always satisfy these criteria. The second test is evidential: is there more than a 50 per cent chance, given the evidence, that the prosecution will be successful? I know nothing about this test; I think there's a points system but I don't know what is included. I'm hopeful. There are two persons alleging rape (my mother and me) and another statement which details physical abuse (my sister). There is the evidence of five years' worth of counselling (if Wayne ever gets round to collecting it), plus evidence from my GP and all the other help I have sought over the years. I stand a chance.

I feel great (in a grubby, sleepy kind of way). I feel powerful. I fucked up his day. He must be worried. I'm proud of myself. Back when the police only had my statement and I didn't think I stood a chance of sending him to jail, I decided that I wanted to do it anyway. I knew that the very least that had to happen was that they'd arrest him and question him. I decided that that was enough. I'd send men to knock on his door as a message from me to him that I wasn't intimidated anymore. Today is a great vengeful, smiling day. It is not the judgement of the court but it is *my* judgement. I am telling him what I think and who I am and what can be done to me and what cannot. And of course, I am telling those things to myself. There has to be a change, doesn't there? Something has happened in the physical world and so there has to be a corresponding change psychologically in me. We shall see.

The Worst Thing that Ever Happened to Me

The worst thing that ever happened to me did not actually happen to *me*. I guess it was morning because I was still wearing my quilted, floral dressing gown, a hideous garment but warm. And I guess it was the weekend because I was not at school. And I know that it was after my mother had left us because of the way I was holding myself, curved and hunched, feet tucked under me so that my body was completely covered and protected from the neck down; no cold could get in, nothing could get in. A grey, terrified, completely hopeless creature of about nine or ten years old, scrunched into the far corner of the sofa, furthest from the two open doors, one of which led, if you turned left, to the glass-panelled door to the street, or if you turned right and walked two or three small steps, to the foot of a staircase leading to three bedrooms, one large, one medium and one small. I was staring numbly, not at the television I think but out of the window, the view from which was the low, red-brick wall which enclosed our not-at-all maintained, small front garden and beyond it the passing traffic, which was frequent. Gaps in the traffic revealed a high, grey, thin concrete wall. Above that wall the infuriating blue-white-grey of a sky that cannot make up its mind.

I was staring very intently, but I don't remember what I was thinking before the crying started. Perhaps I wasn't thinking anything. It was during this period of my life that numbness and thoughtlessness was a condition of great relief and I would cultivate it where I could. I also tried very hard to want nothing, believing as I did, that my wishing for something automatically jinxed it. I even, for a while, began consciously wishing for the opposite of what I wanted, hoping I could trick the jinx – this never really worked out for me.

So I was sat, in a kind of stupor, when the whimpering began. It was my brother's voice and his low cries were punctuated by the cracking sound of a leather belt hitting bare skin. This went on for some minutes, and downstairs, in my world, the tension built in me. I bit my nails and moved my stare, from the window, to the doorway that led to the stairs that led to the crying. The snapping sound of the beating stopped but the cries grew louder, becoming screams and pleadings: 'No...No...No...No...No...No.' And I knew that Isaac was being raped and I located these noises to his box bedroom and the whole scene was as clear to me as if I were in the room and I felt sick to my stomach. And I had feelings. Out of my numbness came fury and I rose without thinking and went to the kitchen, crossed the cold floor, opened the cutlery drawer and took out the sharpest, meanest-looking knife and I set out to murder my father. I got as far as the foot of the stairs, the blood pounding in my ears, the world coloured blood red, and I felt such anger and such indignation on my brother's behalf. I felt the rape in a way that I never did when it was my turn, when the terror and the pain and the humiliation would drive me far from my body and the world of things that exist. I felt it and I felt the badness of it. If I did not protect my brother no one else would. I was the eldest and we were alone now. It was animal-like that anger, natural and spontaneous and demanding. And so was the fear that rose, as my bare foot touched the first step. In my mind the scene went like this: Karl would have his back to the door of Isaac's bedroom. I would push the knife into his back and he would fall down dead; that was the righteous, angry scene. But the fearful one went like this: I push open the door, Karl hears me, he easily grabs the knife from my hand and then he administers what punishment he wants, and it will be terrible.

I couldn't make it up the stairs. In the end I was too afraid and I think I was as afraid of actually witnessing the rape as I was of the repercussions. Some time passed. The screaming stopped and I returned to the living room. Some more time passed and my brother and Karl walked downstairs together and entered the room. Isaac nodded to Karl and said, 'Thank you.' So fucked up. I remember saying it to him myself once after being raped but I do not recall whether we were made to say it or whether it came from us spontaneously, maybe thanking him for leaving us alive, for raping is the closest thing to killing, in its complete negation of the soul.

The puzzling thing is that as they entered the room, out of the two of them, it was Isaac that I hated. I hated the weakness in him that had allowed it to happen, his acceptance of it and thus his complicity in it. I was ashamed of him and disgusted. But then I suppose that Karl was too terrifying a figure to hate. And it is not possible to love someone and have to listen to them being raped. It is not possible to love someone without being able to protect them and care for them. I had weighed and measured it, at the foot of the stairs, and my love would have got us both killed, and so it had to give way. Love had failed and I had failed and that is the worst that Karl did: he separated us from each other and he separated us from ourselves.

The Breakdown

Karl was arrested on the first of September 2006. Now we are almost into October. I don't think I'll ever really be able to explain what I have been through this past month but I will try. The first week of September passed with niggling self doubts but nothing that I couldn't handle. I began worrying about the things that I felt were missing from my life: gainful employment, a boyfriend, the ability to hold a dazzling and informed conversation, a shapely body and so on. By the end of that week my confidence and self-esteem had deserted me completely. The self-hatred grew into a constant, gnawing pain.

I spent a whole weekend alone speaking to various volunteers with the Samaritans. I sat, scrunched into a corner of the sofa, weeping into the phone and I felt I was floating above myself. I didn't believe the girl who was claiming to be in so much pain. She kept saying over and over again that her step-father had just been arrested because she'd complained to the police that he'd sexually abused her. She sobbed like a child who'd lost its mother. In between phone calls I tried to eat but my stomach had become a tight knot that flipped over on itself and I was shaking so badly I couldn't sit still enough anyway. I moved from room to room trying to figure out what to do. The worst thing was I couldn't distract myself. I couldn't concentrate enough to read. The noise of television brought on paranoia that there were people in the room. I listened intently to noises outside my flat and kept my eyes on the door, expecting any moment that it would burst open and the monsters would come in. All this time I was still suffering physical flashbacks – the physical sensations of rape, intense pain in my anus – unaccompanied by any visual memories, they made me feel wretchedly uncomfortable in my body. At night, exhausted, I tried to sleep but instead lay awake, shaking in a cold sweat. My anxiety took physical form. In the darkness it existed as an even darker shape, a sphere that rolled with its own electric energy. The sphere pressed down against my chest and my breathing became desperately laboured and agonising. I hated, hated, hated myself. The sphere would suffocate me for 20 minutes or so at a time and then for a few minutes it would release and hover a few feet above my bed and in those few minutes I'd try and save my life by whispering reassurances into the night. Sleep came eventually but in the morning I'd wake ice-cold and terrified and not knowing what else to do I'd get straight on the phone to the helplines. For five days I cried more than I've ever cried in my life. I cried so much my tear ducts literally ached. In the end I had to go out and ask for help.

I went to a drop-in for women with mental health problems. Someone made me tea and, seeing me about to crack, a kindly woman ushered me into a corner and nodded and 'ahhed' while I cried for an hour and a half and spluttered out bits and pieces of my story. I left with a soggy fistful of fact-sheets containing numerous helpline numbers and tips on coping with trauma symptoms. The volunteers looked really concerned and this was both gratifying and worrying. They kept asking me what I was doing next. 'I'm going to see my GP,' I said and I was but I couldn't quite face the high street right away so I tucked myself down an alley, scrunched down on a stairwell and furtively smoked a cigarette. I fished in my bag for my compact and did my best to create a human appearance but found the damage to be beyond even the powers of Clinique.

At the doctor's surgery I give my name to the receptionist and find a seat on the far end of an empty row, far away from everyone else. An infinite amount of time passes until finally my GP calls me. I leave the surgery, pick up a prescription for Diazepam and sit on some grass in the sunshine. I will myself to enjoy being outdoors but I don't feel safe. People are looking at me; they can see how defenceless I am. I go home and wait for my appointment with Ella. I spend an hour trying to eat a banana. I give up and try to do the dishes instead. I wash up a couple of cups then stop and go to my bedroom and pick up a novel, read the first paragraph and put it down again. I return to the kitchen. I spy the half-eaten banana and even looking at it makes me gag. I wash a couple of plates then abandon the attempt at hygienic living. Smoke a cigarette, check the clock 50 times then make my way to counselling. I hide myself behind a huge pair of sunglasses. I walk quickly. I worry that Ella has forgotten our appointment. She hasn't forgotten, she is there and I collapse into a chair and into tears. I cry from some place deep in the pit of my stomach.

She keeps asking if I can explain at all how I'm feeling and I try but I can't talk through the sobs. We have our first ever three-sentence counselling session and then I have to leave. I cry the whole way home. People on the street pointedly look the other way. A car pulls up beside me and the driver asks for directions. He looks somewhat embarrassed when I turn round to reveal the most tearful girl ever. However, I manage to give him fairly accurate directions and he thanks me profusely and I feel a bit better for having performed a useful service.

Unbelievably, back at my flat I start crying again. My flatmate, newly returned from holiday, sits close and holds my hand tight. I feel like her hand is pulling me from the horror of my childhood into the safe, rational world in which she lives. Eventually she pulls me out (this is what people can do) and I land in the safe world, the one where people can eat and read and watch TV. I eat and read and watch TV.

Narrowed Ambitions

An old friend, Camelia, calls and offers me an opportunity to escape my life for a few days. She's housesitting in suburban London and asks whether I'd like to join her. I say yes. We meet at Brighton station and catch a train together. I have no idea where I am going or how to get there but that's okay because I'm with someone I trust to take care of me. The house is nice: big garden; hundreds of books; massive telly; two silly, affectionate cats – the perfect setting in which to relax. There is only one problem and that is that I have taken myself there, the whole of me, pain and whirlwind anxiety included.

Camelia is thankfully averse to the idea of making a trip to central London. I cannot imagine how I would cope out there; I'm having enough trouble coping with the quiet time we're already 'enjoying'. Any moment that I am not diverted by a book or film or conversation (and sometimes even when I am actively engaged in those things), I am bombarded with thoughts and feelings of the most desperate self-loathing. I am uninteresting, unattractive, thoughtless, a socially incompetent idiot (for fuck's sake, I'm having enough trouble communicating with the friends I have and here I am beating myself up for not having more), and I'm convinced that the feelings I have now are the best that I can hope for in life. I've missed a trick; I've fucked up and will end my days stupid and alone. I don't understand why I feel so worthless. Especially now, after I've made the statement to the police that effectively says, 'He is a shit.' Why am I the shit?

There passes as pleasant a few days that could ever hope to be achieved while one is going through the emotional equivalent of the Somme. I try to pull myself out of it, I really do. I try telling myself positive things – things I am achieving, writing this book; my voluntary work, I throw everything at it, from A Level results on. I didn't know before now that it was possible to have negative 'positive' thoughts but apparently it is because even as I try to focus on my achievements every thought I think wears the same colour (grey) and every feeling has the same weight (heavy beyond endurance).

I do my best to make conversation and I find that I smile a lot as I talk but that I smile from a far-away place, like a person in great pain. I try talking to Camelia about how bad I'm feeling but the right words won't come; I end up feeling like I'm bringing her down. Anyway it's time for me to go home.

I leave Camelia at the house and walk to the train station. I hadn't confided any kind of fears to Camelia about travelling home alone – mainly because I didn't know I had any. However, the further I get from the safe house where I'd had a shit time the smaller and more afraid I feel. At the station I start shaking. I cannot for the life of me imagine how I am going to make this journey. I seem to have forgotten everything I ever knew about my relationship to everything else in the world. People on the platform opposite are looking at me (he wants to rape me; she is laughing at me; those two are talking about me). Not knowing what else to do, I find a bench, sit down, pull out my notepad and start to write:

The world seems so incredibly bright and terrifying and I have a strong desire to take my own life. I won't do it though – never. I'm really panicking – don't know if I'll make it home okay. This is the worst – this is the worst. I have to change at Clapham Junction. I'll look at the nearest departures board to find the right platform for Brighton – walk to that platform – wait for the train. Get on the train – Brighton is the end of the line – it'll take about 40 minutes. I'll get off the train – put the ticket through the machine – walk out of the station – down the hill – I'll put the key in the lock – walk upstairs – open the door to the flat – go to the kitchen – put the kettle on – make a cup of tea – sit down. If I'm freaking out then I can call the Samaritans...Train is coming. Sit here until it stops...Right – on the train – got on it safely. It's okay, it's okay, it's okay, it's okay, it's okay.

It's funny how one's ambitions narrow. Just a few weeks ago a typical list of stuff I'd like to achieve in my life would have included:

- To be a successful writer
- To be fairly rich (though obviously I'd give a lot away to charity)
- To have a holiday home somewhere exotic so that I will never again have to endure a British winter

- To find lovely, smart man – have family
- To live in a nice home, have nice clothes etc.

The revised list looks like this:

- I'd like to be able to use a train.

Dream of Peace

Now that Mum has left us the daytimes are bad but the nighttimes are worse. Without her I don't want to be alive. I miss her all the time, in the very depth of my heart. I will never recover from this. I know I won't. Some pains are too strong. *This* pain is too strong. I am getting bigger now. I am a big girl now and should stop playing with toys. It is time for me to look after my brother and sister. I have to keep them safe. Sometimes he hurts them and then I want to stab him. But I can't do it. I am too afraid he will kill me. He wouldn't need a knife. His hands are so strong he could easily just put them round my neck and do it like that. That's all. It would be over.

I like to be in the woods on my own. Though I am not really allowed, I sneak there anyway sometimes and play in the trees. The trees protect me. The trees mean no harm to me. They don't know me very well but that doesn't matter to them. They don't care about things like that. Trees are my friends. I love them and they love me. And best is that they don't want anything. They don't have to take from me and I don't take from them. We just hang out. I like to make up stories that are set in forests. One day I want to live in a forest in a crooked little house. There are lots of stories about how it's scary and dangerous in forests but they're not true. It's scary and dangerous in houses; that is true. People are scary and dangerous. Trees and animals are okay as long as you don't try and steal from them. Like when you chain up a dog for days and days. That is stealing from the dog – stealing his happy life. I hate it when people do that.

School is harder now than before Mum left because I feel sad nearly all the time. You can't show sadness all the time because people leave you out of games and don't talk to you. So I pretend that I don't feel sad and I don't care about anything. One boy calls me fat and even though I try to pretend not to care I cry in the toilets and won't come out until I stop crying. I wish I was like Leanne who is pretty and nice too. She is like me, she has dark hair but she is slim and she wears nice clothes and she has lots of friends. I'm getting sadder and sadder. I know I am. Sometimes the headmistress looks worried but she also makes me feel like I am doing it on purpose, like I could be happy if I wanted to, so then I feel bad. But I am so tired. He did it again last night. He was on top of me. My face was at his chest. I had his chest hair in my face and a funny smell. He was on top of me and I couldn't feel anything then except that I was embarrassed. But today when I went to the toilet I don't like to wipe myself with the scratchy toilet paper because it is so sore, so I don't wipe and then some pee gets onto my knickers and I worry that I smell so I sit away from everyone.

I wear the same clothes most days. Blue pleated skirt and cream jumper with long white socks and black shoes. They are ugly clothes but no one buys me different. Dad likes me to look ugly and if I try to be fashionable he says I am being

106

worldly. There is no way he will let me get my ears pierced like Leanne.

Nana and Grandpa Rees, Dad's parents, pick us up from school sometimes and look after us when Dad is working. Today they pick us up and take us to our house. Nana makes tea, fish fingers and beans with waffles. We have neapolitan ice cream for afters. We do Bible study and watch telly. Nana fusses around and only sits down when every last plate is dry and put back in the cupboard. Katie and Isaac have their bedtime first and then I have mine, a little bit later. Isaac and Katie are sleeping in the same room now and I am on my own, in the box bedroom, which is decorated with Postman Pat wallpaper, decorated for a boy. In the room is a single bed under the window, a wardrobe and a wooden chair next to the bed. It's a sad room, lonely and cold. The whole house is cold but this room seems the coldest (except for the bathroom which has its own weather system).

I miss my mum. I ache for her. I cry now, safely alone. I cry quietly so as not to wake my little brother and sister. I cry like I have been set on fire. Too late I hear the footstep on the stairs. I have made too much noise. And yet I can't stop. Grandpa Rees enters the room. He sits in the chair next to my bed, holds my hand and says, 'Hush now.' This sympathy is unusual from him and I don't trust it. Usually he is not a caring or kind person. Often he laughs or gets angry if someone is sad. But this night, tonight, he holds my hand and sings a song I have never heard before, like something a sailor would sing to a mermaid, very gentle because that is what mermaids like. I cry and cry in great heaves, I cry out the sickness and the panic.

When, after a long time, my body is empty of sobs and my eyes start to close, I hear a noise downstairs. A voice I recognise, though I dare not hope. Grandpa leaves the room and I hear his footsteps on the stairs. He has left the door open so that a rectangle of yellow light keeps me from complete darkness. The voice again. I sit bolt upright. 'Move out of my way,' the voice says, 'I *am* going to see my children.' Footsteps. I hold my breath. And here she is, like a dream of peace. She fills the doorway, outlined in yellow light, like a halo all round her. She keeps coming. I raise my arms towards her, asking her to hold me. She does. I bury my head in her chest. 'Oh Beth, oh my precious girl. I have missed you so much.' For the first time in months I rest, I rest against her body. She gets into bed with me and now my body is lying, half on her, half on the bed and because I am crying she strokes my hair.

She looks different and I touch her hands to check it is her. Her hair is short and there is fire inside of her, she is different from the one who stared into space, she is alive. It scares me; I am scared that she will get hurt because Dad doesn't like people to be strong.

I rest against her skin, enjoying the feel of it, its rolling landscape. The feel of her hand stroking my hair. Some things I recognise and some things are different. She tells me that she wants me to go live with her. 'I have a lovely flat for us, and a car and a pet monkey.' I don't know about the flat or the car but I know she is lying about the monkey – nobody has a pet monkey. More than the lies, what scares me is the fact that she feels the need to tell them. How can she not know that I would live in a ditch as long as she was there?

Why is she trying to tempt me towards something I've been praying for everyday? How can she not know me at all?

Cold air rushes upstairs as the front door opens. I hold her tighter. I will not let her go. An army of dragons can come through that door and I will not let her go. It is late, dark night now, but the front door opens and closes again and again. A rumble of voices, men's voices. But Mum stays with me and that is all I care about. I lie against her. She doesn't talk anymore, she just strokes my head.

Then footsteps. Dad's shape fills the doorway. 'You'd better come down and talk about this,' he says. 'NO!' I scream. 'You stay in your room or there'll be trouble,' he snarls. My mother untangles herself from me. Till the last possible moment I hang on to a piece of her blouse.

When I hear that they have gone downstairs and into the living room I hold my breath and, quiet as a mouse, I creep down and sit on a step. All I can hear is my own heart beating in my ears, my face glows with heat. I force myself to take short, calming breaths and I strain to listen. It's hard to hear words, though I understand the tone. I pick out the quiet, reasonable voices of Elders from the Kingdom Hall, Alan Blake and Arthur Thomas, others who I can't quite make out. 'They are my children,' my mother's tone sharp, unbending. I am very afraid for her because they won't like that. She says, 'I'm not going without my children.'

'You'll never have your children again, I'll see to that.' Dad's voice.

One of the Elders says, 'You can't take the children Hannah...Your parents are coming to pick you up, you have to go with them.'

My ear pressed against the wall, I don't dare to breathe. There is no way she is leaving without me. Car headlights shine in through the bubbled glass panel in the front door as I walk downstairs and into the living room. The men are rising from their seats. I push my way through their tough arms and legs, seeking out my mother's soft body. Strong arms catch me, as easily as if I were a kitten and they hold me away from her. The arms belong to Alan Blake, old, round and stupid. I kick his stomach (it is like kicking a mountain) and twist round looking for my mother. 'Let me go…Let me go…Let me go…' My mother is being pushed out of the front door. I punch Alan in the nose; he loses his grip and I slide down his body and run to her. I reach out to grab her. 'Take me with you!' I shout. But he catches me again. She is leaving me, disappearing down the garden path. She looks back, her hand trails as though wanting to touch me. I scream. The front door closes and she disappears.

Anger

Session with Ella:

I sit down.

Me: I'm really fucking angry today.

Ella: Can you say a bit more about that?

Me: I'm just really pissed off about how retarded my life is.
      All my friends are having babies and stuff like that and
      I'm just stuck. I just hate everything.

Ella: Would you like to draw or paint how you're feeling?

Ella goes to the corner of the room and fetches a large
sketchpad and felt-tip pens and bottles of poster paints and
brushes of different thicknesses. Using black paint and a
thick brush, I paint Karl's likeness. I picture him standing
sideways, his mouth downturned, his hands tied behind his
back. I always paint or draw him grey or black – ghost-man,
hollow-man, shadow-man. Facing him, I sketch another
figure, the figure is me. I colour myself in the clothes I am
presently wearing (brown fitted sweater, denim skirt). I draw
my arms stretched above my head and in my hands I paint a
thick club. I'm ready now to beat my father to death. With
the brush I scoop up great globs of red poster paint and
apply it to Karl's figure, first and most particularly to his

groin, then his head, then his chest, then his legs, then everywhere. A frenzy of blood spurts from the now featureless outline of the black-red man. There is too much blood for him to be anything but destroyed. It is a great picture and I love it.

Me: I love this picture. I wish I could do it in real life.

Ella: You do?

Me: Yeah, I'd fucking love to beat him to death. I'd do it really slowly, I'd take hours over it until he was just a bloody mess and then I'd have him put in hospital where they could mend all his bones and stitch him back together and do what they could for his damaged brain and then when he was healed I'd do it all over again. It could be like my annual Christmas treat.

A Technical Hitch

15 November 2006

I rush from town to my flat and have just 15 minutes to make myself presentable. I have supervision with the manager of the homeless centre where I volunteer and I'm eager to impress her. I'd been clever and already laid out clothes I wanted to wear but I'd forgotten all about tights and so I spend the best part of ten minutes pulling apart my laundry basket and searching down the side of the bed for a pair. I spend 2 minutes 34 seconds applying make-up (pressed powder; cream eye-shadow; black mascara), and a further minute locating my mobile phone. I check for a message from my boss, I'd hate to be panicking in vain; maybe our appointment has been cancelled. A symbol flashes to indicate that there is a voice message. I press the phone to my ear with my shoulder and dance my way into my coat.

The message is from Wayne Cleaver. His voice is mournful. He says there is a problem with the case. There has been a technical hitch. He doesn't want to go into it on the answer phone. He asks that I call him at the earliest opportunity. He says that he will phone my mother next and explain things to her. Jesus, he sounds mournful.

I decide that I have to go to supervision. My boss will be waiting for me. I walk out of the front door and into the street. My heart is breaking in my chest – a technical hitch! I'm going to be one of those people whose rapist stays smug and safe because the police didn't read them their rights or some such thing. I will go mad if that happens. If that happens I will kill myself because my life will make no sense and the world will make no sense. There is, after all, only so much injustice one person can take. I can see Karl's smug face as he gets away with it, as he always knew he would. I will have to kill him. I cannot bear that he will win. Everything he told me was true. I am worthless. I am powerless.

I keep walking. Salt-water brims in my tearducts but I won't let it spill and ruin my 2 minutes 34 seconds of make-up. I cannot cry now. But how will I focus? How will I speak? What the fuck will I say? I can think only of Wayne and his message.

My appointment goes as well as could be expected; I am jumpy and too loud but it's all over mercifully quickly. As soon as I am back on the street I fish in my handbag for my mobile and my diary and I look up Wayne's number.

'CID,' a woman's voice says. I ask to speak to Wayne. She transfers the call and I hear ringing, then classical music, then ringing again; I bite my lip to keep in the scream; a different woman's voice. Again I ask for Wayne. 'Are you Beth?' she asks. This special treatment is terrifying. She says Wayne will be with me in a second. And then he is. He ascertains that I haven't spoken to my mother yet. He sounds weary. Apparently, there's no easy way to tell me this. I just listen. 'The CPS has lost your file,' he says. He says he has to re-submit all the evidence. He has copies of the main statements but not of the medical evidence. He needs me to give him the list of addresses of my therapists and doctors again because he doesn't know where the old list went. 'But the case is still going ahead?' I ask. 'Yes', he replies. 'And none of this puts Karl at a legal advantage?' I ask. He says it doesn't and regrettably it's my mother and myself who will suffer the disadvantage of having to wait another two months for the CPS to make their decision. He apologises over and over while at the same time making it clear that none of this is his fault.

It doesn't even occur to me to be upset about the added time waiting time, so pleased am I that I'm still in with a chance. I don't care how long it takes. I'd rather go on forever with the possibility of him going to prison than find out tomorrow that he never will. I didn't realise until today how much emphasis I put on obtaining this justice. And even as I live through it I don't quite recognise the toll it is taking on me. For the rest of that day I run around, seeing people, honouring commitments. But when I get home and sit down I find that I cannot get up again. I am literally paralysed by uncertainty and fear.

When my flatmate gets home from work I tell her about the missing file and I start to shout, not about the criminal justice system but about my family, my mum and my sister. I shout about how unsupportive they are (I can only think now that the fear was making me lash out at them). When finally the ranting turns to tears that run molten down my angry face I feel ashamed and I run to my room and scrunch myself into the far corner of my bed. Nancy follows me and sits and holds my hand. With a voice thick with hatred I say,

'He can't get away it; he can't, because he didn't care one bit about me. And he has to care, even if I have to make him.'

And there it is.

After a fitful night's sleep I wake and before doing anything else I phone the Crown Prosecution Service in Swansea. I speak to the secretary of one of the senior solicitors there. She tells me that the file went missing for a month but has been recovered and is being processed. When I ask her where the file could have been for a month, she hints at some incompetence on the part of the police but she will not elaborate. I am heavy with questions and I ask the woman for the name and address of someone who could answer them. I feel too emotional and muddled to hang around on the phone and speak to a senior solicitor, as she suggests, and besides, I have to get to work. Before I leave for work, I telephone Wayne. I tell him that I've gathered all the addresses for my medical evidence again but that the CPS say they've found my file anyway. Wayne rings off to speak to the CPS secretary and calls me back. He says that the original file *is* lost and the one they are looking at now is the 'makeshift' file that he has put together containing the statements that he had copies of but not including any medical evidence. I ask him, 'So you *do* need these addresses?' He says that the CPS can make a decision on the evidence they've already got. I say, 'But what if their decision is not to prosecute and they haven't seen all the medical evidence, could we appeal that decision?' He seems unsure about this. I feel sick. There is so little hope that Karl will be convicted anyway, I couldn't bear it if we didn't even get to court because of something technical like this. I say to him, 'I gathered the medical evidence addresses, I have them here, I could give them to you now.' Wayne says it will be good to have them in case the CPS do request medical evidence and he asks me to put them in the post. I ask him for the address and postcode of his police station. He tells me the address but he does not know the postcode. There's a long pause while I wait for him to find it out but he just says again, 'I don't know the postcode.' I feel too embarrassed to point out that he could pick up a piece of mail, any piece of mail on his desk and it'd be on there. And so I hang up, wait a few minutes, phone the police station back and get the postcode from the secretary. I write a list of addresses for the medical evidence and post them, with them a letter asking him in three different ways to please ensure that the CPS are made aware that the file they are looking at is 'makeshift' (the word plays over and over in my mind, its fragility mocking the weight of importance inside of me) and that important medical evidence is missing from it.

Later that day, in a fever pitch of anxiety, I phone Brighton Police Station's Child Protection Unit – the people I made the statement to in the first place. I ask if I can come and speak to an officer. They say yes, I can come. It's a DC Toft that I speak to and he looks every bit the television historian – handsome face, intelligent eyes, well-cut suit and dark grey hair. By this point in time I'm something of a wreck and what comes out of my mouth is stream-of-consciousness:

'I don't know what's going on. The police say the CPS lost my file but the CPS say it was only missing and now they have it but the police say that's not the same file and important evidence is missing from it maybe and they don't know that and they might make a decision based on that and I'm really scared because I don't know what's going on really and I'm worried that Wayne Cleaver is keeping something from me and shouldn't he have had copies of all the medical evidence anyway, isn't it a breach of the Police and Criminal Evidence Act that he hasn't? It's not. But the thing is that it's hard enough going through this anyway without there being problems.'

At this point I start crying. I'm so ashamed. I make a point of not crying in front of the police, I want them to know that I'm not mad – I'm normal and believable, and deserve their help. (If I am good enough and figure out the right way to behave then I won't get raped – If I'm good enough and figure out the right way to behave then the police will help catch my rapist, and on to infinity.) At the sight of my tears DC Toft asks me if I have any counselling. It's probably a kind question but it feels like a lash, it says, 'This is a place of business, it's not a place to be hysterical.' I force myself to stop crying but then I embarrass myself again by asking the same question three times in a row. 'Do you think I should contact the CPS and make sure they know that the medical evidence isn't in the file? But don't you think I should call them, what if they reach a decision without it? I really think I should speak to someone there about the medical evidence, don't you?'

DC Toft promises to speak to the CPS and to Wayne Cleaver and to try to find out what's going on. He tells me to sit tight and take no action until he gets back to me. He repeats that advice like a mantra, slowly and calmly, as he does so his eyes narrow with the realisation that he is not dealing with a well woman.

Out on the street I sob loudly and openly and I tell myself that it is good, it is healthier to cry than to repress. But the truth is that I have no choice, it is spilling out of me, but it's okay, this is England and no one looks at me.

DC Toft doesn't call me back. I wait a few days and I call the Child Protection Unit and leave a message for him but he never calls me back.

Supervised Visits

Mum is back but we hardly get to see her. Dad tells us that she is a 'dangerous woman'. The Elders have decided that we can only see her for a two-hour visit once a week and that her visits must be supervised and take place in our own home. Dad and Adrian Price, who's here to supervise the visit, stand in the kitchen listening to all that we say to her and all that she says to us. Mostly we just cry. We cry for the whole two hours because we know she will be leaving us soon, we all know about the big hand on the clock and we watch it speed around.

I wonder now if Adrian was there to hear for himself that I didn't tell Mum anything, didn't tell her about him watching me in the bathroom and doing God knows what else. He needn't have worried, back then I kept that memory closed tight in a jar, all I knew was that Adrian scared me and I never could look him in the eye.

Mum brings us armfuls of chocolate. We all sit on the sofa, eating and crying. Katie is sat on Mum's lap, Isaac and I on either side of her; we all want to touch her. When it is time for her to go we don't want her to go. The crying reaches a crescendo and we cling to her, clutch her dress. Dad calls from the kitchen, 'It's time to go. Your time's up.'

At the door Mum looks back at him, her head bowed, her eyes full of suffering. He looks at her, a thin smile on his lips. I don't know which one of them I'm more angry with. I feel completely stuck in this world with these two people who cause me to feel such huge emotions all the time, every day; they exhaust me, they use me up.

When she goes out the door all the beauty goes with her. There is nothing beautiful of me without her because there is no one to tell me I am beautiful or precious. Without her the house is cold. The cold men stand talking in the cold kitchen. I want to go back in time, or forwards. I don't want to be here.

Because Dad hardly lets her see us, Mum volunteers as a helper at our school. This means that she helps the littler children learn to read in Katie's class and helps my class when we paint pictures, helps remind us which colours mix together. I can't concentrate on my painting, I keep looking over to her, checking she is still there. When we have finished she and the teacher peg up our paintings on a line. My mum is thinner than she used to be, I run my fingers along her jutting collarbone. Her hair is short brown with blonde streaks. It's like she is half my mum and half a stranger. But I'm glad she is here. I like to show her off, it feels special to have my mum at school.

She has gone worldly, my mum, and the Elders have disfellowshipped her which is the worst thing that can happen to a person. It means that no other Jehovah's Witnesses are supposed to talk to you. We are allowed to, while we are still young, because she is our mother, but everyone else is supposed to ignore her, even her own parents. I never tell Dad that she comes to school. I don't know if he knows. Whenever she comes to school she brings us chocolate and I share it out with the girls that I want to be friends with. They are friendly to me while I have the chocolate but when it's all gone they go back to their real friends. I want to be like the cool girls in school. They dress in denim jackets like pop stars but my clothes are horrible. Dad makes me wear cotton skirts that go over my knees with long white socks and proper shoes. My hair isn't cut often enough so my fringe is always hanging in my eyes. I'm quite podgy and not pretty like the cool girls; it makes me sad.

On Sunday afternoon I listen to the Top 40. When a song comes on that I like I press RECORD on my tape player and I make a compilation of my favourite songs – it's a pretty cool thing to do. My favourite singers are Kylie and Jason, their song together and their work separately. I've got Jason Donovan's album *Ten Good Reasons* and I play it all the time. I like Bros too, and Roxette but I haven't got any albums by them, just songs taped off the radio. I like Culture Club and the Band Aid song, although we don't believe in Christmas. They show repeats of Live Aid on the telly sometimes and they show repeats of the concert for when Freddie Mercury died. I think they are the best things I've ever seen. Dad likes Queen and Status Quo so he doesn't mind us watching them. We all sit there happy when those shows are on. He told me not to listen to Michael Jackson because Michael Jackson used to be a Jehovah's Witness until he 'turned his back on the truth.' One morning I see Madonna on TV doing her 'Vogue' video and I think she's so cool, I can't believe she actually exists. I want to be her and I pretend not to hear when Dad tells me to switch it off. 'Switch it off,' he says again, and he raises his hand. I get up and walk really slowly to the TV, still watching, mesmerised. 'Now!' he says and I press the button and Madonna disappears.

After three months of supervised visits Mum finally goes before the magistrates' court. They say two hours a week is not enough time for children to see their mother and they rule that she be allowed unsupervised access on Wednesday evenings and every weekend. On Wednesdays she picks us up after school and takes us swimming. Mum plays shark, making the noise of the music from *Jaws* and swimming after us while we scream and splash foam at her. At weekends we visit her in a tiny flat near the sea. We eat chips and play crazy golf and pool. I am the only one old enough to notice that she doesn't eat when we eat, I know she is lying when she says she isn't hungry. I know that she has no money; I worry that I cost too much.

Dad has been talking about moving us someplace far away, like Scotland, and so I tell Mum this, one Saturday while we are visiting her. Her eyes become wild – darting this way and that and it makes me feel afraid. The whole day she watches me intently. In the evening she makes my favourite sandwiches – cheese and salad cream with lettuce and lots of crisps on the side. She watches me eating and I watch her not eating. Isaac and Katie are sleepy after a day of sea air and Mum takes them off to the bathroom to brush their teeth and change into pyjamas. Then she tucks them into the solitary bed (I sleep on the floor) and returns to where I am sat still eating. She kneels in front of me and takes my hands in hers. 'Beth, I have to tell you something.' I move the plate from my lap and place it on the floor. I am already on the verge of tears, I don't want to know, whatever it is, I don't want to know, I am so tired, to the core of my soul I am tired. 'Karl isn't your real father,' she says. I gasp for air as though I've been speared. 'Beth, Beth, look at me,' she squeezes my hands and I force myself to look into her eyes but I can only do it for a moment because I feel so confused like I am falling through a spiral in space. The rest of what Mum has to say is punctuated by my own silent epiphanies. 'You were six months old when Karl and I got married.' (I've never thought it odd that I've never seen their wedding photos – it must be because I am in them.) 'Your real father was married when we made you.' (If Dad is not my dad then Nana and Grandpa Rees are not my grandparents.) 'As far as I know he's still married now.' (Are Katie and Isaac still my brother and sister?) 'We were only together very briefly, he was twice my age. Beth, look at me.' I look into her bright blue eyes, brimming with tears. 'Darling, you were a mistake. I was just sixteen when I became pregnant with you. You were the best mistake I ever made.' (He's not my father; my life didn't have to be like this.)

I get up and rush to the bathroom. I lift the toilet lid just in time. I vomit and vomit, my favourite sandwiches bob on the water, barely digested. Mum stands behind me, rubbing my back, 'Oh, sweetheart, I shouldn't have told you so suddenly, it's just I couldn't bear for Karl to take you away from me, he's not even your father, he has no right to take you away.' I scoop tap water into my mouth and stare hard at the girl in the mirror, pasty white and shaking and someone who is not quite what she seems. 'You must be in shock,' Mum says.

'It's not that,' I say, trying to make Mum feel better. 'I probably just ate too much.' But for the rest of the night I can't stop shaking.

January 2007

Bullshit – waiting – bullshit – waiting. I fucking hate this. I hate the world and all its bullshit. I'm so upset. I've barely slept in days. Just before Christmas Wayne left a message saying that he'd sent the recovered medical evidence to the CPS and that he was expecting their decision mid-January. Today is mid-January – pretty much exactly. It's the afternoon of the sixteenth day of 2007. I hate New Year, I hate time passing – I hate the way nothing ever changes for me. I cried yesterday afternoon as I made my way round the shops and I cried in the evening on a bench as I sat facing the sea (a woman stopped and asked if I was okay – in all my years of crying in public that's the first time anyone's ever done that, I really appreciated it). I cried all night and felt abandoned. I don't even know why I'm so upset – it's like my heart is keeping secrets from me – I guess it's the strain.

The pain, when it comes, is unbearable. I want to unpick my veins. The source of all this pain is my life, my being – it was never Karl's intention to ruin my life – he just wanted to come inside something, or to feel powerful, or whatever it is that rapists want. My life is a by-product. Books and books of writing – more tears than seems feasible – pain – shyness – self-loathing – a fucking prison – my body, not only strange to me but uncomfortable, cumbersome, painful, an enemy – watching other people's lives – other children playing – and now, couples caring for each other and feeling so jealous and separate from them.

And everything turns on this fucking decision that's taking so long because the only acceptable outcome is for Karl to go to prison. I can't live in the world without that. There's not enough room for both of us – I'm trying to kick myself some space – I demand more room.

Aubergines

5 February 2007

Still waiting for the CPS decision. I wake up – I don't want to be awake. I stay in bed. I try to go back to sleep. I nearly make it there, but not quite. I'm starving. I'll have to go outside. I have no food except fruit. I don't want fruit. I want Middle-Eastern potato cakes smothered in hummus. I wonder if they still stock them. I haven't seen them for a while.

I can't go outside. It's too bright and I'm too dark. I want nothing to do with this day. Make it quick. I dress in yesterday's discarded clothes and I hide my face behind a huge pair of sunglasses. Now I feel safer but everyone will hate me because I look like one of those pricks trying to be cool.

In the supermarket I can't see very well in my non-prescription sunglasses. I bump into two people and they look at me like I am dirt. There are no potato cakes and no courgettes or aubergines either. Perhaps they are seasonal. Perhaps everyone knows not to expect courgettes and aubergines at this time of year. I start to panic. I put back the cherry tomatoes and the red pepper and the red onion because you can't have couscous and roasted vegetables with only those three vegetables, you really need a courgette and an aubergine.

Three cans of baked beans for £1. I'll take those. And

strawberries are 50 per cent extra free – I see they're from Egypt. My friends are saying how it's bad for the environment to buy food from overseas. I hesitate for a moment, but strawberries are one of the only fruits I like. I check out the reduced food – there's loads of it today. Chinese ready meals and lasagne, packets of ham and a yellow cardboard box with two custard slices and a sticker on the box that says: REDUCED – WAS £1.09 NOW £0.81. I decide not to buy any of the reduced food. I go to the next aisle and look at the yoghurts but I can't concentrate. I'm imagining the taste of a custard slice in my mouth – the sharp sweetness of the icing – it's divine. I want to taste one for real so I go back to the reduced section. I'm sure everyone is looking at me, watching the crazy girl who can't make up her mind. I add the custard slices to my basket.

Waiting at the checkout I survey my products. Custard slices and chocolate milkshakes are bad but strawberries and cannellini beans are good and baked beans and Greek yoghurt are neutral, I think – it's a fair mix. The girl at the checkout seems off with me. I can't remember if I said hello to her yet and so I do now, halfway through packing my stuff, but after I've said it I remember that I had already said hello and now she seems even more off with me. I can't wait to leave this supermarket and get home. I want nothing to do with this day and this day wants nothing to do with me.

Out on the street the sun is shining and even through sunglasses it seems too bright – it makes me feel dirty, this light. On the corner the ginger homeless man, holding up a copy of the *Big Issue*, looks right at me and shouts, 'Good morning!' All I can manage by way of reply is a watery smile.

As I round the corner the strength leaves my legs and in my chest throbs a grief that's so far beyond tears that I'm not even sure there's a word for it. I look down at the floor. I think I am going to have to sit there with my shopping. I can't go on. I take a breath. I look down the street, a few hundred yards and I'll be home. I will not sit on the ground. I have never collapsed on to the street in the middle of town, I won't start today. I walk on, but it is difficult. My legs feel hollow and my skull pounds gently with madness – I will not give in.

At home I unpack only what needs to be refrigerated, everything else stays in a plastic-bag bundle on the floor. I pick out a DVD and I grab the purple quilt from my bed. I pour milkshake into a tall glass and I drink slowly as I lie on the sofa watching the film and I eat one custard slice and then another.

But I only half watch the film or quarter watch or maybe even less. I don't know what part of me is here today – in the land of the living – but most of me is scared and most of me is really sad and I don't want to listen to that. My legs and my heart and my choking-tight throat are trying to tell me that I feel bad but I don't want to listen – not today – I felt bad yesterday and some of Saturday and a lot of Friday and I don't want to feel bad anymore.

At the same time as watching the film I start thinking about what I'm going to do after it's finished. I think that maybe I'll go for a walk. Sometimes I like walking, sometimes it makes me happy to look at the sea and even at the other people who are walking or running or being together in a couple or playing, if they are children. I think of all these things and I feel very afraid in my chest. When I imagine myself on this walk I feel self-conscious and too vulnerable – anyone could hurt me or scare me.

The film is nearly ending and now I'm really panicked because I haven't decided what to do next. If I go for a walk then maybe I will have a nice time and I will at least have got some exercise and that is good. If I stay here then I will probably stay sad like I am now and it will be bad because I'll be lazy.

As soon as the film finishes I grab my laptop and check my email. I'm excited because there are 23 new messages but then I'm disappointed because they're all from Amazon and other businesses.

And then I open up a new Word document and I write all this. I think that it might change things to write them down – but it hasn't. I still have a sad and frightened heart and a throbbing-crazy head and a choking-tight throat and I bet that if I stood up my legs would want to fall. I nearly cried just now writing that last line. I nearly cried three times while writing this – but I didn't cry. I don't know why. I'm not crying. I just feel bad.

I'm Not as Strong as Her

7 February 2007

I'm at my yoga class and as usual I am rubbish compared to everyone else. I'm just not bendy at all and I can't sit up straight and my hamstrings are too short. I'm getting angry with my stupid body: everyone else in the class can do most of the exercises with ease – and most of them are prettier than me – and they're fucking smiling! We've been doing bending exercises for ten minutes now – *sitting up straight, buttock flesh lifted and moved behind so we can feel our sitting bones.* (Really? Where? How much flesh would I have to move to feel them?) *Legs out straight, toes and knees pointing to the sky, bend from the waist, reach for the toes, chest lifted and breathe.* My body gives me a small range of options here – I can lean forward a little but the pay-off is that my legs bend so that my toes point forward rather than at the sky. Or, I can sit with my legs straight but in that position my torso is actually leaning backwards.

The teacher comes over and adjusts bits of me. He's really kind and gentle and I wish he'd just give up on me. It takes ages for him to get me into anything even resembling a yogic position. Finally the teacher seems satisfied and walks away to adjust someone else. Across the way from me a pony-tailed woman is looking at me with concern. It's then that I feel water on my face and realise that I am crying. I leave the room quickly and I lock myself in the disabled toilet. I can hear the crying now, and when I look in the mirror I can see it on my face. The crying gets louder and I think, what can I do about the crying? I decide that I have to get home. I wait for the crying to pass – this takes ages. I look at my face – it's blotchy pink and red and white. I go back to the class. I tell the teacher that I have to go. I collect my things. He says that I'm welcome to stay in the class and just lie down. 'I have to go,' I say.

Out on the street the situation seems like a maths problem. My thoughts go like this: 'I just had to leave a yoga class because I was crying. That's only happened once before. It was really bad when it happened before. Is this bad? Do I feel bad? Maybe I should ask for help?'

At home I pick up the phone and I dial the Samaritans. A posh-sounding older woman answers. She gets the wrong end of the stick and says, 'So you're worried about your step-father and these allegations against him?' I feel really angry and say, 'No, I'm not worried about him, he raped me for ten years.' I nearly hang up but realise that she doesn't mean to upset me, she just heard me wrong. I cry in big, heaving blocks of pain that punctuate the phonecall like sheets of rain. I tell her about the waiting and how it's making me crazy. I tell her it's like noise in my head and that sometimes I manage to shout above it but it's always there. She asks me if the noise in my head is physical. 'No,' I say, 'it's metaphorical.' She tells me that she's not supposed to give me advice, but if she *was* to give me advice, she would advise that I phone the police and tell them how distressed I am, get them to chase it up. 'Yes,' I think. I thank the Samaritan and I hang up and I dial the number for the CID.

By a marvellous coincidence Wayne Cleaver answers the phone. 'Wayne Cleaver, CID.'

'Hi Wayne, this is Beth Ellis.'

His voice sounds weary as he asks, 'How are you Beth?'

'Actually,' I say, 'I'm tired of waiting.'

Wayne tells me that he understands how I must be feeling – there's a lot I feel like saying to that but I rise above it. He then tells me that it's out of his hands. He says that he's going to call the DP (Duty Prosecutor) and get back to me. I pace around my flat; the phone rings after five minutes. Wayne says he's spoken to the DP, that he's been promised that the file will be read tomorrow and that we'll get a decision by Friday morning.

I explode, 'They haven't even read it! All this time and it's just been sat on a desk. This isn't right. I have been upset for a month, waiting every day to hear something. It's not right.'

Wayne agrees with me, 'I'm on your side,' he says. I ask him for the name of this slack Duty Prosecutor. Wayne provides it gladly: Christopher Talfan Davies. I'm hardly likely to do anything with that information – what strength, what energy do I have to complain with? But it makes me feel better to have it there, to at least know the name of the man who has my life in his hands. If he decides to prosecute then I expect that I will fight and plan and try and work through it like always but if they don't then I am worried about suicide. I make an appointment with my doctor. I'm going to get her to prescribe me something just in case.

I think back to that little girl who existed without prescription drugs, without anyone knowing what she was going through, without help and support and times without any love or kindness. I am not as strong as her.

The Diary

When I am 11 years old Karl reads my diary. I return home from visiting Mum and walk into the living room to find him sat on the sofa, his head in my precious book. I feel a sharp change inside me, from happy to scared – like in a horror film – everything going along nicely, then out of nowhere a monster drops down and blocks the path. I am very afraid (What did I write? What did I write?). And even in that world of him taking huge things away from me, it is a huge thing for him to take away from me.

With a shaking voice I tell him that he shouldn't read my diary, that it is private. He replies that I shouldn't have left it lying around then (it was under my mattress, I would never have left it lying around). At my next protest Karl raises his hand to strike me and so he wins. My throat burns with tears as I take the book that now lies between us – a bridge from his head to mine, I hate him; I wish I was dead. And in great shame I stand outside at the *No Hot Ashes* wheelie bin and tear each page into tiny pieces so that no one will ever get into my head again. And I can't stop the tears now because I loved keeping a diary like a normal girl; and is there nowhere that I can rest?

Mum and Steve

When I was 12 Mum married again. She and Steve have a big 'worldly' wedding. I wear a pink bridesmaid dress with puffy sleeves and a fake flower hair-clip. I hold myself up straight because there are cameras everywhere. They get married at a registry office and then we have a buffet lunch in a hotel. I drink sherry and sashay around thinking I look pretty. In the evening there is a big party with bands and more food. There's maybe 200 people here, nearly all of them are Steve's friends. I dance and have fun. The room is full of curling cigarette smoke and glinting sequins. There is so much goodwill here, people relaxed, men and women kissing and dancing together. I make quite a fuss when we have to leave and when I see Dad I forget to give a disapproving report of the whole thing.

Karl's wedding the year before had been a different affair, cold, awkward, his new wife, Barbara, a bullying crone. His best man was Adrian – hey, who else are you going to choose? Once you've bonded by abusing your daughter in front of a mate then there's really no one else for the job!

The wedding isn't fun, I don't like my stupid peach-coloured dress. For the sake of the photos Dad raises his hand and through gritted teeth he says to me, 'Smile.' I grimace at the cameras. There is a buffet at a community centre. A few dry speeches are made. ('When I first met Karl we got off to a flying start because I asked him what his hobbies were and he said, 'Raping children,' and I said, 'Well now, that's a coincidence' is not what is said.) A small amount of wine is consumed. Dead people have more fun than this.

Dad is married to a 'good' Jehovah's Witness and she is unintelligent, violent and mean. Mum is married to a 'bad' worldly person and he does all the worldly things, smokes and drinks and uses bad language, and he is well liked and generous and non-violent. Barbara tries to get me to call her Mum, I refuse and she hits me. I say, 'You're not my mum.' She hits me again, hard across the face. 'Your mother is a slut,' she says.

I phone Mum and tell her about Barbara hitting me. She speaks to Dad, shouts at him, 'That woman has no right to hit my daughter!' Dad looks weak caught in the middle of this squabble; I see him flounder.

When Dad first took us to meet Barbara, even though she was a Jehovah's Witness, she had brassy blonde hair, curled and bobbed, and wore bright pink lipstick and blue mascara, jeans and a pink tracksuit jacket. Now, stood in our kitchen, months after marrying our father, she is a changed woman. Dad doesn't like that his possessions might be attractive to others so he has stopped her dyeing her hair and now it is mousy-brown and basin cut. He has stopped her from shaving her legs and armpits so that tufts of hair poke from the short sleeves of her dress. She has become fat. She is miserable, dark and fierce.

She is the lightning rod for all my hatred. It is safe (relatively) to hate her. I speak to her with contempt. When she talks to me I drown it out with an internal monologue

('Fuck off you stupid bitch, fuck off'). With puberty came swearing and the growing realisation that they don't know what I'm thinking after all. So when Dad forces me to apologise to her I can still, in my head, say what I really think ('You're a stupid fat bitch and I hope you die'). I start using it on Dad too, so when he tells me to make him a cup of tea, I make it and pass it to him and at the same time in my head I say, 'I hope you fucking choke on it.'

Breasts and blood arrive overnight. I am 11 years old and still at primary school. No one has warned me about periods so when I go to the toilet and find thick red blood in my knickers I think I am dying. There is no one in my house I feel safe to ask about it. The bleeding continues. I worry that I have done something wrong and am being punished. I feel dizzy. I almost pass out. I lean on the cistern. I keep wiping it away but the blood keeps coming. I don't think to put a wad of tissue in my knickers. I go around the next few days, bleeding into my knickers and going to the toilet every few minutes to check myself.

Katie, Isaac and I visit Mum and Steve for the weekend and it's Mum who notices blood on my clothes in the laundry. She takes me to the bedroom with a bowl of soapy water and gets me to strip off my trousers. I feel embarrassed too because the curtains aren't drawn shut, but I'm also embarrassed to point that out so I just do as she says. She washes me down like I am a toddler. She tells me about sanitary towels and she gives me two packets. She adopts a soft, patronising tone as she washes me, 'Oh Beth, look at the mess you're in,' and I feel like I've done something wrong. She manages to impart the information, too late, and without it feeling in the least bit empowering. She makes me feel like I should have known better (from who, Mum? Who the fuck was going to tell me? – But that is my grown-up self asking – back then I just burned with shame).

In Dad's house I am slapped, ignored, both kept on a tight leash and left to my own dreary devices. Karl monitors what I wear, what I watch on television, who I associate with. No effort is made to entertain me and I am just supposed to be good with no reward. But at least now that Barbara is here I no longer have to share Dad's bed.

Most weekends we stay with Mum and Steve. They treat me almost like a grown-up. Steve calls me 'kid' but in a friendly way, not patronising, he says, 'All right kid?' or 'You're a good kid.' They ask me my opinion of their plans. They let me watch grown-up videos, they don't care what music I like.

When I am 12 some school friends ask me to go with them to a park a little way from our house. I know that if I ask permission Dad will say no, so I don't ask, I just go. My friends and I swap gossip, swing from the climbing bars and use our feet to push ourselves on the torpid, lop-sided round-about. I can feel the fresh air pressing against my face. I am utterly free. My friends here look like monkeys, with their cheeky faces and their ears sticking out through lank hair. For them this is just another afternoon in the park. They do not know that I am a revolutionary; they do not know that I am changing the world order. My heart is wide open. I soak up everything, every blade of grass, the rusty swing that hardly moves, the wide grey sky and faintly glowing clouds. Shabby trees with black rubber supports. The space around me and inside of me. I look down to check I am standing on the ground. I am. The sun comes out and shines on our faces.

I hear a car screech to a halt on the gravel waste ground, the squeak and slam of a car door. A long shadow stretches across the lawn and chills me from the inside out. Soft footsteps. I don't look; I won't look. A hand grabs the collar of my coat and drags me backwards. I drink in my five-minute friends; I'm still enjoying their faces even as I am being pulled away from them. He throws me on to the backseat of the car. He gets in the front and he starts the engine. He turns around and checks behind him while he reverses out of the gravel pit. At the same time he snarls at me, 'You are going to be in big trouble when we get home.' All in one fluid motion, the checking, the driving and the threat. I can see in the driving mirror, the rectangle of my face crying, puffed and red, and I don't understand why my heart still feels free. At home I run straight to my room. I know he will be here any minute. And he is. He takes his belt off. 'Pull down your knickers,' he says.

'No,' I say.

He comes closer. I back away until I am scrunched into the corner of the room, as far away from him as I can get.

'Do it,' he says.

'No!' I say and I mean it, he will have to kill me first.

He stares at me; he flounders, seems to understand that something has changed. He leaves the room and I hear him walk downstairs.

As soon as he is gone I run to the phone and dial Mum's number. 'Pick me up,' I say. 'I want to come and live with you.'

Dad towers over me as I talk to her. When I hang up he sits on the stairs and cries, real wet tears. I feel guilty that I have made Dad cry.

I don't pack and I don't say goodbye to anyone, I just stand by the front door until I hear the car pull up and then I leave the house.

Without any belongings I get into the car and we pull away. Steve drives and Mum sits in the passenger seat. She turns around every now and then and stares at me with an intensity that makes me squirm. 'Are you all right? Are you all right, Beth?'

I say nothing; I have forgotten how to speak. I can feel the road moving so fast beneath me it makes me sick. I feel the world stretching to accommodate this new space between me and Dad, me and Isaac, me and Katie. Thinking back makes me confused. Thinking forward makes me confused too. And being right here makes me want to be sick.

At my new home I am numb for weeks, my heart frozen. Mum and I have no method to speak truthfully to each other and even if we did I don't know who or what I am. I am bug-eyed, in thrall to events of my body that my mind has yet to catch up with.

There's just the three of us in this house, except at the weekends when Katie and Isaac visit and Steve's children visit too. I am the eldest and separate from them. I have a lot of space here, a big bedroom with a double bed. Mum and Steve say I am pretty but I don't like the way I look, I don't recognise the girl in the mirror. I spend a lot of time look-ing at her, looking for myself in her; she confuses me. I like my legs; the rest of me is too podgy. I spend a lot of time alone, lying on my bed with my legs up the wall. I listen to whatever music I want to.

There is a musty atmosphere to this house because Steve has so many old things and he's not one for cleaning. In fact, left to his own devices, as he is in his 'study', his possessions sit in toppling piles, rotting and unused, all preserved in a film of nicotine. When he first took my mother home it was so messy she thought he'd been robbed. When they first met Steve was kind and she was broke. I hope there was more to it than that but I don't know. He's nice to me, respectful, but he's not nice to himself, he drinks every night and chain smokes, he works in a job he hates for low pay. He has a lot of friends but he talks about not wanting to impose on them. Since she has been with him Mum has gained lots of weight. We eat a lot in the evenings, eat and watch the television.

A few weeks after leaving Karl's I let myself into the house after school and I make myself a snack. Steve comes home and startles me; I'm not comfortable with him yet and besides he's not usually back this early. He leans against the kitchen counter, my eyes trace him, from the ground up: steel toe-capped black boots; black trousers; black shirt; round belly; grey-black beard; the window behind him, sunshine and leaves. 'Kid, your mum's in hospital,' he says then inhales sharply. 'She tried to kill herself.'

I put down my sandwich, feel my heart stretch heavy like rollered concrete. Steve puts his arm around me, he smells of sweat and I don't want him to touch me but I know he's just being friendly so I don't say anything, just stiffen until he moves away. 'She bought a pack of paracetamol from every shop in the village, took them all and then phoned your grandad.'

I say nothing.

'Come on, kid, let's go see her.'

Steve takes this all in his stride, seems chirpy in fact. I sit frozen in the passenger seat, in my mum's seat. We drive to a great white and windowed hospital and park in the enormous car park. Inside we find our way to an open visiting area, lots of people and chairs. It's easy to tell the visitors from the visited. The visitors are all chirpy; the visited make no effort to be anything. My mother looks like an empty puppet, all that's there of her is meat. I think she's a fake and a fraud. I hate her weakness; I want to hit her. I don't talk to her. I don't play the game. She doesn't look at me. I feel a wall rise inside me. Why can't she stay with me? What is it about me that's so hard cope with?

Steve goes outside for a cigarette and I follow him. 'I wish I could smoke or do something,' I say.

'It only helps if you're used to it,' he says and he offers me the pack.

'No, I'm not used to it,' I say and I wave the pack away. But I like the fact that he offered – treating me like a grown-up.

'We'll get fish and chips tonight,' he says, 'and I'll give you some money to get a video out.'

'Okay,' I say.

Bonnie 'Prince' Billy

9 February 2007

I'm cleaning Cherry's house with my mobile in my pocket, waiting for Wayne to call, like he promised to and tell me whether the CPS are going to prosecute Karl. But no one calls. By 12.30 I am mopping the floor and crying.

Cherry finds me like this and hugs me and asks whether I would like to phone the police while I am with her. I say yes. We sit in her living room and I phone and speak to an officer at CID. He tells me that Wayne is out of the office and he asks me if he can help. I tell him that I'm waiting for a decision from the CPS. He says that most of the CPS haven't been able to get to work today because of snow. I ask him to leave a message for Wayne to call me, whether there's a decision or not.

I cry more and then Cherry offers to drive me home – but I decide to finish the cleaning – 'I have things to do,' I say, 'I cannot *not* do things'. When I have finished the cleaning Cherry offers me lunch – I hesitate – but accept. We eat soup. She asks me questions about my life and I tell her. I tell her so truthfully and unreservedly that I feel like I can breathe and I feel more myself than I have ever felt and it feels more okay to be myself than it ever has before. When I leave, it is with something – with marrow in my bones, with nourishment. I had shared with Cherry my belief that Karl and I are two sides of the same coin – our fates fixed together. I tell her that if he goes to prison then I can get out of prison. Cherry does not think that will happen. She does not think that my freedom is dependant on Karl's incarceration – she says it will take time and therapy to repair the damage he has done but that I will get there.

Later that day I come to realise how much of my energy I expend on worrying about what will happen to him, when really I have no control over that. I realise that I can only really control what happens to me and to my life. And that feels right – I feel free in my body then and I can breathe.

Even though I left a message asking him to call me, Wayne never calls me. It's horrible, it makes me feel like I am nothing.

The weekend passes and I do many things that are brave. It is good that I keep doing things even though it is very difficult. If I live in fear then he will win. I travel to London on Sunday – I have a ticket to see Bonnie 'Prince' Billy at the Shepherd's Bush Empire. When I first arrive at the venue I feel embarrassed because I am on my own. I look around. There are lots other people who are on their own – it's that kind of gig. And there are some very impressive beards on display. I like this crowd: friendly losers – not too cool.

The support act is terrible and seeing as I arrived so early my legs are aching from standing up – I feel depressed – she really is very bad. I have travelled to London – the whole trip, including the ticket, is probably going to cost me £70, and here I am standing on tired legs listening to a badly dressed 25-year-old sing about how we're all going to die one day – as though we need reminding.

I go to the bar. I order a beer and a shot of whisky. I down the shot and carry the beer back into the bearded crowd. I spy a little balcony area – it doesn't look too busy. I get myself over there. It's nice, plenty of elbow room and I can see over the crowd and have a perfect view of the stage.

When the band amble on I laugh – the guy couldn't be less of a pop star – he looks ridiculous in a black and red checked deer-stalker, and even more ridiculous when he finally takes it off to reveal a head that's bald on top and thick with ginger, sticky-out hair at the sides. None of that matters, he is amazing, even his shambling dancing and opaque jokes – whatever. He's one of my favourites, I've listened to his songs in my bedroom for years now and I love them. The band play best in the encore – then they rock and he really pulls it out of the bag, he becomes a front man and it's all the better for being so incredulous. I look over the whole audience. I am the only person there who's dancing – what the fuck do these people think music is for? I can't stop my body moving and I don't want to – I'm glad to be me – I'm glad to be there – I wouldn't swap any of it for any fucking thing. I leave the place feeling very drunk and very alive.

Lots of running and a lucky delay miraculously gets me on to a train that I should have missed by 15 minutes or more. I haven't had a chance to buy anything to drink. I take my life in my hands and drink water from the train toilet all-in-one motion-activated tap, soap dispenser and hand dryer. I drink the 'NOT DRINKING WATER' from my cupped hand until I am sated. And then I find a seat, curl up, throw my coat over me and doze my way home.

I don't remember walking to the flat. I don't remember getting into bed. The first thing I know is that my mobile phone is ringing and it's really loud because I've slept with it next to my head and my stomach flips with the shock. The display says *No number* – that means it's Wayne. I answer. He apologises for not calling me on Friday – he was hardly in the office because of the snow. His apology means nothing to me. I ask him if there is any news. He hasn't spoken to the CPS yet but he's going to call the Duty Prosecutor later. 'There's no point calling them till after lunch,' he says. 'They're usually in court in the morning.' I ask him to please call me whether he gets a decision or not. He says he will.

I'm awake now. It's early and I'm still tired but I'm awake. I wonder what I should do. I potter. I do nothing. I just move stuff around, wash about three dishes, hardly worth filling the sink. I take 2mg of Diazepam. Around 1 p.m. I fall asleep. I've set an alarm so I won't miss counselling at 4.30. The phone rings at 3 p.m. and my stomach leaps to my throat. Wayne says he's been promised a decision tomorrow morning. He apologises, he says the system is unfair – it's always the victim that suffers. I hardly know what I say.

I don't know how to cope with another 'night before'. I can't stay here. I can't be at home. It's too depressing – here – with my thoughts – and my room that's barely habitable right now, the floor full of papers and books and clothes and tea mugs, the bed I get into every night all scrunched-up, the sheet come undone so it's only half-covering the mattress and a smell that I can't quite pin-point, and that might well be me – and there's not an ounce in me of the stuff that makes people sort these things out.

I am getting ready for counselling when my mobile rings again. It is Wayne. He sounds very grave and very official. He has heard from the CPS. They have decided to take no further action on either statement. I don't say goodbye before I hang up.

12th February 2007

Dear Ms Ellis

Re: R v Karl Rees

The South Wales Police have sent me the file relating to your allegation of rape against Karl Rees since the CPS is now responsible for deciding whether or not charges should be brought against him. As the Crown Prosecutor responsible for reviewing the file, I have to make that decision. I am writing to explain the reasons for my decision not to proceed with this matter further.

When deciding whether or not to prosecute, I have to follow the guidance set out in the Code for Crown Prosecutors to ensure that our decisions are both fair and consistent. Crown

Prosecutors must consider whether there is sufficient evidence and whether it can be used in court and is reliable. If there is not a realistic prospect of conviction, the case must not go ahead, no matter how important or serious it may be.

I have carefully reviewed the papers sent to me by the police and have decided that there is insufficient evidence to proceed further with this matter and have informed the police accordingly.

Rape is an extremely serious charge and on many occasions the prosecution case has to rely on one person's word against another as it does in this instant. Therefore any other evidence that assists the prosecution case is very valuable. Equally if there is evidence that undermines that case, this too has to be taken into account when making the final decision whether to charge or not.

I have read all the papers in this case and have had access to some of your psychiatric notes. In the file of evidence there are other witness statements, the contents of which do not corroborate your assertions and in some instances plainly contradict what you state. There is no evidence that actually supports your allegations, other than your own statement. I do not wish to outline all the problems in this letter as there are many intimate and personal details in your evidence, which the defence would inevitably bring to a jury's attention. Whilst I appreciate that you may be disappointed with the decision that has been reached I hope that this letter will help you to understand how I came to my decision.

If you have any queries relating to this letter or any other matter, or if you would like a meeting with me please telephone Mrs Linda Davies who could arrange such a meeting. I would *ask that DC Wayne Cleaver attend also. However I should point out that I have made my decision and all I can do is explain my reasoning for that decision.*

Yours sincerely

Christopher Talfan Davies
Senior Crown Prosecutor

I Don't Know How to Carry this

I don't know how to carry this. The world changed shape again today – and still there's no room for me. I keep opening doors and behind every one there's either a monster – or fuck all – fuck all for me. I'd be better off dead. I tried to do something about it, I try to show people what he did and they say there's no case to answer – two statements alleging rape and there's no case to answer – there are people in prison for not paying their TV licence. I gave everything to this and I put too much on it. I didn't know. I would never have put myself through this if I'd known. It hurts so much. I don't know where to go now – that was my road. Even in a world of huge things being taken away from me it is a huge thing that they've taken from me. I am in so much pain and for what? For nothing. It was always for nothing – I could just never get used to that idea – it's for nothing – it means nothing – he loses nothing. I don't know how to carry this.

I wanted to fix it. I don't have a plan B. I don't know how to heal it now. It's as if I've been told that I have a broken arm and that I'll always have a broken arm – every day it will hurt and every day I'll see people doing things that I can't do. I wanted to make everything right for her – for that little girl – alone in the dark, crying and sore – aching and dreading the next day. I wanted to fix it for her – make it right – make the world safe for her. Now it will never be safe. Karl is subject to the same random kindnesses as I am – he enjoys the same sunshine days and sometimes people look at him and they smile. I'm not tough enough for this. I'm not tough enough to live in the world with monsters.

I can't get out of bed. I wake up crying. I phone Stuart. He comes round. He climbs into bed next to me and puts his arm around me and I lay my head on his chest and cry for three hours. I say to him, 'If I ever become terminally ill I'm going to kill him. If you were terminally ill would you kill him?' Stuart says, 'I'm thinking of ways I could kill him now.'

Because I feel suicidal I phone around to make sure there can be someone with me all the time – otherwise I'm scared that the images in my head will become real – the image where I sit in the bath and unpick the veins of my wrists or the image where in the same bath I take the meat cleaver to my throat or the image where I collect together all the pills I can put my hands on and I swallow them down and never wake up again in this stinking world where a man spent ten years raping me, another man spent a few days investigating it and another man a few hours reading about it and a few minutes telling me no – you cannot have what you want. I'm dead anyway. This has killed me.

I have an appointment to see Cherry – I barely make it there. I can hardly walk. There is nothing inside me. All the marrow has drained from my bones and I am all edges – I am hollow now. My mother is talking about fighting it and now Cherry is saying the same thing but with what – I gave it everything I have – there's nothing left inside of me. Her office looks beautiful – the real-looking fake fire is lit and the scene is so pretty that it seems silly, absurd that it should have any part in this day. I cry of course and I am angry and I tell her that I feel like a stupid girl for thinking that things would be different. 'I wanted him to go to prison.'

Cherry says I still have the book – that I can get him with the book.

I feel feverish with grief. 'But the book was supposed to be about what it was like to face your abuser in court. It was supposed to end with Karl going to prison and with the judge saying how brave I am then banging his hammer and sentencing him to life. I don't want to be here. It's not supposed to be like this.'

Cherry says the book is important, whether Karl goes to prison or not. She says that I am talented, she says it over and over and when she says, 'I never say that unless it is true.' Her tone is almost angry. There she is again, drawing me back into the world when I want out – telling me I can have what I want in the face of incontrovertible evidence. But there's a part of me that believes her and that wants to believe her, in the pretty office with the magically real fire. And when I hobble from her office it is not with marrow in my bones for they are still empty but with a tiny piece of fire, fierce and bright, that I carry in place of a heart. The fire fragment shifts its shape. Sometimes it is molten-hot and it burns down old things to make room for new. Sometimes it is a safe-warm light that shows truth against the shadows. And sometimes it is cold and hard, a jewel resting inside me, waiting for the next touch. It is all I have in this new world. But it has not been touched by him. Always it is mine. This is bottom – and this is what I have found here.

Paula

I keep myself alive somehow. I take Diazepam – I stay in bed. I try not to be awake. I've called an emergency session with my friend Camelia and at 7.30 I leave my house and begin the sea-front walk to Camelia's flat. I'm halfway there when my legs seize up. I turn from my path to look at the sea. It looks so inviting – indifferent – peaceful – black with white stripes: simple, knowable. I consider doing a Virginia Woolf – filling my pockets with stones and walking onwards until my head is covered up and my pain is no more. The only thing that stops me is the thought of leaving him alive. If I go – he goes.

I keep on my path but it's so hard and I'm crying now. I'm crying when Camelia opens the door. She takes my hand and I cry for two hours and say all the 'why's and 'how's and 'what now's. Camelia says that people love me – 'So many people care about you and you'll have that no matter where you go in the world. He will never have that.'

I ask her to promise to kill him if she ever becomes terminally ill. She says, 'Perhaps we should both start smoking again, speed the process up.'

'At least if one of us does get diagnosed with cancer something good will come out of it,' I say.

And we laugh. I am fed and given wine and we talk about people we fancy and films and normal stuff. Drunkenly, I fall into a taxi and then into bed and the hangover the next day doesn't help matters – but what can you do!

Over the next few days I go to the Survivors' Network drop-in and to their closed support group, which I am participating in for the second time and which is far smaller than the group I did with Katharine. I take my place in the circle of seats, everyone knows the news I've been waiting for. As soon as I'm sat they ask me, 'Did you hear anything?' It's awful to have to tell them and watch their faces crumble. If only one of us could beat one of them – just once.

Over the next weeks Paula, a fellow participant in the group, takes it upon herself to phone me and send me text messages, sometimes two or three times a day. Asking if I need anything – shopping? Someone to listen? Wise and funny and rude, Paula takes the time to step outside of her own life and into mine. She listens while I loll, slumped on my bedroom floor, and simply cry down the phone, my tears washing clean rivulets along the dusty receiver.

'I don't think I can make it,' I say.

'I know Beth, it's so hard. I can't really imagine what you're going through right now.'

'I just don't think I can live with this.'

Sometimes we talk like this for an hour or more at a time. I wish I could say that I would have been so generous, had the roles been reversed, but I don't know. Just a year ago Paula changed everything in her life, she rose from the dead, and pushed away the tombstone that kept her from life. She gave up her thankless but well-paid care job to follow her heart's first ambition – to become an actor. Every day at acting class she is implored by her teachers to be authentic, to reach into her own experiences and so every day she has to look inside and see what's really there – much of it heart-breaking: abuse; neglect; betrayal. She cries for weeks before a performance and doesn't sleep, and then, on the night, she pulls it together and is brilliant. I've never seen anyone run at their issues like she does. Paula is one of my heroes.

You Explain it to Her

A tiny part of me understands the decision of the CPS. The cold-rational adult part – the one that studied a degree in law – the one that argued for the rights of defendants – the one that read thousands of words in hundreds of books – about *The Law*. But it was not her who was hurt. Try explaining to a five-year-old who has just been raped that nothing will happen to the monster who tore her body from soul and took pleasure in doing it – you explain it to her.

I live in the place where terrorists are born. With too much breath and no one to shout it at: disallowed; disenfranchised. Politicians, society, laws – they do not speak for *me* – they do not protect *me*. I am an outlaw – I could do anything now. It does not matter whether I am good or not. It does not help *me*.

Istanbul

I phone Katharine who's in Istanbul, teaching English, to tell her of the CPS decision. I know, because of our shared experience of the Survivor's group, that she will be one of the few people to really understand what I'm going through right now. I am beside myself with grief. She says softly, 'My flatmate is going away soon, why don't you just come?'

Within the hour I am booked on a flight and within a fortnight am there with her, in the most different place I have ever been. A patriotic, self-referential place – from the shops and bars of the absurdly crowded streets, float pop songs about 'Istanbul', so that over and over in my head, like a football chant I hear, 'Istanbul!...Istanbul!...Istanbul!...Istanbul!'

I feel drunk. I love Istanbul, a city split by the sea, with its curvaceous skyline and its street-hawkers and singing buildings. I spend a few days on a wide-eyed breakneck tour of the city, hanging on Katharine's arm, safe and happy, with aching legs.

And then I am left alone. Katharine has to go back to work. And so we compile phonetic lists of useful words and make idiot-proof maps. I am given keys and sent on my way – out into the world. I manage to find my way by ferry to a quiet town called Eyup and I walk (all alone) up the hill and to a famous café with a famous view of Istanbul. When I am finished with my drink and with the view I walk very quickly down the winding hill, not wanting to miss the ferry and on my way I refuse the assistance of a taxi, but without confidence – though in the end I do make it – only just.

On the ferry where I sit (deliciously alone) the sun is beginning to set and a smiling, thick-set man offers me a glass of tea from the tray balanced on his arm. I accept and I pay him a coin. The glass is curved like a woman's silhouette and presented on a shiny-gold saucer with a spoon and a cube of sugar. I drop the sugar-cube into the steaming tea and I break it with the spoon and watch it dissolve. I pass the glass from hand to hand, keeping my palms warm. I sip the tea and it is delicious – dark and bittersweet. I look up at the sea that is now streaked with pink reflections of sunset. I feel a kind of happiness spread inside of me that plays not only in a different note from any I have felt before, but in a whole new key – a secret locked inside of me (a good secret for a change) – sent flowing by the combination of a city divided by water and the habit of a civilisation to drink tea from small glasses.

On my last night in Istanbul I cook a roast for Katharine and me. A miracle to produce anything from that mini-oven – but there it is – perfectly good roast potatoes and veggie sausages with onion gravy and boiled carrots and green beans. When Katharine arrives home from work, I am distracted with last-minute gravy making and carrot draining. And when we sit down to eat I don't really enjoy the meal – though I am satisfied that all turned out well. I guzzle wine. I drink five glasses to Katharine's two and I start to cry and we talk about the 'war'. I cry like a little girl and I feel like a little girl. Bewildered by the wine, thin raspy sobs come from a place underneath my stomach – an old, old place.

'I wanted him to go to prison,' I say.

Katharine shares my outrage and she talks of her own failed reporting – to social services – she had worried that her father might be abusing her young sister as he had abused her. Social services looked into it and found nothing. Katharine was left feeling disbelieved. She also lost her sister, her father won't allow Katharine to see her again.

I cry a lot. 'I wanted him to go to prison,' I repeat.

'And they just ignored you,' Katharine says.

'No, they didn't just ignore me,' I slur. 'They sent me a letter of explanation. I got a letter.'

I drift from Istanbul then and back to my childhood and the letter left on the mantelpiece (behind the carriage clock) in explanation of my mother's absence – in place of her – how woeful it was as a substitute. And the new letter – a woeful substitute for a prison sentence. I am numb with the pain.

Katharine holds my fierce gaze as I say, 'How can it mean nothing? How can being raped for ten years of my child-hood mean nothing?' She doesn't know but at least she holds my gaze.

Drunkenly, I propel myself from the sofa and towards the bathroom. I collect a wad of toilet tissue and I blow my nose into it. Carefully I re-close the wood and glass living room doors, the better to keep in the heat of the gas-bottle fire. Between blowings I say, 'It won't do for me.' I realise how pompous I sound. 'I'm sure it won't do for anyone,' I concede. 'But it really won't do for me.'

Katharine talks about a Danielle Steel book she read about a rich woman who is raped in Central Park. Her family rallied around and got her therapy and in time she recovered. Katharine says, 'I read it and I just felt like...' She doesn't have to finish her sentence; I know exactly what she felt.

I start to cry again. 'I wanted a Hollywood ending,' I say. 'I have to do something. I have to avenge myself. I guess I have the book but I wanted it to have a different ending.'

'It will have a real ending,' Katharine says. 'It is a book for me and all the other women who don't have Hollywood endings.'

Then I get angry. 'It's just, you know...I wanted something more substantial than sitting in circles talking about my feelings. I didn't want the ending to be me making some bullshit piece of art that represents my anger. I don't want to make a fucking angry quilt.'

Laughter bubbles out of Katharine, 'My God, that's funny...Jesus Christ, even when you're crying you're funny. That's quite an achievement.'

I want to live in this sudden warmth, so to make it last a little longer I exaggerate my slurred speech: 'Instead of being a book about justice it can be a book about how I became a drunk and a quilt-maker.'

Katharine cackles and I feel pleased with myself.

I shake my head, 'What are we going to do?'

'Live', says Katharine, eyes flashing, hard as steel. 'We live the best lives we can.'

'Right,' I say and I start to cry again.

162

The Summer and David Leigh

Back in Brighton I feel crushed by the CPS decision. I feel cynical, bruised, let down. I sit in Cherry's study and tell her how shit life is – how impossible – how pointless, awful, fucked up. She suggests that I take a break from writing the book. 'Perhaps you should take six months off,' she says and she shoots me a pained smile.

I am stunned into silence and I sit with my mouth agape. 'But, but, but...I don't really do anything else.'

It's true: I clean a couple of houses; I work one day a week with people who don't have adequate accommodation, people less fortunate than me, which helps give me some perspective; I cry and I write my book. That's it.

'It's up to you; it's just a suggestion.'

'But you think I should?'

'It's up to you to make that decision, but I do think it's important that you know that you have that option.'

I worry that Cherry will go away if I stop writing – that she'll lose interest in me.

'I'll be here,' Cherry says. 'I'll still be here.'

Over the next days the idea grows on me and I speak to Cherry. 'Yes, yes,' I say, 'I think I will take the summer off.' I imagine spending time doing physical things – walking, swimming and yoga – getting back into my poor body. I tell

Cherry. We have our final meeting and to quell my anxiety over losing her we make a date to meet again in September.

In June I move out of my shared flat and into a studio flat – completely independent for the first time ever. All of my belongings fit into it perfectly and there's a desk at which I can write and built-in shelves for all my books. I have hardly any money so progress is slow in decorating it. But I find things in the street – a cream rug, slightly clawed; a small round table that sits in the bay window. One day, when I'm picking up a dress from the menders, the Chinese seamstress, to make up for the fact that the dress isn't ready, tells me to pick out whatever buttons I like from a tupperware box that sits in the window. I do. I diligently sort through handfuls of buttons and after ten minutes she says, 'Why don't you just take the lot.' I carry the heavy box through town, cradling it, leaning it against my body. It comes with me on my chores through the shops. In the supermarket I joke with a cute cashier about paying for my groceries with them. He picks out a bright blue and a brass button. 'This should cover it,' he smiles.

At home, I spend two days totally absorbed – sorting the buttons into piles of colours, and on the wall, over the fireplace I start to stick them on with blu-tac till a shape starts to emerge, a butterfly with a black button body and colourful button wings. It's very me, this buttonfly, in some primary colour arts and crafts way that I hadn't known about before. I don't know if I've ever really played before.

I discover that I love flowers. I start visiting the park near my house, a walled garden, full, this year particularly, with

164

hundreds of flowers. I don't know any of their names, but I explore them. I smell them, every one, and I feel their leaves, gently touch their petals. If they are trumpet-shaped flowers then I crouch down so I can look up into them. If they are planted along a path then I sit in the path – the better to look at them – it doesn't matter, hardly anyone comes here anyway. It's a kind of meditation, this time with the flowers, when I forget myself and the constant soundtrack – who I am, how I compare, blah, blah. It's a cool feeling, and exciting at the same time. The same thing happens every time I walk, from the lawn of the greater park, under the low stone doorway and into the walled garden – an exhale – ah. And for a moment, sometimes a few minutes, sometimes an hour or more, I am happy – if happiness is to forget the self and discover something wonderful then I am happy.

Out of the blue Cherry calls me. She asks if we can meet. 'Certainly', I say. It is lovely to see her and to be in her house. I am feeling fine, calm, happy even. I sit opposite her and she tells me excitedly that she had lunch with a friend of hers last week. 'An investigative journalist, David Leigh, he writes for the *Guardian*. He's been working for ages on a big corruption piece and feeling burnt out with it and wants to write something more human interest. I told him what's happened to you with the CPS decision and he'd be interested to know more. It's not certain that he'd want to investigate and even if he did there's no guarantees that the *Guardian* would want to run the story. But what do you think? Can I tell him a little more about you? Perhaps show him some of your writing?' She fixes me with a quizzical look.

I squirm in my chair. 'Of course it's what I want ultimately with writing the book, you know for this to be exposed, and not to feel ashamed. I mean I'd really like to be the kind of person who could do that...it's just...well, I don't know.'

In the end I tell her that I will think about it. I sound out a few friends. I nod appreciatively at the ones who think I should do it and ignore the ones who voice caution. I email Cherry and tell her that if her journalist friend is interested in writing about my story then it's fine with me. It's ridiculous making decisions like that, about things that are so utterly unknown. But yesterday I'd reached the end of the road and today someone's laid down another step and I have to walk it.

Cherry phones and asks me to pick out a few pieces from my book so that David can read them and get a sense of my story. Immediately after I hang up the phone, I pick up my laptop and read page after page of my story (these pages, this story). I start by reading with one eye half-closed – in defence against the expected rubbishness. But that's not what I find. I see myself in December, January, September and February – standing outside of a police station, chain-smoking cigarettes and crying on the phone to the Samaritans – waiting for phone calls, praying for phone calls – numb, traumatised, hot-cold, a broken toy, a plaything gone mad, trying so very hard to be civilised, to NOT MAKE A FUSS. God bless me. I wish to hold myself – and the wishing is *like* holding myself; it is in fact love.

Cherry says she will phone me after her meeting with David on Friday. Friday comes and I am out most of the day – where,

I don't remember. I do remember getting back to the flat and nonchalantly picking up the phone (I may even have put the kettle on first so little do I care). I listen aghast to the unbroken dial tone; the charade comes to an end (I do care, I do care). I fidget and pout, sit on my bed and then on the chair. The phone rings. It is my mother. We don't talk for long.

It's late and I'm getting ready for bed when I remember that I need to call and check tomorrow's plans with a friend – she's a night-owl, she won't mind me calling. I pick up the receiver and hear the broken purr of the dial tone. I call the message service. Cherry had called – at the same time as my mother had – she had called and left a message during the only ten minutes that the phone was in use. 'David and I just had a wonderful meeting,' there are train station noises in the background. 'He loves your writing and he's really interested in investigating your story. I think we should all meet soon. Well done, well done for being such a terrific writer.'

How exciting. I sit on the edge of my bed and listen to the message three times and beam and kick my legs. I do the only thing that feels appropriate in the circumstances – I take down my new sun-hat from the wardrobe and put it on. I pull down one side of the brim in a chic 1950s style. Elegantly, I sit down and I flick out my wrist as though holding a cigarette holder. I say to no one in particular, 'David Leigh *loves* my writing,' and I laugh and feel the happiness.

The next week I walk to Cherry's house to meet with her and David. I am very nervous. I feel silly and inconsequential. I sit down with them and Cherry introduces us. 'As well as writing for the *Guardian*, David is professor of journalism at City

University,' she says. 'You might want to think about going into journalism one day,' and she smiles at me brightly.

'Beth is a real writer,' David says. 'She won't have to do that.'

His words are a marker in time and life after he says them is subtly but tangibly different than life before. Despite the praise, I feel out-classed by these two power-ful and intelligent people. To be fair, they are twice my age. Both of them brown-haired and brown-eyed – Cherry petite and David slight to medium build. They would be woodland creatures rather than safari ones, but the wiliest and sharpest in all the wood.

We sit in the conservatory, surrounded by growing pots and with the doors open on to the cheerful patio-garden. For an hour or so David asks me questions and I answer as fully as I can though by the end I am exhausted and say less and less, like a clockwork doll winding down. I produce the CPS letter informing me of the decision not to prosecute and both David and Cherry are shocked by its rude, abrupt tone. The letter provides me with the option of meeting with the decision maker, Mr Talfan Davies, and hearing a full explanation. I tell David that I've already written requesting this meeting and am awaiting a reply. We discuss the possi-bility of David coming to the meeting but he's concerned that he'll be rumbled as a journalist. Cherry volunteers to come with me instead and pretend to simply be my friend and take notes for David. I'm overwhelmed by her offer.

David clasps his hands and taps his fingertips together in a rolling motion. 'You've taken on some very disagreeable men,' he says and smiles. 'We can do one of two things, or perhaps both. I could try to put pressure on the CPS to change their decision; or I could write an article exposing Karl.'

He may as well have said – Would you like this pot of gold or would you prefer a bag of diamonds? I'm not sure what the word is for what I felt, sat between two competent, intelligent and powerful adults, both offering their help. It's not a position I've ever been in before. It wasn't a big feeling – quite restful, one part shock, two parts relief.

The next day I'm sat on a plane heading for the South of France, on one of those super-cheap flights where the airline is practically paying me to get on. I am meeting a friend there, he's convinced me to join him on a big organised walking holiday. 'You'll love it,' he said. It is only when I am on the plane that I wonder what on earth I am doing – I've never been on that kind of holiday before and camping and eating with loads of people I don't know – the dreaded hairless monkeys. Oh well, I think as we pass through a cloud, it's already happening now.

For the next week I live an utterly different life. Every day I walk, with a hundred or so other people, through the French countryside, mainly trails through forests, soft underfoot. Our heavy rucksacks and tents are carried in vans so we walk lightly, carrying only drinking water and a waterproof jacket should the weather turn. Even when it does rain we are mostly protected by the trees. Every afternoon we stop somewhere pretty for lunch and a van turns up with boxes of foot-long baguettes stuffed with salad and Brie. We take two-hour lunches that give time to nap or explore or chat. Some days are so hot that it's all we can do to pull our bodies to the shade of a tree and lie down to sleep. The afternoon walk, on country lanes and trails (we hardly ever see a car), brings us to our camp for the night. A different spot every night, always near water, a lake or a river. The crew have been there all day, setting up a kitchen and digging pit toilets.

For the trip I've brought a pop-up tent that's super-easy to put up every evening and take down every morning. And for me, that's the most satisfying part of the whole trip. After a 7 a.m. breakfast, standing with the strangers, some of whom I'm getting to like, standing under trees, in the mist, queuing at great vats of porridge and coffee, with tin cups and bowls, we take down the tents. Because we have stayed for only one night the grass springs right back up and there are no markings to show that we've been there. We leave no trace, the toilets are carefully covered with earth, the surroundings checked for rubbish. We take forest paths to our next destination. We are silent mainly as we walk, contemplative, the forest forces us to engage with it, to find our way around temporary collections of watery mud. When I see blackberries I pick them and eat them.

For the first few days, as I begin to feel safe, I feel anxiety pour from me like water. I do wobble – the despair grabs me even there, maybe even especially there, without the usual distractions. But I talk about it – I confide in a couple of the strange hairless monkeys and it gets easier.

I make friends easily, like I exhale and there is a friend and I exhale again and there is another friend. One gloriously bright afternoon we stop for lunch near a stone bridge over a river that looks like something from a painting or a dream. Blue dragonflies skim its surface and in shallow places it becomes a water-garden of soft green moss, long and flowing with delicate white flowers. My friend and I cross the stone bridge and eat our lunch quietly away from the others. We dip our feet in the cold water – it feels delicious. People are starting to get in and swim. I curse; I've left my swimming costume in my rucksack. I spot my new friends standing under the stone bridge, singing siren songs. It is too much for me to have to watch this. In a practically unheralded act of unselfconsciousness I strip down to my bra and pants and I jump in the water and swim under the bridge. I explore the water with my friends, splashing and testing the sand floor with my toes. I pick white river flowers and stick them behind my ears. I explore on my own, finding a place where the stones are so high and the water so shallow that I can sit cross-legged in the warm sunshine while the water rushes past me on either side. I laugh. Magic dragonflies dart past me and there is sunshine everywhere. When it is time to go I dry myself with a shawl and I put on my T-shirt and cut-off jeans and walk underwearless through the cool shadowy forest enjoying the jagged and erratic light display. That evening, as the sun sets, we erect our tents in a big circle around a lake. As a child of the 1980s I thought that what I wanted out of life was a penthouse apartment, a leotard body and a fiancé who looked like Alec Baldwin. But now it seems that all I want is a pop-up canvas home, a bowl of rice and a tree to look at. I have never been more content than this.

Thursday, 2 August 2007, 11.20 a.m.

Hi Cherry,

I just had an upsetting phone call from the CPS prosecutor – trying to put me off coming I think. He made it very clear that he's not going to change his decision. He said, without my asking, that a rape specialist has looked at the file and made the same decision – he made reference to the fact that my mother had affairs and how that would undermine the case – and less insulting stuff like my brother's evidence. He hammered on about the sensitive psychiatric evidence that undermined our cases but when it came down to it he said actually there was nothing that he thought undermined my evidence and just one ambiguous sentence in one of my mother's reports. He says he doesn't believe I could remember abuse that happened when I was two or three years old and that I should remember more about abuse that happened later.

Anyway. We're still on for the 21st at 2 p.m. He's worried about speaking about sensitive abuse and psychiatric issues in front of third parties (i.e. you). I don't mind if you don't. People can leave the room if needs be.

Oh I hate him – I hate the way he was just talking to me like he was doing me a big favour – actually protecting me from court. He actually said that a failed case can be more traumatic – but he didn't finish his sentence – more traumatic than what? Not going to court – how could he possibly know? Horrible, patronising man – no reference at all to the fact that he's just taken something very important away from me – no, just that he'd stepped in and stopped me doing something very foolish and harmful to myself. (I was polite enough to him though.)

Excuse the rant – going cleaning now.

Bx

Thursday, 2 August 2007, 11.39 a.m.

Hi Beth,

Picked up your email and was shocked, so I phoned hoping to catch you before you left for cleaning. Anyway, I have copied your email to David, hoping to catch him before he leaves for Scotland. I'm really angry on your behalf. As you say, he sounds as if he is trying to put you off. Horrid man. And we will not be put off. Good news is that the meeting is confirmed for 2 p.m. That also gives me plenty of time to get there by train.

Give me a call later. I haven't got patients today.

Love, Cherry

Paper Wings

I wake in fear. A terrible dread in my chest, I'm so terrified of going home to Wales for the CPS meeting. I feel so utterly and desolately alone. I feel desperate. I move from bed to desk. I hope to write out the fear – write some sense in. Two pages of adult irritations and worries and then a little fist taps against my shoulder and I turn around and I see *her*.

...with no thoughts of love I bang my paper wings against the glass dome of my cage – the enormous world. All night I cry into a hole in the world – but one which I cannot squeeze my wings through – I wish more than anything to be gone from this place. This world of plates and cups and false smiles – smiles that are not meant for me – smiles that do not signify my happiness. My little heart beats so fast – it will break inside my body – I am sure of it. I only wish it would be over sooner – I want to get out, out of this world – he is nearly here – he is nearly on me – shadow-man – hollow-man – reaper-man – Dad. There is no way out of this life – nothing for me to do but pray to die. Please, God let me die, please, God let me die, please, God let me die, please, God let me die, please, God let me die, please, God let me die. I can't take any more, God...

I feel as though my stomach has been eaten out, leaving a bottomless chasm through which my heart falls. I will never have a normal life. I will never be happy. All this badness is stuck to me – grafted on. If I could pull down the moon I would use it to smash my head against. I want to spill my brains – I want to, I want to, I want to. I could spray black blood from my arms – I imagine the gush would bring coolness and relief. Stain the solar system. My whole world is rape-coloured. I see no way out. There's no way out of these rooms with men, rooms with men, rooms with men. Looking, prodding, deciding. Deciding for both of us. If I could sick it up I would. But I can't. I can't live with it inside me and I can't get it out. I don't want this life. I don't want it. I keep making mistakes – I mistakenly am alive – I don't want it, I don't want it, I don't want it. Nobody understands. I can't do this. I swear to God I can't.

Monday, 13 August 2007, 11.37 a.m.

Dear Cherry,

I'm worried about how desolate I feel. I'm still not sleeping properly and my body feels awful – tense and painful. I cancelled working at the homeless centre today because I felt too vulnerable. My life feels really hard – I hope it will get better. I've lived through these feelings so many times but each time it seems like I can't possibly bear it. I feel lonely. I feel really angry at people for being happier than I am. I am in bed writing about these feelings for my book. I have my curtains closed. I know I'm probably not helping myself but it's hard to know what to do.

None of this means I want to give up fighting the CPS or writing my book. Nor do you have to reply – I just wanted to tell someone. But if you do have any suggestions they'd be most welcome.

Bx

Monday 13 August 2007, 12:05 p.m.

Dear Beth,

I'm really sorry you are feeling so bleak. But I am not surprised all these bad feelings have come back to the surface this week. After all, you are about to go back to Wales, which is bringing up so much stuff for you, both from the distant past and recent stuff to do with the case. Also, knowing that the meeting with the CPS is going to be a horrible experience isn't helping – that was the idea of his phone call to you, of course, he wants you to cancel so he tells you it is pointless going, nothing will change his mind! But as you say, you are not going to give up fighting, or writing your book. Also you are not so alone in the fight this time round, you've got some big guns on your side. I know that's so hard for you to take on board. But I have to keep saying it until one day you can hear it and believe it without all the turbulent feelings that we talked about last week.

I'm concerned about you not sleeping. It may be worth talking to your GP. The important thing to remember is that although life is really hard at the moment, it will get better. I am sure of that, meanwhile look after yourself.

Love, Cherry

Meeting with the Crown Prosecution Service

17 August 2007

On the train on the way to the dreaded CPS meeting, two stops from home, I pull out my notebook and I write these words:

The clouds are dark grey and the mountain is dark green – against it stands twisty tubes and stark steel shapes, machines or buildings, I don't know which. Water-cooling towers made of ridged concrete – accidentally beautiful – a giant's flower-less vase. And the industrial smell, here unlike anywhere else. I don't know how people live here – I guess they get used to it. In Brighton, along the alley that leads to my street, a heavy honey-suckle bush cascades down the wall. I like to imagine that even with my eyes closed I could find the way from the cornershop to my flat – I could smell my way. And now, on this train, even if I had my eyes closed I would know where I was. It stinks.

My mother is there to greet the train and so are the shiny, expectant faces of Jasmine and Tim, my little brother and sister. There is no time to be maudlin now; all the usual questions have to be answered (yes, the journey was fine –

no, no delays). And at home Jasmine and Tim have a host of things to show and tell me. Tim demonstrates his recently perfected sofa somersault and Jasmine reels off a barrage of really awful homemade jokes. (How do you get a lion into a freezer? Ask the giraffe to get out first.) At the end of which she wiggles her eyebrows in a zany manner and asks, 'Get it?' – not in the least perturbed by the groans of her audience. They are such fun it would take some effort to remain completely depressed while in their company.

Days pass and for the most part I am okay, except the day before the meeting with the CPS. It's a horrible day – I wake like thunder – late, 11 a.m. – and I shuffle downstairs and collapse on to the sofa. Mum tries to rouse me but her attempts just infuriate me. I tell her, 'You're such a pain in the arse.' I still have a pile of little yellow Diazepam pills but I don't take any – I don't want to numb myself before tomorrow. Mum fusses around me, offering this and that to eat and drink. We have a fight. 'Stop trying to make it better,' I say.

'I'd do anything Beth, believe me I'd do anything to make it better,' she says and she looks at me with such intensity that it sets the floor swimming. 'I love you, Beth.'

'This is me!' I shout and I jab my forefinger into my chest.

'And this is me,' my mother says quietly, tears brimming in her eyes.

She and the rest of the family go off in the car. I can't deal being with them. All I can think to do is walk. I follow a footpath well worn from teenage days, with the canal on one side and the fast-flowing river on the other. The far side of the canal drips with a cornucopia of wild flowers, pinks and purples. I focus on my feet – feel my feet on the ground.

The canal deposits me smack into the centre of the village and I walk the length of the High Street, which takes all of three minutes. With nothing else to do I turn around and walk back home – off the main road, past the chapel – up the winding street, past the house with the rickety boat parked outside – the boat's name, *Whirlygig*. Flowers everywhere. Delicate blue flowers poking from the cracks in the rough stone walls, flowers in the kempt and the unkempt gardens, in hanging baskets and pots, in wild meadow-like lawns – flowers and grey stone. The people seem incidental.

At home I make myself a drink and a sandwich. A friend arrives – there is a baby to admire – I admire and tickle and ask the feeding-sleeping questions. In the evening I stuff down a pizza and three desserts – making myself sick with food – old habit, oldest habit. Outside the sun is setting and opposite us a crescent moon sits atop the ramshackle council house. The street lamps, which just moments ago were clear glass, now glow sherbet-orange. In the fading pink sunset we play a complicated game involving three hoops and four balls of different sizes. This game (at which I do badly) is punctuated every so often by Tim or Jasmine calling out, 'Chase me, chase me.'

I make the same reply every time, 'You must be mistaken, you must be thinking of someone else. I never chase people.' And with that I run like hell up and down the street trying to catch them. If I succeed then they get tickled but if they're touching the wall that means they're in the den and I can't get them.

I sleep fitfully. I wake from dream after dream where people have stolen things from me – burgled my house – stolen my jewellery, precious letters. Not difficult to decipher the symbolism of this, today, the day I'm going to meet the man who's stolen justice from me.

Out of bed I take a notebook and myself straight through the garden and into the Wendy house. There I sit on a pile of old sofa-cushions, Jasmine, pottering around, picking armfuls of sweetpeas, is framed by the heart-shaped window. I write myself three pages of love and hope. Three pages of 'you can do it'. I try to meditate for a while, just breathe in and out. I sit with myself through muscle spasms that shake my whole body and through layers of heart-grinding despair and self-loathing. I sit and I breathe in and out.

Mum calls up the garden that I need to get ready and so I head into the house and bathe and dress. I'd picked out a dress for the day – the one that Katharine gave me – apron-shaped and alive with bright pink flowers. I check and re-check my reflection. Maybe this dress isn't sober enough, I think. And then, fuck it; I'm dressing for myself, not for them. And besides I want to take Katharine with me in some sense, I want to speak for her too. I want to take Ella with me too and so I pocket the turquoise stone that connects us – the sister stone to the one I gave her.

The day is over-bright; I feel exposed, nowhere to hide. Mum brings the car round and I get in. She drives us along miles of motorway then turns off for Swansea city centre.

As we wheel our way towards the train station I glance up familiar streets and try to decide whether or not this is a nice city. But the streets are clogged with bad associations and there's no way for me to judge objectively.

I get out at the station and Mum drives off to find a parking space. I stand nervously anticipating Cherry's arrival, I feel sickly unsure about mixing together these separate elements of my life. Here, in Wales, I am surly, awkward, out of place. Back in Brighton I try my best to be something else, something more. Cherry appears; she looks like herself but smaller, less certain. We hug and I take her outside to meet my mother. Mum is nervous too, she said to me earlier, 'I just hope she likes me.'

'What's not to like?' I'd said and then guiltily started to compile a list: the melodrama; the lack of focus; the swirling emotional torrents of words which occasionally appear and disappear, apropos of nothing at all; the lipstick on her teeth; the haphazard grooming, hair patchily home-dyed…

'I'm sure she'll like you,' I said.

Mum arrives and greets Cherry with the special-strength warmth that she reserves for people who have been kind to her children. We walk together through the city's heart. I try to think of something interesting to tell Cherry. 'Anthony Hopkins grew up in Port Talbot,' I say and Cherry raises both eyebrows. I walk ahead, leaving them to get to know each other; I suddenly feel very young.

We locate the CPS office then head into the pub next door. Karen, Mum's friend and support, has arranged to meet us here. It's lunchtime, Cherry orders bacon, egg and sausage. I order a pot of tea; I'm too nervous to eat.

We find seats in the paving-slab and pot-plant beer garden, chunky wooden chairs with great thick armrests that rather get in the way. The sky is white. I sit in my girlish Katharine dress and quietly search for a foothold; I am waiting for my courage to arrive. Karen finds us. Mum rises and gives her a hug. When everyone is introduced Cherry says, 'It's important that Teflon-Davies, or whatever his name is, doesn't suspect that I am taking notes on behalf of the *Guardian*. It's very unlikely that it will even occur to him but if he asks then I will just say I'm Beth's friend.' Her mobile phone starts buzzing and she answers. Cherry catches my eye and covers the receiver, 'It's David, do you want to talk to him?'

'Sure,' I say and she hands me the phone.

'Hi David, how are you?'

'Fine, fine, how are you feeling?'

'I'm okay now. I was nervous earlier but I feel better now that Cherry's here.'

'Good, that's good. Now it's not going to be a pleasant meeting, Teflon has already said that he's not going to change his decision so we just need to hear what he has to say and give him enough rope to hang himself with. So there's no need to be nervous but try not to lose your temper, no matter how unreasonable he is.'

'Okay.'

'We don't want to give him a reason to end the meeting before we've heard everything he has to say.'

'Okay.'

'And don't worry.'

I laugh, 'Okay. Do you want to talk to Cherry again?'

'Yeah, put her back on. Good luck, Beth. I'll see you soon.'

*

It's time. We leave the pub and walk the few yards to the tall office block. We press the buzzer and announce ourselves. I push through shining doors. We are directed upstairs and into the building's library, a long room with a large lightwood table and walls of books encased in glass. Hand-shakes, formalities, I introduce Cherry as 'my friend' and no one queries it. We disgruntled women sit on one side of the table, they sit on the other. Christopher Talfan Davies, Senior Prosecutor, soft-bodied, red-nosed, grey-haired, affable, takes the central seat, the seat of power. To his right he introduces, 'Katrin Atwell, our specialist rape prosecu-tor,' stocky with a blunt-cut fringe and heavy glasses; she could be my age but it's hard to tell because she dresses old. 'And of course, you already know Wayne Cleaver.' Wayne has had his hair cut short since last I saw him and he's put on weight, less club-singer now, more ex-army gone to seed.

Mum and I take the central seats on our side of the table. Cherry sits to my right and takes out pen and paper. Karen sits quietly, hands folded on her lap, next to Mum. The courage I've been waiting for arrives in a great sheet of energy that straightens my back and lights two tiny fires in my eyes. I take a deep breath and turn the fire towards the decision-makers; I take each of them in, one at a time. Talfan Davies takes this in his stride – he almost chortles, he under-stands me and my anger so well. Wayne, however, drops his gaze to the table. I can't tell if this penitence is real or just for show, I have no faith in him anymore. Miss Atwell stares right back; she is having none of it.

'Are there copies of mine and my mother's statements, as we requested, for us to take home?'

Talfan Davies pushes the books of horror across the table. 'The rest of the evidence will be sent by secure mail to CPS headquarters,' he says. 'I know you've requested access to all the documents but it's for them to decide how much you're allowed to see.'

I take a deep breath. 'We've never been given a full explanation of what happened to our file when it went missing. Can you tell us now?'

Wayne speaks up. 'I did give an explanation at the time,' he says and looks upset. 'I don't understand this change Beth; you and I always had a good relationship.'

I stifle the urge to meet his passive-aggression with aggressive-aggression. What I want to say is: 'We don't have a fucking relationship. All I ever wanted was for you to do your job.' Instead I ignore him and look right at Talfan Davies.

'In October Wayne Cleaver sent me the file,' he says. 'I never received it, I don't know why. Copies of the evidence were made and a second file submitted, by which time the original was found.'

'So the file was lost between October and mid-November. And no one knows where it was,' I say sharply.

'It's a horrible feeling,' Mum says, 'to know such sensitive material about you is out there, God knows where and God knows who has seen it.' Mum speaks softly, vulnerable to these people.

On the other side of the table there is silence.

I take charge. 'We think it'd be clearer if you spoke about the reasons why you turned down each case

185

separately. If it's okay with you, Mum, perhaps we could go through my case first.'

Mum nods, 'That's fine.'

'My job,' says Talfan Davies, 'when I review a file, and I can only make a decision based on the file the police submit to me. My job is to consider whether there is a likely prospect of conviction in court. The jury need to be convinced of the defendant's guilt beyond all reasonable doubt. So when I look at a case I need to consider whether there is any evidence that is likely to cause a doubt.' He takes a breath and lets it out slowly. 'The days of letting the complainant have their day in court are long gone.' I double-take and think to myself, so things are *worse* than they used to be! 'The problem with your statement Beth is that there is no corroborative evidence.'

'Isn't that the nature of the offence?' I say and I cross my arms defensively.

Talfan Davies huffs, 'There is also evidence which contradicts your statement. There's the problem of memory. I've taken a lot of cases to court but I have never heard of anyone remembering abuse from two or three years old.'

There is a chorus from our side of the room, mixed voices contradicting him. 'There's plenty of research, if you would care to read it, which accepts that people can remember that far back.'

Talfan Davies shakes his head, 'This is not as important as the other objections so I'm going to move on. Beth claims to have been abused when Adrian Price was present in the room. He denies that totally.'

Mum says, 'It's not something he's likely to admit to, is it?'

Talfan Davies expertly ignores her. 'In your statement

Beth, you refer to physical abuse towards your brother Isaac. You claim that,' he flicks through a pile of papers, 'you say here that he got it even worse than you did. And yet he has no recollection of physical abuse.'

The words overwhelm me with sadness; I feel sad for Isaac. 'Katie,' I say, 'in her statement talked about the physical abuse that went on in our house.'

'So we have two people who say A and two people who say B. Is there a reasonable prospect of conviction on this basis?'

'Mum and I were both raped by Karl Rees and Katie has testified as to his physical abuse, so there are in fact three of us. Isaac is protecting him. He has never lived a life outside of the Jehovah's Witness religion, he's brain-washed, he...'

'Here we have people from the same family giving entirely different accounts. How is a jury going to decide on that basis?' He sounds so confident and reasonable as he says this that on our side of the table we entirely forget that that is what juries are asked to do every day. 'They are bound to be left with doubts. In a case like this the defence would trawl through every detail of the family background...'

'That would be brilliant for us,' I say. 'That's exactly what we want, we have nothing to hide.'

Talfan Davies raises an eyebrow, 'Psychiatric reports would come into it.'

'I wanted my counsellor's notes, seven years' worth of sessions, to be taken into account but they were never collected.'

'I wrote to everyone on the list that you gave me,' Wayne

says. 'And I always returned your calls as soon as I could,' he adds in a hurt voice. My mother and I roll our eyes. He actually wants us to feel sorry for him.

'Your counsellor's notes are not evidence; they are not eyewitness evidence.'

'How often do you have an eyewitness to a rape? It generally takes place behind closed doors.'

'True, but the people here,' he taps his pile of papers, Karl's statement and Isaac's and Adrian's, 'they deny what you say.'

'But you must expect the abusers to deny they did anything and my brother, well, it's not just my word against his; there's my sister's statement too.'

Katrin Atwell cuts me off, 'You can't just cherry-pick the bits you want to rely on. Your sister does not support your account. She didn't witness the incidents that are claimed in your statement. So she doesn't help your case enough.'

'It took a lot of courage for my sister to make that statement. It was a very serious thing for her, she knew she might be called to give evidence in court. It's upsetting to hear her dismissed so lightly.'

I look to Talfan Davies, everything about him is so patronising, there is no point in being here, yet I have to carry on. I take a harsher tone. 'In the decision letter refusing my case and again when you telephoned me a couple of weeks ago, there was the implication that there was undermining evidence in my psychiatric notes. Can you clarify whether that is the case?'

He sighs and shuffles his papers, 'With this case I had to join the two allegations together. In fact there is not much in your file that would be damaging. In the letter I don't in fact make reference to undermining medical evidence, I merely say that I have had access to some of your psychiatric notes. I must come back to the point that members of your own family dispute your version of events.'

I feel weary. 'On the phone you also expressed concern at my ability to withstand trial. Did this affect your decision?'

'It wasn't a factor that I took into account but I have seen complainants badly damaged by going to court and losing the case. I don't like to see people damaged like that but it's not a reason for turning down the case.'

'So when you mentioned this on the phone it wasn't in your capacity as decision-maker, it was extra-curricular, more like charity.'

Talfan Davies either ignores or fails to see the irony, 'That's right,' he says solemnly.

I've run out of steam and look down at the list of questions David's compiled for me.

'Your letter seems to say that your decision is final. Is there a mechanism by which to appeal?'

'I see no grounds to appeal, the case has been viewed by myself and also by Miss Atwell, who is a rape specialist. She could have questioned my decision if she thought it was wrong, but she agreed with me entirely.'

Miss Atwell looks at Talfan Davies and nods her dour head.

Cherry, who until now has been scribbling away, pipes up, her voice is strong and her strength is infectious. 'Miss Atwell, have you ever had any successful rape prosecutions?'

You can almost see the steam leaving Miss Atwell's nostrils, 'I don't know why I should have to be questioned in this way.

I certainly have brought successful prosecutions. But in this case I agreed with Mr Talfan Davies on every point.'

'On every point?' Cherry asks.

'Yes!'

Impressed with her verve, I look over at Cherry who raises her eyebrows at me and starts scribbling again.

I continue to work my way down David's list. 'Why was there such a long delay while you made your decision?'

'As I recall I had a heavy caseload at the time, a case involving a young child which I'm sure you understand had to take priority,' he says piously, 'and a murder case. That took me until the end of January. It was only then that I was able to deal with the file.'

A young child and a murder case, there's not much I can say to that. I'm done. I wish I wasn't but I am. 'Mum, are you ready to move on to your case now?'

Mum sighs and bats her eyes, 'I don't know what to say, or if there's any point in carrying on. It's clear that there's no justice for us here.' She looks at Talfan Davies, 'Karl Rees raped me and he raped my daughter. He's a dangerous man and God only knows who else he might hurt.' She looks at Wayne Cleaver. 'We put our trust in you Wayne. You told me that you thought we stood a chance. We thought there would be a different outcome.'

'I wanted there to be a different outcome,' Wayne says, avoiding the prosecutor's eyes.

Talfan Davies sits smug and snug, delighted that the attention is away from him.

I agree with Mum, I don't want to be there anymore, it's too sad. But I want to hear what they have to say. 'Mum, it's taken us a long time to get to this point. For me it's taken seven years. Five years of counselling before I found the courage and now this, hanging over us for the last two years. This is the end for us, the end of the road and I don't want us to leave now and then regret not hearing in full why our case was turned down. If you can stand it then I'd like to stay.'

'Okay,' she says. 'Okay.' And she shrinks back into her seat.

'I'm worried about this becoming personal,' says Talfan Davies. 'Is everyone okay here?'

Mum nods, 'You can say what you want.'

'There is a lot of evidence in your file which might cause a jury to have a reasonable doubt, medical notes, evidence of sexual relationships outside of your marriage to Mr Rees. There is disputing evidence as to the cause of the family breakdown; Mr Rees and your son both say you left as the result of an affair, that you abandoned your children and went to Devon with another man. So your version of events, your claim to have left as a result of a breakdown, is denied by these other witnesses. The issue for the jury when they hear this is, is this rape or a woman who leaves willy-nilly?' The sentence hangs in the air like poison. 'It's your word against that of Mr Rees and the only thing against him is what you say. This is the background that will be dragged through the courts.'

I feel awkward because I know that my mum did have an affair while she was married to Karl and Katie was the result of it.

Mum looks at the table. 'Does my morality, or lack of it, mean that my daughter also should be punished? Should she lose the prospect of justice because, in your opinion, her mother is promiscuous?'

'Your case and Beth's are two separate issues but I cannot ignore this evidence which undermines your statement. As well as what we've already discussed you left your children knowing that they were being physically abused by their father.'

Mum doesn't look at him, or at anyone. 'I left because I had a breakdown, I would never have left them otherwise.'

'Your son says you left due to an affair with another man.'

I interject, 'My brother was seven years old when our mother left us. The only things he knows are what he's been told by Karl. It's in Karl's interest to make him believe that Mum left for another man.'

Mum says, 'The reality of my marriage to Karl Rees was that I was 17 when we married and he was very controlling; he controlled all aspects of my life. The Jehovah's Witness religion is very male-dominated. I was totally isolated. He told me that I'd be better off dead. I left because I felt my only alternative was suicide.'

Listening to my mother, I feel ever so small and helpless.

'There is still a credibility issue,' Talfan Davies adds.

'I did not know that my children were being sexually abused by Karl until Beth told me when she was 18. I immediately went to my solicitor and cut all contact between Katie and Karl.'

Cherry cuts in, 'Would it make a difference if we could track down the solicitor's letter severing access?'

Talfan Davies shrugs. 'It would be normal for a mother to take action against the father, if one of the daughters accuses him of sexual abuse, to protect the other daughter. It wouldn't make any difference to my judgement.'

'Well, what evidence would make a difference?' Cherry asks, exasperated.

'Physical evidence,' Talfan Davies says cruelly, 'or if Isaac changed his statement or another witness came forward.'

It's so frustrating sitting here, I feel entirely deflated, all the courage used up, the marrow sucked from my bones. I can't speak now, all my attention is focused on keeping the tears from spilling out.

Miss Atwell eyeballs me, 'Do you have any further questions?'

We've been here for an hour and a half. All the questions are used up but it's so hard to leave. I wish I had a million more questions, and I wish one of those questions would contain the words that would work like a key on this bar against justice.

'Do you have any more questions?'

'No. No, thank you for meeting us,' my words trail off into the ether.

When I stand to leave I find that I am shaking. I hold the tears in until we get onto the street and then my mother holds me against her chest and I dissolve.

What a horrible world we live in.

We wander back to the beer garden to re-convene. My mother and Cherry go to the bar while I sit crying and I say to Karen – say to the world, 'It feels absurd that all that's happened should end in that room. I needed something else to happen.' I look up at the white sky. 'How can you not need what you need?'

Meeting with David

12 September 2007

Cherry and I take the train together from Brighton to King's Cross where we will be meeting David Leigh at his flat. We walk for ten minutes or so through streets so noisy it's impossible to have a conversation. I feel nervous today, shy, unprepared for this. I imagine David lives in a very grand flat – all glass and angled lighting. But when we are nearly there I realise something else too. I realise that this invitation, to meet at his flat, shows that he's not afraid that I'm a madwoman or a liar. Not afraid that I should know his address.

David Leigh's flat isn't all that grand. There is a glass dining table in the kitchen but it's not terribly clean. In the hallway and in the living room there are tall shelves of books but they're not intimidating; I notice with pleasure that I've read a fair few of them. Perhaps clever, successful people are not of a different species after all. Three sofas surround a coffee table that's laid with biscuits and chocolates and fruit. David warns us that the sofas are worn to varying degrees of decrepitude and discomfort and I have to change places halfway through the meeting for fear of disappearing down the side of one.

We talk for a long time. I talk mostly. David by now has read my statement and that causes some embarrassment for me but it is gratifying for me to hear him say, 'It's so clear you're telling the truth.'

David asks me how I wish to proceed. I stress how difficult it will be for me to go through with exposing Karl in an article because it will also mean exposing myself. I will do it, however, I will go through with it. But I make it clear that I don't want to do anything that might jeopardise the possibility of Karl being prosecuted, if by some miracle the CPS decision was overturned or a new witness was to come forward. David talks about naming Karl in the article. I am worried about this. I'm worried about a vigilante attack that might lead to a third party getting hurt; I am even worried about Karl getting hurt. Cherry says this is because I have an oversized sense of responsibility. But I say no, it's a practical consideration. I don't want to harm myself further. I am a pacifist – quite deeply so. But there's a balance here. Karl is an Elder in the Jehovah's Witnesses, his being named might protect people. Also any other people who might have been abused by him, it might encourage them to come forward, to move out of his shadow.

The phone rings and David rises to answer it. My head is full of the shards of my life and I scan the room, looking for a different focus. I spot a black and white photograph of a young woman on the piano across from me, David's daughter, I guess. I have a flash of what it would be like to be her, to be loved, to have piano lessons and to be listened to; to have stylish photos taken of me so I might be adored in my absence, to hang out with friends after school and sometimes have sleepovers, to tut at parental concern and roll my eyes, 'Yes, I have my scarf.' It's all there in the beautiful smiling photo and its placement for optimum viewing from any point in the room.

David sits down again. He says he's planning a trip to Wales soon so he can speak to my mother. 'Also I'll confront Karl.'

'What?' I exclaim and my stomach lurches at this dip in the rollercoaster. I feel fear, for myself and for David, fear of the monster-catching, harpoon-required variety. And I feel something else too. How long have I waited for this? For someone to confront him. For someone to stand up to him. Someone to say they believe me. Someone to take him on. Someone willing to take a risk on my behalf. Someone stronger than Karl. Who better than David Leigh, the liar-catcher who helped bring down a government minister?

How spectacular it would be to finally get what I want, even in this roundabout way. It seems impossible to really live my life without it, but at the same time it seems a miracle that I should get it. How do we live – we without truth or light? Perhaps we manage because we do not really live; we stay small, expect little, and get less. We play dead. I always wanted someone to find out and make it right, to break down the wall between society and me, between life and me. It was supposed to be the police who did that – but they're just doughnut-eaters, incompetent, self-serving and dumb. Could it be that David will take their place? For the moment it's a relief just to be in the same room as someone who's got more about them than Wayne Cleaver.

The meeting ends at the absolute limits of everyone's

schedules and we walk out still talking. Cherry and I stroll down the street and into the noise and nonsense of King's Cross. I feel taller, rangy almost. And I feel my age. I feel like a young woman rather than a tired old woman or a confused child. There is light both around me and inside of me, space between my cells. Hope returns.

Thursday, 20 September 2007, 5.00 p.m.

Hi Beth,

I've lined up Nicole Westmarland, who is a criminologist at Durham University and chair of the Rape Crises Centres, to say that your recollections are classic of a trauma victim. I'm going to send her your stuff anonymised, if that's okay.

I've also been chasing all the things the government says it's doing for rape cases – and discovering that none of them actually happen on the ground.

Why didn't Talfan Davies interview you personally if he was concerned about your credibility?

Answer: There is an archaic rule (only in England and Wales, not Scotland, Northern Ireland, Canada or the USA) that bans prosecutors speaking to witnesses. In 2002 Lord Goldsmith, then Attorney-General, said this was ridiculous, and should stop.

Nothing has yet happened. Defence barristers complained it could mean 'coaching' of witnesses. There was a consultation, some pilot schemes. The CPS says it is still thinking about it, five years later!

Why couldn't your case be supported by expert evidence that your psychological injuries are consistent with such a trauma?

Answer: Another archaic rule bans this in England and Wales. In 2005 the Solicitor-General, Mike O'Brien, said this was ridiculous and should stop.

There was another consultation. The judges objected, saying it would prolong trials and cause rows between experts. It all ran into the sand. Mike O'Brien got moved. Now the new Solicitor-General, Vera Baird says she's thinking about a new scheme, in which juries would get a booklet exploding rape 'myths'.

Bottom line: Nothing has happened. It's all talk.

I'm getting quite angry about all this. Not as angry as you I guess...

Best, David

Thursday, 20 September 2007, 5.34 p.m.

Hi David,

Wow, I'm surprised even 6 per cent (or whatever it is) get convicted. The law doesn't work! The terrible thing is that most people blame themselves anyway and this just compounds it. I am angry and I'm glad you're on side. I reckon you've spent more time working on this in the last couple of weeks than the police did over a whole year – in fact I'm sure you have!

I've come to the conclusion that if you do wish to name Karl then that is fine with me. I spoke to a few people who I am close to and asked for their opinions. My favourite reaction was from my friend Paula who said, 'They hardly ever get killed', which made me laugh because she sounded so disappointed. But it was Angela from the Survivors' Network who really made me think because she said that if he or his family were being harassed, he could put an end to that at any time by taking responsibility for his actions and making a confession. Duh! Never even occurred to me – I guess that's what Cherry meant when she said I had an oversized sense of responsibility. I guess it's kind of absurd that I've spent more time thinking about his human rights than he ever did about mine – but that's right too – I don't want to be like him – not one bit.

Regards, Beth

Normal

The Nicole Westmarland report arrives in the post. Westmarland has three degrees; she is some sort of super-expert on rape. I make myself a cup of tea and settle down to read about myself. David has sent her my statement and some of my writing and asked her opinion about whether my symptoms fit with a classic rape case and what chance I would have in court. I have butterflies in my tummy. I am about to be characterised – described – assigned a place in the scheme of known things. I take a deep breath and start to read.

Dear David,

Thank you for requesting my advice…All of what I have read is characteristic of traumatised rape victims. The flashbacks, change in eating habits, problems going to the toilet, sleeping difficulties, smoking, realisation of abuse point – where nothing is ever the same afterwards, panic attacks, psychosomatic pains and depression are particularly common.

It's at once kind of great but also kind of deflating to be 'normal'. Normal is standard, unfreakish – it's not special. For a long time I've harboured my pain as a unique, unknowable, delicate thing – my pain. But it seems not my pain – it's *the* pain; it's the pain of being raped. Which is great because as I'm able to experience the human pain of being raped then most likely I'm also able to experience the human joy of having a family or whatever – I don't have to live forever behind this glass.

Denial or minimisation is very common in sexual abuse allegations. It is likely that her brother's life is based on a different reality and he is not able to confront the abuse; it does not fit with his life plans.

Why don't the CPS know this? I wonder. Where are they getting their information from?

From my experience, even knowing how many cases are dropped, I am surprised that this one was. It would seem to me that there is compelling evidence, even without the brother's statement. It is unlikely that the mother's previous sexual history would be allowed into the court so it is unclear why this informed the CPS decision.

It's just two pieces of paper but it's so good to have this input, flowing against the direction of the stream – it makes my heart dance; it gives me hope. I am not mad. I am not alone.

David Confronts Karl

Hi Beth,

I'm planning to drive to Wales tomorrow and I've written the following letter to Karl – for legal reasons – if, as I guess, he isn't too keen to have a conversation then I will put it through his door. Could you read it and let me know what your views are?

Dear Mr Rees,
I am in charge of investigations at the Guardian *newspaper in London. We have been looking at the way allegations of rape are handled in this country.*

One of the things we intend to refer to is the accusations that have been made against you by your two step-daughters and your ex-wife.

We are aware that you were arrested by South Wales police last autumn, and questioned. We are also aware that prosecution was not proceeded with at that time. We have since made further inquiries and obtained further evidence. We also possess copies of the statements made to police by your step-daughters Beth and Katie and your ex-wife Hannah.

We should like to give you the full opportunity to comment on these allegations before publishing this material.

The information which we have obtained is as follows:

1. *You denied these allegations when you were arrested.*
2. *You are an Elder of the Jehovah's Witnesses and at all relevant times were a practising member of this sect.*
3. *Your sect teaches, among other things, that the husband is the head of his family, and that his wife and children must obey him.*
4. *Your sect also teaches that its members should not go to college, should not vote and should not join the police force or other official bodies.*
5. *Your sect also teaches that its members should avoid contact and co-operation with 'worldly' people, and that in some circumstances it is permissible to mislead or conceal facts from the authorities. They claim the world will end shortly and only members of your sect will be saved.*
6. *Your sect has also been involved in several accusations of child abuse. Its published policy is that unless there are two witnesses to any alleged act of abuse, the alleged perpetrator is to be treated as innocent. Furthermore, such allegations are not to be repeated to outside 'worldly' people.*
7. *You are accused by the three women of acts of violence against your family. These include beating the children with a leather belt or a wooden spoon, punching your step-daughter Beth in the face and slamming her face into a wall.*
8. *All three women say that they went in fear of you and that you demanded obedience from them. They say you beat the girl children on their bare buttocks.*
9. *Your step-daughter Beth alleges that you forced her to share your bed when she was a child.*

10. She alleges that you deliberately stuck your fingers into her anus when beating her.
11. She alleges in detail that you sexually abused her whilst a child in the bathroom of the family home and in your bed; and that she has suffered severe psychological injury as a result.
12. Your ex-wife Hannah alleges that you anally raped her a few days after the birth of Katie and continued to force yourself on her thereafter. She says, as do both your step-daughters, that you refused to allow members of the family to visit a doctor alone, and that you refused to allow her any money for housekeeping.
13. Your ex-wife alleges that she became so depressed that she fled the family home for a period of several weeks; and that when she returned and demanded a divorce on the grounds of your unreasonable behaviour, she was 'disfel-lowshipped' and ostracised by your sect, to whom you falsely alleged that she had 'run off with another man'. Your behaviour caused her, too, severe psychological injury.
14. Your ex-wife and step-daughter also allege that you have continued to make false statements to the police about the circumstances of your marriage in order to mislead the authorities; and that you have been aware of these allegations since you were confronted with them by Hannah in 1998.

We should be glad to know which of these specific allegations you deny and which you accept, if any. I can be contacted either by mail at the above address, by phone, or by email. I should very much like to discuss this situation with you personally and hear your side of the case. But if we do not hear from you, we

shall proceed on the basis that you have no dispute with the
above facts, and no comment you wish to make.

   Yours faithfully,
   David Leigh

As I read about the rapes I start to feel the physical sensations of them and I know that that's my evening over.
However, as much as I wish it weren't, the letter is accurate
to the best of my knowledge and so I phone David and tell
him so and I make plans to be in touch with him the following afternoon.

The next day is strange. I go across town for a morning's
training with my voluntary work with homeless people. The
session is entitled, 'How to deal with difficult people and
situations', but there's nothing in the booklet about how to
deal with the difficult feelings that arise on the day a journalist is going to confront your paedophile father. I get
home from training around 2.30 p.m. and immediately
phone David. He's still driving, he's just crossed the border
into Wales, and he says he'll call me as soon as he has something to tell me. I consider my options. I reckon I have a
couple of hours before David calls back. I can't bear the idea
of just sitting around and watching the phone, so I take
myself to the cinema. The film, *Control*, is a really good one
but probably not the best choice seeing as it's about the life
and suicide of the singer Ian Curtis. I really identify with his
sense of entrapment and hopelessness. I feel that I know why
he commits suicide. I leave the cinema shaking – the world

which has been shrouded in grey cloud for days has been coloured in a garish, mocking Technicolor while I've been sat in the dark. I walk home shaking. I have to stop for breath. I hold my tears until I am home and then I sit in the armchair hugging my knees and I cry and cry. I'm crying when the phone rings and I'm crying when I answer it and I don't stop crying while David Leigh describes his fairly anti-climatic contact with Karl.

David called at Karl's house but he was not home, so he put the letter through the door. David telephoned Karl a little while later and when Karl answered he asked him if he had received his letter. Karl said he had and that the accusations in it were 'outrageous'. Karl said he would be contacting his solicitor. David says that Karl was very calm throughout. I cry and cry. David says, 'I really don't think that Karl will come after you or anyone else in the family...' I keep crying. 'He's just a little man really. I'm sorry this is so difficult for you.'

'It's like turning the world upside-down,' I say.

Bert and Ernie

I am woken by the phone ringing. It's 4 a.m. – someone must be dead. Oh God, I don't want to know. No, it's best to know. I get out of bed, knock a glass of water over and get to the phone just as it stops ringing. I stand there, in the darkness, staring at the phone. It rings again. 'Hello,' I say, breathlessly.

'It's me,' Stuart's voice. 'Claire dumped me,' he's crying, 'and I'm locked out of my house and I don't know what to do.' Sobbing now.

'Come here,' I say. 'Just come.'

I put on some clothes and boil the kettle. When the doorbell goes I try to tiptoe downstairs so as not to wake the neighbours. Stuart looks broken, dark circles under his eyes, his skin flaxen in the artificial light. 'Come in, come in,' I say and put my arms around him.

'Sorry,' he says, his voice muffled by my shoulder.

'Don't be sorry, come in. I'll make you some tea.'

Confused and weightless like a paper doll, I have to lead him by the hand to the sofa and sit him down.

'What happened?' I ask. 'Or maybe you don't want to talk about it?'

'What's wrong with me?' he says, the words slurred by crying. 'Why doesn't she want to be with me? Why does nobody want to be with me?'

I kind of blink-stare back, my brain numb from lack of sleep, unable to dredge up the right words.

'And I stormed out,' he grabs his head with both hands. 'Claire said she wasn't sure if she wanted to be with me and I said to her – "Well, you obviously *don't* want to be with me then" – and I stormed out and left my keys there, so now I'm locked out of my house as well.'

'You know you can stay here,' I say and conjure every break-up cliché in the book to try to make him feel better. 'She wasn't good enough for you. I always thought that.'

'You didn't even know her,' he says, not lifting his head from his hands.

'Exactly!' I say. 'That means I can be more objective. I didn't even know her and yet from everything you told me, I sensed she wasn't right for you. I have a very strong sense for people, remember the fish man that I had a bad feeling about?'

Stuart sniffs.

'And what happened to him?' I ask and pass Stuart a box of tissues.

'He got shut down for selling dodgy fish,' he concedes and honkingly blows his nose.

'Do you want some tea?'

He shakes his head. 'Sorry. I'm keeping you up. You should go back to sleep; I'll be okay.'

'Are you going to come to bed too?'

'I will in a bit,' he says with false cheerfulness.

'Okay, well, I'll sleep on the far side and you can just climb in with me and don't worry about waking me up, I sleep like a log.'

'I know you do,' he says, 'I do remember.'

But he doesn't come to bed and every time I stir, I catch

a glimpse of him, sat on the sofa, cigarette smoke curling around his hand, staring into space. When the morning comes, the real morning, the one with sunlight, that's how I find him – hollow-eyed, smoking and obsessively chewing events over. In the place where most people would say, 'Good morning', he says, 'I think I should go and get my stuff, what do you think? Do you think I should?'

'Urr, I could make us some breakfast first. Could you eat?'

'No, I can't eat,' he says angrily, gesturing with his hands, as though I must be the stupidest person in the world for asking.

'Then yes, you should go. If it's making you crazy then go, get it over with. But come back here, don't go home, don't be on your own.'

'Okay,' he says and looks relieved.

From the window I watch him walk away and I hop into a pair of jeans and run my fingers through my hair and rush into town to gather emergency break-up provisions: comfort food (bangers and mash); alcohol (four bottles of brown ale) and a DVD box-set (Ray Mears' *Extreme Survival*). Back at the flat I have a tidy-up and set up the sofa with cushions and blankets so that when Stuart arrives, angrily clutching a box of CDs, he sits down and sinks into womb-like comfort. I sit across from him. We talk for hours. Mainly he just tells me that he's shit and I just tell him that he's brilliant.

By the afternoon he's exhausted and sits, agog, watching Ray Mears make a shelter on a desert island out of bamboo and his own spit. I stand in the kitchen mashing potatoes and calling out, 'I couldn't remember what ales you like so I got a selection. You can have a Bishop's Finger, a Haymaker, a Suffolk Strong or a Crop Circle.'

*

We get into bed early and sit side by side reading sections of the newspaper. Later, as I'm drifting off to sleep, I get a fit of the giggles.

'What is it?' says Stuart. 'What's funny?'

'Oh it's nothing, it's stupid,' I whisper.

'No, go on.'

'Okay, but I've never told anyone this,' I take a deep breath. 'You know that film with the talking computer that everyone loves? The Kubrick film?'

'Yeah, *2001*,' Stuart says. We are both sitting upright again, in the pitch blackness.

'I think it's shit,' I say and I burst out laughing and cover my hand with my mouth.

Stuart laughs too. We laugh for ages and trying to stop makes it worse; we're like kids at a sleepover. 'I think it's shit too,' he whispers. 'That bit with the bone, where the monkey throws the bone into the air and it becomes a space-ship.'

'That's the worst bit,' I say.

'I know, everyone thinks it's amazing and it's rubbish.'

'This is so liberating,' I say. 'This must be what it feels like to come out.'

'Why are we whispering?'

'I don't know.'

I settle back down to sleep, pull the duvet up to my chin. 'You know, this is nice,' I say. 'If the worst comes to the worst and we're both still single when we get to 50 we should move in together and get twin beds like Bert and Ernie.'

Stuart laughs, 'Okay, it's a deal, Bert and Ernie.'

Autumn 2007

I suppose it must have been David confronting Karl that has led to this latest bout of post-traumatic stress disorder symptoms. Because for the last few weeks, every night on returning home, I have looked up at my window, imagining that I will see Karl's sharp face staring down at me. And when I unlock the door to my flat I leave it ajar, the quicker to escape. I inspect each room: kitchen; bathroom; living/bedroom then finally, I check inside the wardrobe. I am 28 years old. Only when I am sure I am alone do I close myself into the flat. If I did find him here, hiding in the wardrobe, or behind the kitchen door, my only chance would be to run; I would not be able to scream, the scream would get stuck in my throat. If he raped me again it would finish me. He would not have to kill me, it would finish me.

I have a meeting with Cherry, an all-day meeting where we discuss the writing I've done so far, and what pieces of the story are missing and how we want to present my book for hopeful publication. It's a wonderful day. I'd woken up terribly depressed but leave her house full of vim. I think to myself, *I wish all my friendships were like that,* but then realise that would mean all my friends just focusing on me all the time and talking about my writing and how brilliant I am, and that probably wouldn't be very healthy. The meeting has left me, though, with a to-do list that I'd really rather not do. My schedule reads: Monday: Describe first meeting with police officers who ultimately failed me – try to include the hope that I had in them at that time; Tuesday: Bring to life the experience of growing up in a weird religious cult; Wednesday: Descriptively recount being abandoned by Mum; Thursday: Scream. Scream and scream till someone comes and makes it stop.

I imagine the job description typed up and pinned to a board at the job centre:

Job Description: Excavating Hell
Pay: Only if you're very lucky
Side Benefits: Slow but inexorable descent into madness

I'd like to know of someone else going through this, some-one else who's entering the third year of a battle to get their abuser jailed (eighth year if you count the five years of coun-selling that gave me the courage to go to the police in the first place – but let's not, it's too sad). It's not that I'd want to talk to them, I wouldn't want their advice particularly. I'd just like to be able to pass them in the street and to nod and for them to nod back and for us just to *know*. The way the VW camper van drivers toot at each other or old-fashioned bankers used to touch their bowler hats in acknowledgement of each other, or like an Antarctic explorer might find a flag. I want living-proof that this is possible.

Out on the street the Post Traumatic Stress Disorder fizzles all over me like a coat of electricity. With each person I am about to pass, I visualise them punching me in the face, or pushing me or kicking my legs from under me. But then they just pass and I breathe a sigh of relief, until the next person comes along. This *is* post-traumatic stress disorder and not morbid daydreaming because I cannot reason with it – I cannot make it go away, it's just there. For much of October the daytimes go on like this and the nighttimes are little better. At night there are no visual torments at least (none that I recall anyway). But each night I wake and sit bolt upright, gasping as strong hands wring fear from my heart. One night I am woken up by the sound of screaming. It is me; I am screaming. I trundle to the doctor's, back on the pills, yellow Diazepam and white oval sleeping pills. My first, uninterrupted night's sleep is like a lottery win. Fizzle-fizzle, I go about my day. I don't get shut in – there is that at least, and I don't feel suicidal. These are, by anyone's standards, low expectation measurements of life, but there they are, they are mine.

I am so lonely but there are only about five people in the world that I can stand, and three of them are fictional, (thanks to Allan Gurganus' incredible book, *Plays Well with Others* and its three central characters who've become my new best friends). One of the non-fictional characters, Paula, hands me a mountainous plate of dinner. She has been experimenting with wheat-free Yorkshire puddings (not to be recommended). She has a joke today, she keeps calling everything 'the silent killer', so that you'll be talking about something like apricot jam and she'll adopt this super-serious public information film voice and say, 'Ahhh... apricot jam...the silent killer!' or 'Family values...the silent killer!' or 'Amateur dramatics...the silent killer!'

Anyway, it's very funny the way she says it.

When we've finished eating I try explaining to Paula these feelings of dissatisfaction I'm experiencing. 'I just feel, I have these feelings, restless feelings, I think maybe I want to have sex.'

Paula crosses her hands on her lap and adopts a faux prim voice, 'And when was the last time you had sexual intercourse?'

'Oh I don't know,' I say. 'Long, long ago, before the concept of time was even invented.'

'Seriously, how long ago?'

I scan recent memory with a rising sense of panic. 'Oh my God, it can't be...Paula, it's been two years since I had sex. Two years! No...wait...remember that one-night stand I had in January? It's not even been a year, that's okay, that's fairly normal,' I exhale.

'I thought you said he couldn't get it up.'

'No, he was too high to maintain an erection so we didn't have penetrative sex but we did lots of other stuff.'

'But you didn't actually have sex so I'm afraid that one doesn't count.'

'It totally counts, I'm counting it. We met at a club, went back to my flat, took loads of E, listened to Screamadelica and went at it for hours. A classic heterosexual encounter. '

'But if you didn't have penetrative sex then it doesn't count as sex.'

'That's rich coming from you.' (Paula is gay.)

'There are different rules for us, in hetero-world "sex" means penetrative sex.'

'How dare *you* disqualify my solitary, squalid one-night

stand when you...' I point my finger and raise my voice in outrage, 'you have betrayed me by finding happiness with your new girlfriend. I...(I beat my chest) I would never betray you by becoming happy.'

Paula looks genuinely sheepish. She allows a decent interval to pass before asking, 'Why don't you just go out this weekend, take loads of drugs and have non-sex sex with a stranger?'

'Because...because I was hoping that the next time I wake up with someone I'll feel more of a sense of affection and closeness and less, you know, confusion and shame.'

'Ah, shame...the silent killer.'

'Actually shame really *is* the silent killer.'

Finally something we agree on.

Mum is being brilliant. When I've phoned, or she's phoned me and I've been crying, she's really listened; she doesn't sound scared of my grief any more and I feel like I can really let go, can imagine her chest in the place of the phone and me sobbing, releasing into it, as if no time had passed between now and those nights after she left, the long, long nights. She just listens mostly and that's the big difference, she doesn't try to fix me anymore. Most times, after we've spoken for a while, she passes the phone to Jasmine who reels off a barrage of terrible and often quite cryptic jokes and everything feels a bit better for a while.

I hate this time of year anyway, the furthest point from summer. My walled garden has been desecrated; it has no defence against the ravages of autumn. My beautiful haven lies mostly now against the ground, a collapsed heap of brown fronds. There are no bees, but robins instead. Not all is yet dead. Cliques of feathery bulrushes conspire around the gateway. The mulberry tree has turned yellow. Flawless round cream roses spot an otherwise barren trellis. I choose the fattest rose and push my nose into its centre; the scent is paradisal. The yellow poppies alone seem to be thriving; there are more now than there were in July. The pond has retained its lily-pads but lost its flowers. A lonesome hollyhock stands in a mulching bed, its single flower ragged and torn. The chrysanthemums and dahlias have survived well. I spend some time with two particular individuals, crimson dahlias; they stand haughtily, a little distance from the crowd. I look from the earth upwards, 50 careworn leaves supporting each flower. And the flowers, what to say of them, perhaps a hundred petals on each, each petal folded with great care into a cone and placed one next to the other, round, fat, wine-coloured cones ring the outside, growing thinner and more richly coloured towards the centre; a dream of beauty. They say that plants have no consciousness but that's not true: these flowers know that they are beautiful.

Big Guns

Back in August, after the meeting with the CPS, David advised me to write a letter of complaint to Talfan Davies, which I duly did. After all, there was plenty I felt I had to complain about. The months passed without my receiving a reply. When David Leigh writes to him, making much the same complaints, the response is a little different. David forwards me an email he received from CPS headquarters and for the first time I get a taste of what Cherry meant when she said I now have some big guns on my side.

Wednesday, 10 October 2007, 6.25 p.m.

From Julie Seddon@CPS

Hi David,

I think I can now finalise our arrangements for the briefing on rape. I have arranged for three of our specialists to be present. They are:

Charlotte Triggs, head of the unit responsible for implementing the recommendations from the recent joint inspectorates' report on the handling of rape offences;

Jonathan Bushell, CPS policy lead on sexual offences;

Claire Ward, special casework lawyer in CPS London's

Special Casework Unit. She will be able to talk from the position of an experienced lawyer in these cases.

We have decided not to agree to your request for an interview with Christopher Talfan Davies. The Chief Crown Prosecutor for South Wales, Christopher Wooley, will give you a written response instead for you to use as the CPS response letter. Christopher Wooley is currently looking into the case himself, following receipt of your letter and the points you make.

Regards, Julie

It's shocking that there is such a disparity in how an ordinary person is treated and how it is when the press is on side. But it means that my case is not dead. It seems, despite the head shaking of Talfan Davies, that there is an appeal procedure after all; my case is being 'reviewed'. Dare I hope? David is pessimistic, he says Christopher Wooley is almost certain to close ranks and uphold the original decision. Mum, on the other hand, is pleased, 'It's not a no, is it?' she says.

A week later it *is* a no. Christopher J Wooley, Chief Crown Prosecutor for South Wales, writes:

After reading the file I agree with the prosecutor that there is not sufficient evidence to provide a realistic prospect of conviction...If the defendants are unhappy with the result of my review of the case they can contact CPS Headquarters which will refer the complaint to the DPP (Director of Public Prosecutions) or Chief Executive...

David rushes around now compiling an appeal to send to the DPP. The work he does now is way beyond his remit or responsibility to me, the cover letter alone runs to seven pages, attached to it a fat dossier of evidence collected by him which the police did not bother to gather, including an interview with a witness who met my mum on the train the day she fled the family home and who testified that she was alone, that the 'other man' Karl claimed she had run off with did not exist. The breadth of the appeal and the strong tone that David adopts throughout it really bolster my faith in humanity. I actually 'whoop' as I read the closing paragraphs:

These facts suggest that the case has been handled so far in an unenthusiastic manner, without sufficient regard either to the rights of the victim or the danger to the public from such a man being left free.

You hear that? You hear that DP fucking P? Now account for this mess.

The Guardian Canteen

I recognise David when I see him but I find him difficult to describe. I remember him wrong. For instance, I remember him as short but now, as I walk into the lobby of *Guardian* HQ and he stands to greet me, I see that he is not short. And later on, when we are sat at a small round table in the *Guardian* canteen, I listen to David's anecdotes and try to take a memory-snap of him. I know he's older than Cherry, which would make him 60 or more, but he doesn't look that old because his hair is still brown, and he doesn't have an older man's paunch, but his skin is a little loose around the jowls. Just as I'm getting somewhere David takes off his glasses and rubs his eyes awake and he's a different man again. I see that his eyes are blue and not brown, as I'd earlier described them (some detective I'd make). I'm starting to wonder if David Leigh really exists, or that if he does then maybe he's a shape shifter. Or maybe it's just me, maybe I have David Leigh blindness, maybe I don't really believe he can exist. He does seem too good to be true. I'll just leave it at this, this I can say for sure: The main thing about David is his intelligence; even his soul is smart. Over the telephone, without the accompanying softening smile, he can seem terse. He tends to bark questions and before you've finished answering he asks another, holds your answer up to the light, turns it round and round.

One thing's certain, I must be telling the truth to have got past David. Not that I've ever disbelieved myself, not really, though sometimes my breath gets stolen by a sense of general disbelief, like I can't believe these things actually happen. When I started unpacking my life story I was no better prepared for the realities of child rape than anyone else. When the memories came, they came at me like a pack of wolves and dragged me to the floor. And the difficulty is this: How to live in the same world as child rape? How to bring light to the shadow-lands? Not through ignoring it and not through violent repression, those methods are well tried and tested. Right now I've landed on the side of reasoned, informed debate. The lights are our eyes; we look.

And here I am in the *Guardian* canteen sipping tea from a cardboard cup with my very own reasoned debater. I look around the canteen expecting to see famous journalists at every table. Then I realise that there might well be famous journalists at every table – I don't actually know what any *Guardian* journalists actually look like, except maybe Simon Hoggart and even then I wouldn't be sure. I feel very nervous of saying something stupid and chasing away my good fortune, so I don't say anything – but that's wrong too because I realise now I'm just staring at David and so I rouse myself. 'Have there been any developments?' I ask.

David explains about the legal wrangles going on over naming Karl. The *Guardian*'s lawyer, Nuala Cosgrove, is dead against it.

I visibly deflate. 'But you'll still be writing the article?'

'Oh yes,' he says, and he shoots me a smile. 'I'll still

be writing the article. And I'll still be using extracts of your writing. And we can use your name because you changed your surname years ago so it's not connected to Karl but we won't be able to specify the area of Wales and we won't be able to use a proper picture of you in case it's recognised and people put two and two together.'

I feel the loss of not being able to tell my story – the full story, my truth. 'I guess the problem is,' I say, 'and it's not a problem that's your responsibility, but if the *Guardian* won't name him then I'll come up against the same problem at a publishing house. I'll have to change my story to protect him; it seems really unfair. And to have to have one of those silhouette pictures, again it seems really unfair considering that I'm prepared to reveal my identity.'

David shakes his head. He says he feels foolish for raising the expectation that he'd be able to name Karl. 'The only other paper to do this,' he says, 'was the *Daily Mail* when they named the Lawrence killers.'

'So there's no precedent for this?'

'No.'

'And the lawyer's worried about libel?'

'Yes, but I don't think Karl would sue. If he did that he'd have to take to the witness box and so would Isaac and I don't think he'd want to do that.'

'I don't either.' I say. 'And besides the standard of proof would be lower than in a criminal court so we'd have that on our side.'

'The lawyer says that the standard of proof would be pretty much a criminal one because of the seriousness of the allegations.'

222

'And we've already failed to satisfy to criminal standards so basically it's a Catch-22 situation.'

'That's what I'm arguing with the lawyer about, this Catch-22.'

I feel as though I have wandered into a maze. Karl is actually protected by the awfulness of his crime; there's no way for me to get at him. I take a deep breath, 'I know that some people, most people maybe, they learn to live with injustice, to live their lives alongside it. I'm not one of those people.'

We take each other in. 'It's very hard to live with injustice,' David says and he looks gutted.

'If he's not named then it takes away the protection element, people still won't know who he is and others who've been abused by him in the past won't come forward. That was partly what this was about, you know, to show the others that it is possible to stand up to him and not get killed, that they can move out of his shadow.' I take a sad, wavering breath. 'Also it takes away the revenge element. It really sticks in my craw that he might get away with it; it's very hard to live with that.'

David continues to look gutted and partly for his benefit and partly because it is true I turn the coin over and look for a while at the flipside. 'But I am glad that at least it hasn't gone away for him. He was probably just starting to sleep again after the CPS decision and then he got your letter. It feels good thinking of him taking it to a solicitor, having to sit there while the solicitor reads it, reads all those things that he'd done...and they'd have known, they'd have had a feeling about him I'm sure.' I sink back into my chair.

223

'And his threats of taking action have come to nothing,' David says, spreading his palms. 'I've received no letter from him or his solicitor, despite him threatening to take action. I'm sure he is more scared of you now than you are of him.'

'Well,' I say, unconvinced, 'either it's that or his solicitor advised him not to worry and that the *Guardian* is very unlikely to print his name.'

'Yes, they might have,' David says and we slump again. 'But, I was thinking, in consolation to myself...there's no reason why we can't print his name at a later date. Say, for example, the DPP denies your appeal, which he probably will, and you meet with this solicitor I've found, and she brings a case of judicial review against the decision. There's no reason why I couldn't name him then, as part of reporting on the case. The problem is that I could name him now if I was prepared to write a more balanced piece, give Karl's side of the story and water down your side. But I can't do that and include extracts of your writing because they are so powerful that as soon as anyone reads them they are immediately on your side, and the only thing that everyone has agreed is that we must use your writing because it is so good.'

I beam with pleasure. 'It's very gratifying that anyone at the *Guardian* has even read my writing, let alone that they're having arguments over me.'

'If your writing wasn't so good there'd be no problem, we could just water the piece down.'

Well, I could just sit here all day listening to this, unashamedly lapping up the praise. But unfortunately David's schedule is a little tighter than mine and though he seems incredibly tired he rises to return to his work. We part company. 'Ciao,' he says and he disappears down the corridor. On the way out the door I bend to pick a free newspaper from the stack on the floor. I see David's name above the headline story and I feel a smile spread inside of me, from my toes to the roots of my hair.

I walk to Farringdon station and jump on the next train home. I don't know if it's my mood but these commuters are the friendliest I've ever come across and they make all sorts of efforts to ensure that I'm able to squeeze my way into the only available seat. I sit there, as cheerful as the most cheerful thing imaginable. I smile at the lady opposite and, what do you know, she smiles right back – can this really be London? The only thing is that I'm starving so as soon as I'm through the door I race into the kitchen and cook up some pasta, and I pour myself a long glass of red wine from a posh bottle that was given to me, so posh in fact that I was going to save it and use it as someone's Christmas present – fuck that. I fill the fireplace with tea-lights. I feel like singing and that's exactly what I do, for hours and hours. I get pissed, play my favourite albums (Nick Cave, Johnny Cash, Talking Heads, The Pogues…lots and lots of The Pogues) and caterwaul along to them for all my life's worth (my poor neighbours). Every now and then the phone rings and three…count them, three…people whom I love and who've been really mean to me lately phone me and apologise and are lovely to me. Is this how life works? Months of shit then you get one diamond-shaped day where everything is brilliant.

Saimo Chahal

27 November 2007

David has hooked me up with a solicitor. David's wife, who is a barrister, told him that this lawyer is the toughest operator she'd ever met. Her name is Saimo Chahal and she is said to be the top lawyer specialising in human rights and civil liberties law. I feel ill on the train to meet her. Ill and tired, as though I'm suffering the after-effects of a blow to the head but without the preceding violence. My appointment with Saimo is at 4 p.m. The light is already fading as I find my way to her office on the ugly Gray's Inn Road.

Saimo Chahal is a British Asian woman in, I would guess, her late thirties. We get off to a bad start. There's some confusion about which seat she wants me to sit in and there's an embarrassing scene in which I shift myself and my thousands of layers of clothes round and round the office like some idiot in a farce. I try to laugh it off but my laughter is met with a stony silence and I plop down into the correct seat, a silly child in front of an adult.

Saimo opens by saying that she found reading the notes quite traumatising and, 'I understand why you would wish to pursue this case. There are, however, a number of problems with the case. Huge challenges in terms of the law.' I feel tears rise to the surface and I will them back down.

'The best course of action will be to challenge the decision-making process, argue that there is evidence that hasn't been taken into account. Even with this course of action there are difficulties because judicial review has to be brought within three months of the decision and the original decision was made by the CPS in February so we are already out of time.'

I chug down tears. 'What about the appeal that David has handed to the DPP? If the DPP upholds the original CPS decision, as David says he probably will, then won't that count as a fresh decision? Can't we bring judicial review of *that* decision?'

Saimo wrinkles her nose and leafs through the thick ring-binder file in front of her. 'Hmm…I'll need to ensure that I have everything that David submitted to the DPP. I'm sure he's well intentioned but he's not a lawyer; we need to bring a *legal* challenge of the decision.'

I shoot her daggers. I think of David spending his time compiling the appeal, his own time, protecting my interests well above and beyond the call of duty. *At least he has heart*, I think to myself.

'To bring an action for judicial review one must bring evidence that the decision made was either "irrational" or "unreasonable". The problem we face is that it will be almost impossible to prove that the CPS made an irrational decision so what we need to do is *revive* the decision by digging up fresh evidence. You see the CPS has to make its decision on two bases: firstly, whether it is in the public interest to prosecute, which your case would certainly satisfy. And secondly, the evidential test, the prosecutor has to decide on the basis of the evidence before them whether a jury would be more likely than not to convict.'

'Yes, I know all that,' I puff out my chest and adopt what I think of as a middle-class way of speaking. 'I have a degree in law.'

Saimo arches an eyebrow and proceeds to wipe the floor with me by coming out with a string of very basic legal norms which any law graduate should know of but which I clearly do not. All stuff that I should have studied in the first years when I was busy getting pissed and trying not to remember being raped. Of course, I can't say any of this to Saimo because that would involve us both acknowledging the fact that she's wiping the floor with me. So I just nod and grimace, nod and grimace. Besides she's far too expensive to mess around with. We both know how much she costs and so we both say everything we need to say really fast.

Saimo asks a load of questions that I have no answer to. Was there anyone that I told about the abuse as it was happening? A school counsellor perhaps, or a teacher or nurse?

'No, I don't think so. There wasn't a counsellor at any of the schools I went to and besides I made it my business that nobody ever found out, because of the shame and because of the threats.'

'What about the incident where you say that Karl picked you up and slammed you into the wall? Do you remember any injuries? Did you see a doctor? Do you remember anything else about the incident?'

'What I said in the statement, that's all I remember. And you know Karl would have made it his business to make sure I was kept away from a doctor. The problems with my case are problems inherent to being...'

Saimo cuts me off with another question. It feels as though she's not interested in hearing about the law as it should be, she's only interested in working with it as it is. I guess that's her remit, her contribution, but the way the law stands I'm pretty much fucked and I feel it, my body aches and bends with the pain and I do not like this woman and the things she is saying. We agree that I will apply for childhood medical and educational records. I do not think there will be anything in them. But I will collect them just in case.

'But surely if someone had suspected I was being abused they would have done something about it.'

'It's worth applying for them so as to make sure every avenue is explored,' Saimo says. 'I'd also like to apply for notes from your counsellor. I'll need you to write me a letter of authority granting me access to them.'

'What about bringing a civil action?' I ask.

'Well, firstly, is there any point bringing a civil action against someone if they do not have the money to pay damages?'

'It's not about the money, just another way to get at him. You know it's very hard to live with the fact that he might get away with this.'

'There's also the problem of time limits. One can only bring a civil claim within six years of the injury. In your case the time limit was 1997.'

'So my right to sue ran out before I even realised I'd been abused.' I spit the last sentence through gritted teeth.

Saimo looks away. 'However, recently the House of Lords did allow a case which gave the right to a woman to sue her rapist, even though the rape had taken place 20 years previously. I am not yet familiar with the details and would have to read up on it. The only other option available to us would be to pursue a claim for criminal injury compensation but the time limit for that is even stricter, two years, again I'd have to look into it.'

Saimo and I sit and stare at each other. For the first time I notice how very pretty she is, petite and elegantly dressed.

Making a huge effort not to cry, I launch into the little speech I gave to David at the *Guardian* canteen, no less true for being once worn. 'I know some people, perhaps most people, they learn to live their lives alongside injustice. They learn somehow to live in parallel to their pain. For some reason, and I do not know why, I am not one of those people. I cannot just accept what was done to me. I need something to happen that has not yet happened...I need it.'

Saimo's eyes remain stern, 'Then perhaps you will be the person who changes the law. Because that's what it takes, someone who refuses to accept the way things are.'

As I get up to leave I offer Saimo my hand and she replies with the lightest of touches.

Back on the street I discover, not for the first time, that London is a tough place to be harbouring tender feelings. I limp away from Saimo's office feeling like an old fighting dog with lumps of flesh torn from my side. I have to decide now whether to catch a train home (at rush hour) or whether to keep my plan to have dinner at Natalie's flat. I decide to stay in London and that means I have a couple of hours to kill. I ponder over museums. The Tate Modern being the obvious choice because it's closest to Natalie's place but I settle on the Natural History Museum, choosing animal bones and crystal formations over the output of fucking people. Stinking world, stinking people.

I drag my bones to the tube station and get on the right line for Kensington. I feel tears pressing against the backs of my eyes and I will them to stay put, for a little while at least. I have an image of myself sitting on a bench, weeping next to the bones of some great dinosaur. But my grief has no regard for the cinematic and the tears just cascade down my face. I wonder then, is it this that makes us human? This consciousness of the discrepancy between what we have and what we need? If so, then surely a definition of grace is born from how we cope with the lack.

Later that evening I arrive very despondent at Natalie's. We order Thai food and curl up on the sofa and she asks me all about the article and the case. Natalie spends three hours buoying me up, saying things like, 'It's amazing that you're doing all this.' And, 'You've written fifty thousand words of your book, that's amazing.'

I hang my head, 'I guess I worry that I'm a bit single issue. I mean, this is the focus of my whole life. From the outside my life must look very flat.'

'I always think how interesting you are,' she says softly. 'You're always trying new things and you don't do a boring nine to five like most people. How are you feeling about the article coming out?'

'I don't know. I mean I'm very pleased that people at the *Guardian* have even read my writing let alone that they're having a big fight over it. I guess the only obstacle is the shame, people knowing those things about me.'

'But nobody would think you're bad, everybody would think what you've done is amazing.'

I'm glad I decided to stay for dinner. Natalie is just what I needed and I feel very different by the time I leave. She does a very convincing job of loving me, that girl.

Birth Weights

Mum calls me early one morning, her voice brittle. She has been awake, crying all night. It is hard for her. She lives a few miles from the man who raped her and raped her children. It is slowly dawning on her now that most likely nothing will ever happen to him. She is having to come to terms with the unimaginable. We all are. She says, 'You know Beth, I was so stupid. When I came back I could have just taken you. His name wasn't on your birth certificate and he'd never adopted you,' she sobs. 'I should have just broken into the house and taken you. I'm so sorry, I'm so sorry I left you with him.'

I don't know what to say, I can't say it's okay, so I make a soft cooing noise.

I can feel the wetness of her tears, though I cannot see them. 'He had no right to keep you legally. But he told me that if I made a fuss and social services got involved you'd be taken into care and I'd never see you again. And no one told me any different.' Her voice takes on a different quality, an edge of anger cutting through the grief, 'not my solicitor, not my dad. He had no right to keep you from me. There was a conspiracy, a conspiracy to destroy me as a person. And it nearly worked. It got so that I would lie in the darkness and I couldn't remember anything about you except your birth weights; that was all I had to hang on to. I'd lie there and repeat them to myself over and over and I'd say to myself, I *did* give birth to these children, I *am* their mother.'

Andrew Caldecott QC

12 December 2007

I'm on the train, gliding towards London, on my way to meet the top libel barrister in the country. I am to be cross-examined by Andrew Caldecott QC at his chambers and my performance will, in part, inform his advice to the *Guardian* on whether or not they should name Karl in the article (so not really a big deal then!). It's a cold, bright, wide-skied day and the sunlight reflects off London's power and its shapes. I smile as segments of the Millennium Wheel are revealed at twists and turns in the tracks. The Thames, grey and unbeautiful, wide and self-important, ripples with mini-waves.

I meet Cherry and David in Farringdon and I drink herbal tea while they do their best to be cheerful and comforting and bring my anxiety levels down. When it's time to go David hails us a black cab, which swooshes us through working London, past generic coffee shops with tasteful logos and newsagents and bars and into shushed old London, all cobbled, tall and enchanted. The Gothic Inns of Court are a sight to behold, elegant, thick-walled; the street lighting respectfully dimmed. Outside each old building stand stubby, conical Christmas trees lit with pin-prick white lights.

We locate the offices we need: One Brick Court. On one side of its doorway is a long reel of lawyers' names and on the other, our lawyer's name, on a big plaque, but all by itself: Andrew Caldecott QC.

We take a wooden staircase to the first floor where we're shown into a beautiful waiting room with a grand fireplace and flickering fire and a whole array of seats ranging from comfortable to really fucking comfortable. The atmosphere is such that I half-expect to be handed a glass of sherry and for someone to propose a toast. I visit the toilet. I note the designer soap, which costs more than my weekly shopping budget, and I eye up a basket of fluffy white hand towels. I wrestle with my conscience but in the end decide that it's probably best not to steal one, especially since we're here to establish my excellent character.

When I return to the waiting lounge Nuala Cosgrove has arrived and she introduces herself. I'm not really sure how to interact with the woman who's advised against naming the man who raped me for ten years, especially as I've been told how pissed off she is that any of this is happening. We are here today because David is trying to get Nuala's advice overturned; he desperately wants to name Karl. Nuala is blonde and very slim, too slim for her personality, which spills out of her and takes up twice the space her body does. She takes it upon herself to sit beside me and tell me a little of what to expect. It's quite jarring because she is trying to help me, but at the same time she's quite palpably angry. Not knowing how to handle her I revert to the safety of smiling and nodding, smiling and nodding.

There's a flourish of activity when Caldecott appears and politely introduces himself and ushers our party into his office. I follow everyone in but then have to run outside again because I've forgotten to spit out my chewing gum. There is no bin and so I have to spit it into a tissue and hand it to Caldecott's secretary who looks at me unkindly. I feel like Eliza Dolittle.

Here we sit, Caldecott at the head of the highly polished oval table, I am seated to his right, my legs dangling inches from the ground (or perhaps just feeling like they are). David is to my left and Cherry is sitting directly opposite me, a seating plan that I'm sure they worked out before I met them today. Nuala is seated furthest from me and out of eyeshot unless I turn my head; she has pen and paper ready to take notes. Caldecott is extremely friendly. If his niceness is faked then he is very good at it. He makes it clear that he understands how difficult this is for me. 'So anytime you need to take a break just ask.' He has a friendly face, and an Oxbridge-plummy voice. His features are a little sharp but softened by friendliness, head balding with gingerish side hair and shiny blue eyes.

The interview begins and Caldecott transforms into a legal machine. The pertinent parts of my life lie ring-bound and sectioned by colour-coded dividers in front of him. My life has never looked so neat. My stomach tightens and I grip the seat of my chair, I know I am in for a ride. Caldecott only holds eye contact with me for one protracted length of time, at a place where he obviously needed the clarification of trying to 'see' whether I was lying. When he did I defiantly held his gaze; I felt as though we were in a light-sabre contest – my green eyes against his blue. Other than that mostly he looked the other way, at Cherry. He'd make some great, perfectly worded statement then sweep his head dramatically in the direction of Cherry. I suppose because this is how he is used to performing in court: asking questions of the witness but directing his attention the other way, towards the jury. Most everything he says is a statement, he hardly ever asks questions which leads me more than once to defiantly counter, 'I have an answer to that if you're interested in hearing it.' The second time I say this Caldecott answers, 'Of course I am interested, that's why we're here.' And I finally twig that he *is* asking questions, it just doesn't sound like he is – that's his job too.

Just two days ago I'd been crying with Ella, saying, 'I don't want to do it, I'm really scared.' Now here I am doing it, a watershed in my life, being examined by a top lawyer, standing my ground. This is my version of court and I am as interested as everyone else to see how I will stand up to questioning. Ella said something to me then that I now know to be true. She said, 'You'll find that there's something about telling the truth that gives you confidence.'

The first thing Caldecott wants to know is whether I am writing a book.

'Yes I am.'

'How did you get the idea to write a book?'

I tell him about wanting to make the statement and looking for a personal account by someone that had been through the process and not being able to find one. It was then that I knew there was a need for such a book. Also I have always wanted to be a writer.

'Did you get the idea before you went to the police or after?'

I think carefully. 'I first realised that such a book didn't exist before I went to the police but my writing one didn't actually become a firm idea until after I became Cherry's writing student, which was after I made the statement to the police.'

'The prosecution will say that you only made the statement in order to write a best seller.'

The idea is so leftfield and preposterous that I don't give it any credence at all. In a world where that's what's going to undermine this case we're all fucking fucked, aren't we. Although I do have to say that when I took on cleaning work it was all part of a grand plan to become a writer. I thought to myself, if I announce myself as a writer to enough employers then eventually one of them is sure to take me under their wing and help me write a book about my abuse experiences. The idea is only plausible if we disregard the long chain of history that lead up to me writing the book (I thought I'd live on benefits and pay for counselling by cleaning people's houses for six years – not because I needed to – I just sensed it would lend my book that gritty authentic edge). I wouldn't be writing it if I hadn't meet Cherry and I wouldn't be sitting in this office at all if she didn't know David. It would take some fucking foresight to predict this chain of events.

Another problem, and I don't think this is my problem, is Caldecott's querying of my nervousness the night before I made the statement. 'It says here,' he picks up a high-lighted extract from my book, '"The night before had been dreadful...If the feeling had taken physical form it would have been a thousand lacerations a second..." You drank a whole bottle of wine in an hour. Why were you so nervous? Perhaps because you knew that the statement you were to give was not true.' And he sweeps his head dramatically towards Cherry.

I explain to him the anxiety I feel at every telling, 'Because I was threatened from such a young age. Karl used to tell me that if I ever told anyone he would find me and kill me. The fear, it runs in my blood, it's part of my DNA.'

'Have you read many books about abuse?'

'About half a dozen probably.'

'It could be that reading these books has informed your memories, that the harm you claim is actually self-caused.'

'I had most of the memories before I started reading about abuse.'

'Which memories came to you after you started reading these books?'

'The memory of being orally abused when I was two or three, that came to me as a flashback some months after I started counselling.'

'How sure are you of that memory?'

'Very sure.'

'And the other memories, the point where you claim to have realised you had been abused, you describe here, the quite hallucinatory incident with the insect: "I'm lying face-down on a wicker basket...Karl is staring coldly at my body...his friend, Adrian, is coldly staring at my body." There's no mention of abuse here, is there? This could be merely an uncomfortable voyeuristic experience that you beefed up in order to get revenge for what was, by anybody's standards, a very miserable childhood. No Christmas, no birthdays, not even allowed to celebrate Easter.' This is the point where we clash light-sabres.

'In your statement you claim to have heard your brother screaming and you say within it that he was being raped…'

I interrupt him, 'I said that I believed then and I believe now that he was being raped but I was not in the same room and I never claimed to know for sure.'

'But in the version written for your book you describe hearing your brother being hit with a belt which puts a very different slant on why he might be screaming. There's no mention of hearing the belt in your statement.'

'I didn't mean to leave that out. It was an oversight,' I murmur and my heart drifts away and back to the cold house, the slaps and screams and the terrified me.

Caldecott is talking but I can't hear him, I'm not back yet. Cherry interrupts him, 'Are you okay Beth?'

I look at her and she stares back with eyes filled with compassion entirely focused on me and they nearly do me in.

'I'm fine. I would rather get this over with than take a break.'

'Are you sure?' Caldecott asks, assuming his human form again.

'Yes, I want to keep going.'

'You give a very vivid account of when you say you realised you were abused. You were at university; there was a girl, in the book you call her Jo, in the statement she's called Jenny.'

'Jenny is her real name but I didn't want to use it in the book.'

'You claim that she told you that she was abused. Do you know where she lives now? Did you keep in touch with her?'

'No.'

'So, you're in your room, listening to the same song over and over. Then you're trying to get to sleep and this memory is going through your mind and you realise that an event you have labelled one way, that you believed to be one thing, is actually something else. I think that's understandable, you've vividly described that process. And you go on to say, just here: "I take a look around the new world and fuck, there's toxic waste all over the place." I have to say that this is fantastically well written.'

I burst out laughing at the juxtaposition between being praised and cross-examined at the same time.

'But what of these memories: "The times that I shared his bed and would scrunch up as close to the wall as possible…", these are memories that you always had but you didn't label them wrongly. Explain that to me.'

'I just didn't think about them. It was like they were there but I didn't go into them. I can't describe it better than that.'

'I think that would be very confusing for a jury. They like things to be clear. The different ways that you dealt with your memories would be a real problem in court. The incident with your brother: you believed he was being abused yet you told no one. You left him in a situation where you believed he was at risk of being greatly harmed. You left him behind.'

That one fucking hurts. There's nothing I can say to it – or rather there are things I could say but it would take hours.

How can I tell him that just weeks after I left Karl's house to live with my mother she attempted suicide? How can I tell him that all through my adolescence I was literally afraid of my own shadow, afraid of what was under my own skin? I thought the bad was in me. How can I tell him that I wasn't allowed to have a brother or a sister, wasn't allowed to love? How can I tell him that this is love, this right now? That I took the earliest possible opportunity to rescue my brother – it just happened that that was 20 years after hearing him be raped. How can I tell him that this is for them, this right here, that what gives me the strength to sit here is to think of them (they were so little) and all of the children who cry in the dark, I want to save all of us. Cherry catches my eye and this time I nearly dissolve. 'It's the same as with the other memories.' I say. 'I always remembered it but I just didn't go into it, didn't look at it. So, there was nothing to tell as far as my conscious mind was concerned.'

There are other problems, but also, Caldecott admits, things that are in my favour. For the time being though he thinks he's heard enough from me and I am massively relieved as he turns his attention to David. David asks Caldecott whether the libel defence would be allowed to bring in expert evidence as regards to whether my symptoms and process of remembering are concurrent with a typical rape victim. Caldecott is not sure. David says, 'Well, I went to see Vera Baird, the Solicitor-General, the other day (at this point I have an overwhelming sense of how incredulous it is that I am here, at the centre of these events) and she thinks that you can introduce psychological injury evidence because she has done it herself in domestic violence cases.'

Caldecott says, 'Beth's counsellor won't be able to say though that she is telling the truth.'

Cherry pitches in, 'In my own experience as a therapist it is very difficult to maintain a lie over a very long period and Beth has been seeing her therapist and talking about the same issues for more than five years.'

'So far the counsellor's notes have not been seen? Is that correct?' asks Caldecott.

I nod.

'I wonder whether I should delay advising the *Guardian* until I have had a chance to read over them.'

Nuala interjects, 'Five years' worth of counselling notes are going to take you a considerable time to read.' She looks at me, 'Andrew is very good but he's also very expensive.'

Money! I wonder how much *her* dignity is worth.

In the end it's decided that Caldecott will give his opinion tomorrow as planned and do without the counselling notes as, in his opinion, they'd be unlikely to make him more 'bullish'.

As a parting shot he says to me, 'If you don't get this book published then you must write another one. Seriously, you have a gift.'

I laugh again and glow with pleasure at the praise.

In the corridor we bundle up in coats, hats and scarves and Nuala says, 'He was very easy on you. It wouldn't be like that in court.' David gives her the brush off, excluding her from our gang; It's a very weird feeling being on the inside of a gang, I kind of like it but I feel sorry for Nuala too because most often I've been in her place.

David congratulates me, 'That was a brilliant performance. At least he won't be able say that we don't have a good witness.'

Cherry asks him how *she* did.

'It wasn't about you,' David says, and they start bickering and that makes me laugh. I feel incredibly happy. Partly because I survived that ordeal and partly (mostly) because Caldecott liked my writing – he has no reason to lie about that. He wasn't able to trip me up because I am telling the truth. All the problems with my case are either inherent to the ways memory reacts to trauma or inherent to the legal system itself. I feel pure and shiny-clean.

When I've said goodbye to Cherry and David and am at the platform waiting for a train, I spontaneously start up a conversation with the woman next to me, just mindless chit-chat. Noteworthy not in itself but by the fact that it is happening at all. The woman wanders away and I find myself gazing at my own smiling face, reflected in the dark window of the train. I feel utterly comfortable in my skin. So, this is how it feels to unclench. I review the meeting. I did well. I stood my ground. Maybe it's going to be okay after all, to be in the world and be me.

On the train home I play over Caldecott's praise and I imagine him giving a good opinion to the *Guardian* tomorrow. I imagine him saying, 'Yes, name the bastard!' I will him to help me. I will him to be one of my champions.

Sunsets and Crystals

I answer the doorbell to find two ladies clutching familiar *Watchtower* and *Awake* magazines, I recognise the low-quality paper and the soft-focus, wispy-bearded Jesus. One woman hangs back, her face a mixture of hopefulness and shame, she is thin as a whippet with clipped brown hair and holds her handbag up high to her chest. The one nearest me, the one door-stopping me, sports a helmet of silver-grey hair and an air of determination.

'Would you be interested in learning about...'

Without thinking I cut her off, 'I was abused for years by Jehovah's Witnesses, so no, I don't want anything to do with you.'

The woman behind looks crushed, heartbroken for me, while the one nearest says, 'Well, I wasn't there!' And I don't know whether she means that she wasn't there so she doesn't believe me or if she had been there it would never have happened. My heart's hammering in my chest, I'm so surprised by my outburst. Helmet hair grabs the other by the arm and guides her away. I catch them looking back, making a note of the house number so they can warn the others not to call here.

I run back upstairs and into my flat. I worry about what I have just done – have I sign-posted myself to Karl? Will it get back to him somehow? Have I just told him where I live?

I phone Cherry and ask her, 'Do you think it's just a coincidence? Am I being paranoid?'

'I'm sure it's just a coincidence,' she says. 'Try not to worry.'

I hang up the phone, move to the desk and check my email.

Hi Beth,

As I feared, Caldecott QC said it was all too risky unless it was anonymised. He said you were articulate, bright, feisty and obviously talented — and there was no reason to think you weren't telling the truth. But there wasn't enough corroboration to be sure a jury wouldn't end up having a doubt. In a situation where expert evidence is not allowed...

To my dismay, he said he thought any counsel for Karl would make a lot of play with the idea that you only decided to go to the police in order to be able to write a best-selling book. I told you your obvious writing talent was going to be a double-edged sword!

Nuala Cosgrove is swanning around angrily saying all this money has been spent in a vain attempt to overturn her original legal advice. But Alan Rusbridger wanted me to tell you that he was happy to spend the money in an attempt to get your story fully told, because the *Guardian* did care. I suppose he's right, but I'm feeling very gutted. I may go home and get pissed.

Cheers, David

For the first time in months I turn towards the cool, dark comfort of suicide. I picture myself opening up my arms. I fight the desire (Why do that honey, why hurt yourself?). How can Karl win? At every turn, how can he win? I conjure meditation techniques I've been learning lately, ones which enable you to live with pain, cope with difficulties. But by difficulties I think they mean a sore knee or an argument with your partner. Here is my difficulty: I am screaming in the dark. The scream is inside of me. He is there. He is doing what he wants. I am not even human. They say this is okay.

Many of the women I know, women I have met in therapy groups and drop-ins, they cut themselves. They slice into their own arms or thighs, burn themselves in places that can be easily hidden from others. For them the outer pain is preferable to the inner. Their bodies are maps of pain, they offer an alternative geography of this liberal country; if only they would roll up their sleeves and you would see. Courage has a different meaning in our lives. What we overcome, and the energy it takes, is rarely noticed by others. We were invisible to our fathers and uncles who raped us, invisible to mothers, either abusive or indifferent or powerless, and invisible to the law. We live outside of the world.

I take a walk in the park, walk amongst the trees that, even though they are bare, try to cheer me. 'Fuck off,' I say to them. 'You don't know what it's like for me.' I settle on a bench and consider, very seriously, the implications of suicide. The worst thing would be Mum having to tell the children; they wouldn't understand for ages, she'd have to keep saying it. The good thing would be the peace. If I do live then I will have to find a way to exist alongside this pain. I don't know if I can do that.

I look up. Someone has set the sky on fire for me. I sit still, my body compact against the cold air, and I stare as the fire gently dampens down and the clouds glow lavender in the ashen sky. I suppose I have made my choice. The sky chose for me, me and the other women; if it weren't for sunsets and crystals and inspirational poetry, we'd be fucked.

I trundle home and open a bottle of wine. When Stuart, my forgotten dinner guest, arrives it's only just gone 7 p.m. and I'm half-pissed already. I pour him a glass of wine and I bash around the kitchen cobbling together a dinner. I chop with rage, bash tins on the kitchen surface, throw my knife down. I collapse into a sob and Stuart puts his arms around my waist and hugs me from behind. 'How's anyone supposed to get on in a world like this, eh?' I ask. 'How's anyone supposed to get on?'

I calm down after a while and we sit and eat and talk about lighter subjects. But every now and again the pain and anger bubble to the surface. 'How can the world be like this? How can he win?' And later, when we're properly pissed and we're laughing and talking nonsense, I suddenly erupt, 'I'm gonna have to kill him! I'm gonna have to kick him to death! Will you help me? Will you come to Wales and help me kick him to death?'

Stuart looks down at the floor. 'I'll have to change my shoes first,' he says.

I look from his tattered yellow trainers to my faux-sheep-skin slippers and I sigh, 'Yeah, me too.'

Different

Saimo Chahal is very good at her job and I am convinced that with her on the case no piece of evidence will slip through the net. Unfortunately for me that includes all the evidence that *I* can provide her with and I spend the dying months of 2007 searching out documents for her. I look under my bed, through thick files, in the bottom of my wardrobe, all the while cursing my casual record keeping. We need fresh evidence for the DPP. We need something, some small thing, to change the 'no' decision to a 'yes' decision.

With little hope of success I sign a million data access consent forms which get sent off, little wishes disguised as legal documents, blown off on the wind, the many miles back to my childhood schools and doctors. Nothing comes back, nothing we can use, anyway. One record keeper phones me direct to tell me the bad news. 'I'm so sorry,' she says, 'the covering letter said why you needed the information, I'm so sorry.' I say, 'Thank you,' with tears in my throat and only when I've hung up the phone do I let them fall.

In the end the only extra evidence that we have to send to the DPP is a letter from Ella confirming that I have received counselling from her these last seven years and another confirming that I attended two support groups with the Survivors' Network. There is not the contemporaneous evidence of injury in childhood that Saimo had been hoping for. It doesn't look good for us.

We forge ahead anyway. Saimo asks me to write a letter for the appeal detailing all the ways in which I feel I've been let down. I sit down at the computer and it pours out of me. I start by complaining:

Throughout the whole process it was made very clear to me that, as our case was 'historical', it was not considered high priority and its investigation would have to give way if any contemporaneous events arose.

And four pages later I close with the words:

I lost all faith in the police. To that I can now add the justice system as a whole. I thought it would be different. I cannot adequately express how much I needed it to be different.

To my relief the letter meets with Saimo's approval and she sends it on to the DPP.

Beth Ellis

10 January 2008

Not only did Caldecott advise against naming Karl. Not only did he charge £20,000 for that advice, he also stole my fucking name. David went to Caldecott hoping to overturn Nuala Cosgrove's advice and we ended up actually losing ground. Nuala at least was going to let the article name me (because I changed my surname from Karl's years ago). David asks me to think of a name in a hurry. There, Beth Ellis. There. It doesn't mean anything to me, I can't think of anything profound. Here is a list of things that, at one time or another, I find myself deeply afraid of:

- Hands
- Washing-up liquid
- Walls
- People, especially men – especially men in suits
- The outside of my body
- The inside of my body
- My mind
- My feelings
- Belts
- Not knowing who is behind me
- The sound of car doors slamming

- The sound of keys in a lock
- The sound of footsteps
- Raised voices
- Whispering
- Swallowing
- Eating slimy food
- Children playing
- Feeling cold
- Having to stay in one place
- My own voice
- Sexual feelings
- Going outside
- People knowing me

Whatever my name, this is what he did to me.

The Prayer

GUARDIAN SPECIAL REPORT: RAPE
Errors, delays and finally rejection: One woman's ordeal.
A year after Beth Ellis told police she had been raped as
a child the CPS dropped the case. She wanted to know
why. DAVID LEIGH AND CHERRY POTTER

Beth Ellis is an unusually determined person. Last year she
nerved herself to tell police she had been repeatedly raped as
a child by her step-father.

But local prosecutors refused to do a thing about it.

After that decision Ellis, now 28, might have turned into
another unhappy statistic – 94% of British women who
report rape of all kinds fail to see a conviction result. She was
not prepared to give up.

Ellis took an undercover *Guardian* reporter with her and
travelled back to her home town to demand an explanation
from the prosecutor. She also kept a journal of her experiences at the hands of the authorities, which the *Guardian* is
publishing today.

What she discovered demonstrates why so many rape
victims are wasting their time.

After more than a year's delay the prosecutor:

• rejected her credibility without speaking to her;

- gathered no expert evidence about her trauma symptoms;
- rejected her mother's supporting testimony because of her sexual history.

He also lost her file and later wrongly claimed she had no right of appeal.

More than 14,000 women a year come forward to report rape. But hardly any of their cases are resolved. The biggest single cause, recent Home Office research has found, is because prosecutors claim there is insufficient evidence to bring charges.

In recent months Britain's notorious rape 'justice gap' has come to the fore politically – the Conservative leader David Cameron has seized on it, and ministers are struggling to make changes.

But the Ellis case reveals that many of the government's trumpeted initiatives are so far making little difference on the ground. The *Guardian* hired a QC to question Beth Ellis. He reported that she was a candid and articulate witness. But CPS lawyers had been forbidden to speak to her before deciding to drop her case.

The then Attorney-General, Lord Goldsmith, called for the scrapping of this archaic rule against speaking to victims four years ago. But only now has an agreement been made to train prosecutors to do so.

The directors of public prosecutions, Sir Ken Macdonald, and the then Solicitor-General, Mike O'Brien, also attempted to abolish another legal ban, on the use of expert evidence in rape. This would have helped Ellis in particular, as an alleged 'historic' child abuse victim for whom other medical evidence would be absent.

The *Guardian* commissioned an expert criminologist and Home Office adviser, Dr Nicole Westmarland, to examine Ellis's case. She reported that Ellis's panic attacks and flashbacks were entirely consistent with childhood sexual abuse.

But ministers have lost their nerve about introducing such expert evidence, after judges objected.

Ellis's mother agreed to testify in court that she too had been raped within marriage by the same man, and the *Guardian* unearthed evidence which supported her story. But she too was dismissed by the prosecutor. Irrelevant cross-examination about women's sexual history is now supposed to be outlawed, but the prosecutor said her evidence would be rejected by a jury because she had an extramarital affair. It is CPS policy that police and specialist prosecutors should work together from the outset to build rape cases, and support victims.

But none of this actually happened in the Ellis case. A detective constable spent nine months intermittently collecting statements. A written file was then sent to the local CPS. It was at first lost, and then put aside for months because the prosecutor said he was too busy.

When Ellis and her mother protested at his decision, and said the suspect could be dangerous to children, they were told: 'The days of letting the complainant have her day in court were put to bed many years ago.'

Last year the chief constable of Surrey, Bob Quick, accused prosecutors of blocking uncertain cases in order to meet central targets. He said: 'Victims want to see perpetrators in court.' He claimed there was 'a risk-averse culture where only dead certainties are prosecuted'.

Ellis says: 'A man spent ten years raping me; another man spent a few days investigating it; and another man a few hours reading about it and a few minutes telling me, "No. You cannot have what you want".' Her step-father simply denied the allegations and his son claimed to police they had a happy family.

The prosecutor said Beth Ellis's word was not enough. Like so many other women, she was left voiceless.

Although she is fully willing to waive her anonymity, the *Guardian* is unable to identify her or her alleged assailant for legal reasons. Her name has been changed.

The local chief prosecutor said: 'I can only apologise on behalf of the criminal justice system. I do not dispute that the complainants have been caused great distress by the decision not to proceed. I recognise the whole process has been a painful ordeal for them.'

14 January 2008

This is not only a newspaper article it's also a prayer. A prayer that I might find something better in the world than what stalked my childhood, something better than the drippy detectives who turned up (late) on my doorstep, something better than what I found in that CPS meeting with its un-listening decision-makers. The scream is outside of me now. There is room for other things to come in.

The sea is majestic today. Strong winds blow irregular

lines of white-tipped waves towards me. Sea spray makes the pebbles gleam, and the sky, which graces the turbulent sea with sunshine, sits slate grey over the city, in an apocalyptic forewarning. I sit heavily on the glistening rocks, in a collapsed courtesy, mere feet from the breaking waves, ready to receive their wisdom. I'm with the sky on this, the real wisdom's over here, that lot's fucking doomed.

I hold my hat against the whipping wind and think back to a summer's day in 2001 when this day was inside out, when the sky and world were calm – and me? Every cell was anguished and not one part of me was still or sure or felt that it ever could be. I prefer this day, where things are the other way round. It took everything for me to take that first step, to ask for help, ask for directions right back to here, to this very same beach, but different, a different girl, not a girl at all, a woman now. The years in between have taken every ounce of grit, all my own and some I had to borrow. I start to cry. Not for now but for then. I am so fucking glad to be on the other side of that journey. I am proud of myself. I have taken every opportunity to help myself and others. I didn't know then that I could do this. I have. I have done it.

My ears begin to ache from the sea-wind and so I rise in slow-motion from my crumpled heap. I nod my thanks to the sea and go on my way.

Help

My experience of NHS mental health services over the years has been chequered to say the least. Since I first asked for help in 2001 I've attended a variety of assessments, generously spaced at a period of two to three years. After initially waiting two years I was assessed and then offered nothing – no help. Around this time I changed GP and my new doctor, not knowing what to do with me (I would not take medication – I remembered too vividly my mum, numb, zombie-like and un-helped), they referred me back to mental health services and I patiently waited for another assessment. All this time I was living on benefits, paying to see Ella and cleaning to earn the money.

The second assessment came just after Christmas 2005 and led to me being put on the waiting list for cognitive behavioural therapy. A few months later I was sent to Hove Polyclinic and saw a CBT specialist. This woman agreed that CBT would be useful in my case and said that when the time came I could expect to be offered at least six months' worth of sessions if not more. I really liked her, Scandinavian, with smiling eyes; she seemed to know something of happiness. When she asked me if I would like to see her when the time came I said, 'yes'. I was duly put on their two-year waiting list.

In 2006, around the time of Karl's arrest, a locum doctor

I saw and who was troubled by my expression of suicidal thoughts, arranged for an emergency Mental Health Team assessment. I was angry and scared the whole way through it; having to talk about my history to a guy I didn't know. He had me fill in a questionnaire. I scored 15 for depression – just one point below what is considered severe – one point off needing urgent help. At the end of the assessment, when I was still visibly distressed, the man sat next to me and put his arm around me. I found this terrifying. I'm not implying for a moment that he intended to make me feel like this or intended anything other than to offer comfort, but for God's sake, he should have been trained at the very least not to make physical contact with a traumatised rape victim. I didn't say anything to him – I just stayed frozen till he moved away.

In November 2007 it seemed I'd finally hit a stroke of luck when I was called back to the polyclinic, it hadn't even been two years! But it wasn't luck after all. The therapist I saw (who was not my laughing-eyed Scandinavian) explained that they were streaming some of their patients off the CBT list and instead offering them a six-month period of counselling. I was furious because I'd been paying for my own counselling for nearly seven years and furious too that this change of tack had not been indicated in the appointment letter. I was in a horrible quandary because I was really not coping financially and seeing Ella less and less, so the idea of getting help for free, even if it wasn't the help I'd been put forward for, was very appealing. The therapist explained that I had to decide there and then whether I wished to take up this offer of counselling or whether

I wanted to return to the waiting list for CBT for an unspecified period.

'I can't think about it for a week?'

'No.'

I decided to go with the counselling. But then, when I went for my first session, it seemed there was plenty of time to decide after all and the therapist encouraged me to think again, which broke my trust with her so in the end, even though both Cherry and Ella were dubious about its effectiveness in such a deep-rooted trauma as mine, I decided to wait for CBT. It was something that I hadn't tried yet. And I would try anything. I just want to change my life.

In early March 2008 a letter arrives inviting me to an appointment with a CBT practitioner. Again this is not my smiling lady but a man instead – Laurence Kind – good name I thought. I go along to the first appointment, in a handsome building opposite a church, I feel small, scared, and vulnerable in front of this man. Laurence Kind, Australian, startlingly blue-eyed, tall and slightly chubby, looks like an athlete gone soft. One of the first things he says is that he's not sure how long he's going to be in the country for.

'Sorry, can you repeat that?' I shake my head in disbelief. 'Are you kidding me? I've waited seven years for help and now I'm being palmed off on someone who might leave any minute. You must know how long you'll be here.'

Laurence seems surprised by my outburst, 'I'm really not sure at present but I'd say it'll be a number of months.'

'Do you think you can let me know as soon as you find out?' I ask, huffily.

'Of course,' he says and he slumps back into his chair.

With Laurence's approval I keep seeing Ella, though this is now fortnightly or monthly, depending on when I have the money. Laurence is so different from her, he asks lots of questions, he challenges me and interrupts me if he feels I am repeating myself. 'It's scary working with a man,' I say.

'What is it that scares you?' he asks.

'That I might be raped.'

We begin to explore my reactions to trauma. He asks me if I self-harm. 'No,' I say. 'I just tend to do nothing. When things are tough I just close down, stay in bed. Days can pass where I can't go outside.'

Laurence explains that as well as flight or fight there's a third recognised trauma response: freeze. He goes on to illustrate his point by telling me about experiments done on dogs years ago, before such experiments were considered inhumane. The dogs were kept confined and beaten, 'When the dog's attempts to improve its situation continued to fail it would eventually suffer from a learned helplessness so that it would no longer try to help itself even if released from that situation. Do you have any idea how difficult it would be to retrain that dog?'

I shrug, 'No.'

'Very,' he says and he looks at me intently.

Great!

In a similar way as happened when I attended the first Survivors' group, my life (which was not action-packed to start with) starts to shut down. The sessions with Laurence occupy my thoughts, at night the bad dreams return and by day I am troubled and distracted. With each therapeutic encounter a mirror is held up awfully close and brightly lit and it's frightening. It's frightening to see a woman who can't contemplate being intimate with someone without the aid of drugs or alcohol, who spends most of her time alone, whose grand dreams of an adventurous future are so at odds with an inability still sometimes to negotiate a visit to the cornershop. I want to try though and so I keep going. I want so much to push through to the place on the other side where there is (there must be) something better waiting for me.

The DPP's Decision

15 March 2008

Dear Ms Ellis

I am writing to let you know that I have now received a response from Chris Newell, the principal legal adviser at the CPS.

You will find the reply deeply disappointing.

In summary, Mr Newell has decided that the case should be referred back to the South Wales CPS and Police to reinvestigate. However, he gives no indication of what further issues are to be investigated.

So far as the procedural complaints are concerned, which you set out in your letters of November and December 2007, he deals with these and confirms that those complaints, which are against the police, cannot be dealt with by the CPS. This is technically correct.

So far as the complaints against the CPS are concerned, you will find what he says in relation to each of these of little comfort.

There is nothing we can do with regard to his decision to refer the matter back for reinvestigation. I do not think that a reinvestigation is likely to yield anything further.

I will update you as soon as there is any further news.

Yours sincerely,
Saimo Chahal

I am completely shocked. I wasn't advised that this was even a possibility. I thought the DPP would either say yes to the prosecution or no. What does a reinvestigation mean? Has it been ordered as a time-wasting device in the hope that the *Guardian* will lose interest and I will give up? Mr Newell deals with my complaints point by point and the basic tenant is this: He has not found any wrongdoing on behalf of Mr Talfan Davies or the CPS in general in their handling of my case and is unable to deal with my complaints against the police. Of the decision before him he writes:

I turn first to the decision not to prosecute Mr Rees in relation to Ms Ellis's allegations against him…I have to say at once that I do not think I am in a position at this stage properly to take a decision in relation to Ms Ellis's allegations against Mr Rees. The substantive decision, as originally conveyed by Mr Talfan Davies in his letter to Ms Ellis of 12 February 2007, was based on an investigation by the police that was, in my opinion, incomplete…The statements are badly written, not in chronological order and do not put forward Ms Ellis's case in the way that they should. The quality of Ms Ellis's own statement is poor and the same applies to the statements of her mother and sister.

In my opinion, the investigation was not as thorough as it could or should have been; and the product of such investigation as there was, was not of an acceptable standard.

In January 2007, HM Crown Prosecution Service Inspectorate and HM Inspectorate of Constabulary published a report on their joint review of the investigation and prosecution of rape offences. The report emphasised the importance of 'case building' in rape cases; and of the CPS providing advice to the police as to how this should be done. Following publication of the report, the CPS has developed a much more proactive role in working alongside police to 'build' cases. Clearly, this approach was not followed in Ms Ellis's case. I believe it now should be.

I wonder what all this means. I feel terribly jaded and angry that this might all be for show. What will they put us through? I remember then that I am not alone this time round and I pass the documents on to David. He emails the South Wales Police to try to get them to clarify whether or not they will be reinvestigating. He forwards their slippery reply to me:

South Wales Police is clearly concerned that this individual is unhappy with the investigation and the way she was dealt with by the Crown Prosecution Service.

As far as the investigation is concerned we will make every effort to ensure that her concerns are addressed. To this end we confirm that we have instructed our Major Crime Review Unit to undertake a thorough review of it. We are also in discussion with the Crown Prosecution Service so that a way forward can be agreed.

We will be in contact with the person concerned at the very earliest opportunity and will keep her informed of developments.

David phones me and points out that the police seem to be saying that I'm unhappy with the way I was treated by the CPS while the CPS is blaming everything on the police. He says that a 'review' of the case is very different from the 'reinvestigation' that the DPP has called for. He tells me he's going to write a follow-up piece about the decision and tells me not to get my hopes up about all this.

The Propaganda War

Back when I still lived with Karl, when we were first allowed to visit Mum at the weekends, when we'd be dropped off from these visits, Karl would like us to say bad things about her. We tell him bits of information, like about her friend that swore while we were there. We tell him that she goes to pubs and dyes her hair. If we tell him enough then we get a treat, a Chinese takeaway or a bag of crisps.

There is a propaganda war going on in the Kingdom Hall between Dad and Nana and Grandad, Mum's parents. Dad hates them and is trying to get them in trouble. He says they haven't been obeying the rules because they've been helping Mum out, even though she's disfellow-shipped. Grandad says his daughter had nowhere to live when she first came back and he couldn't let her sleep on the street. Dad says he should have let her sleep on the street. Those are the rules. When the Jehovah's Witnesses disfellowship a person no one's allowed to speak to them, including their parents.

Occasionally we visit Nana and Grandad's little flat, deco-rated in red flock wallpaper and stuffed to the rafters with little china figurines, donkeys pulling carts of flowers, knitted tissue box holders. Mum is never there when we visit because if she was and Dad saw her there when he was dropping us off then he'd report it to the Elders. With the red wallpaper, the smell of wee and lavender and Nana's scattergun anger, I feel the walls closing in on me.

Nana pumps us for information she can use against Dad. 'He's a wicked man,' she says. I love my grandad who is quiet and straight-backed and leaves me be, but Nana gets on my nerves. She's horrible to me sometimes. 'How are you going to find a husband when you're so over-weight?' she says. I am ten years old and I hold the tears tight in my throat. Like Dad, she disapproves of 'worldly' music but I am not scared of her, like I am of Dad, so I just keep on listening to it and behind her back I stick my tongue behind my bottom lip, in a mong face. The atmosphere around Nana is always cloying; I feel choked, as though I can't breathe. She is always complaining. She has never been well for a single day of her life. I tell her things about Karl because she wants to hear them, nasty things he's said about Mum, but we don't get any treats for it, we just play to the audience.

Nana goes into tirades against Dad and how bad he has been to my mother. How hard she worked to clean up that council house when we first got it and it was filthy. How he would put her down, never help her, never give her enough money for shopping. Sometimes I start to cry thinking about how sad Mum's life was and then Grandad speaks up, 'That's enough; you're upsetting the girl. That's enough now.'

After months of this tug-of-war the Elders decide not to disfellowship Grandad as Dad wants, but instead they demote him from being an Elder. This means that although he can stay a Jehovah's Witness, he can no longer give talks or be included in making important decisions about the congregation. Now he is stripped of his status and is just ordinary, like any other baptised Jehovah's Witness. If this bothers him then not a word of it passes his thin lips. Nana though, she complains bitterly and re-doubles her efforts to pump us for information that will help her regain her social status. Me, I can't bear her. Even looking at her makes me angry. I hate the way she says my name, her mouth soft and wrinkly. If I answer her by just saying 'yes', she makes me say it again, 'Yes, Nanny', she says and I have to parrot her.

She's small, really – the different parts of her body all collapsing into each other, she resembles nothing so much as a bowling ball. How can someone so small take up so much room? She disapproves of everything, says all TV is 'rubbish'. She reads historical romances and watches the news every evening, so that she can tut over all the 'worldly' problems. Her feet and ankles are knotty with varicose veins, blue and green and red and black. Her kitchen smells of vitamins and Marmite. She is always on at me, from the moment I walk through the door. All the while Grandad sits quietly in the corner, thinking what, I don't know.

The Double Agent

25 March 2008

On the train heading home, trying to figure out how I feel. Welsh accents now – past Bristol – almost over the border. I can see the Severn Bridge. I feel a mixture of things – of what I was and what I am now – or am becoming.

I feel tense – I keep holding my breath. I'm wondering how it will be, speaking to Grandad about the past – Cherry thinks it might be interesting for the book – but I'm imagining how sad it will make me. And angry. I'm angry that he didn't take responsibility – I'm angry that I have to do all this.

A pioneer. I'm ready to stop feeling sorry for myself now. A woman. I'm a woman now! I do feel different. Even in the panic. Yesterday I spent a whole day feeling panic about coming home and then righting myself, soothing myself. Today I feel purposeful but heavy-hearted – coated in sadness as a fish might be coated in breadcrumbs – the sadness is sealed in, but it is not at my core now.

When Mum picks me up from the station I try to be in a good mood. I hate myself for being such a snob but I can't stop sneering at this grubby town. I feel like putting on a white glove and running my finger over the stone terraces,

269

the concrete flyover, the enormous Tesco. The only good things are the things that were already here: the sky and the trees; the people have brought nothing beautiful.

The snobbery and anger stay with me all that first evening and as I negotiate my way into the child's bottom bunk bed, I wonder how I will last the week. I cry a few vinegary tears into a pink *High School Musical* pillowcase over the unfairness of a life where I feel lonely in Brighton but overwhelmed here, with my family. Where on earth am I supposed to be?

The next day Mum brings Grandad over for dinner. Faced with him, the suit-jacket, flat-capness of him, I slide automatically into politeness and flattery. 'You're looking very well, Grandad.'

'Thanks love. Yes, I'm feeling well. I've had the flu that's been doing the rounds, but I'm feeling much better now.'

He speaks so clearly and loudly. He must weigh something. Thirteen stone, I would guess. He's not one of those old men that you worry will disappear, all skin and bones, he's always had presence, though never been fat, just thick-set. I asked him a while ago what was the worst thing about getting old. He said the worst thing is not being able to stand as straight as he'd like to. It's true, time was you wouldn't have found a straighter back (or thinner lips) and I look at him now – sat on a wooden dining chair (though I have offered him the armchair) and his back is a few degrees off vertical, just a few – not slumped or hunched – he just doesn't have his military precision anymore. It's the knees that make me wince and fuss around him. He doesn't walk now so much as shuffle, as though his thighbone were fused to his lower leg, and in truth it might as well be because his legs won't bend anymore without forcing his tight lips into an even tighter line.

I take him in and I wonder how to do it. How to move out of the small talk and into something bigger. I sent him a letter last week asking if he'd speak to me about Karl's campaign to have him demoted from being an Elder. It takes me half an hour of stalling and pussy-footing around (What am I so worried about?) before I say, 'Have you had a chance to think about talking to me about Karl?'

Grandad's eyes dart from one side of the room to the other; I feel him stumbling on the inside, as though he doesn't know where to place himself.

'Urr,' he clears his throat, 'will it be made clear that Karl is a Jehovah's Witness?'

'Yes,' my eyes flash, the whole room comes alive; we are living in present time. 'Well, he is.'

Grandad shifts in his chair. The clanking sounds die down in the kitchen as Mum listens to us instead. 'That's the reason I didn't suspect him for a moment. I never suspected that a Jehovah's Witness would be capable of such things.'

I suppress the urge to scoff and remind myself to soften and listen, soften and listen.

'If I had known,' he goes on, 'then most likely I would have killed him.'

My pupils dilate at this cheap thrill. A thrill because my grandad loves me so much he says he'd kill anyone who'd hurt me. Cheap because I don't believe for a second that he would. It's just what men say, isn't it? What the good ones say about the bad ones.

'The Bible says that God will repay harm done,' Grandad says, and the words float around the room but they do not penetrate me.

'Well, I just want to make doubly sure,' I say, sarcastically. 'You don't have to talk to me if you don't want to. I merely want to flesh out pieces that I've written anyway. I've written about the Elders' disfellowshipping Mum and about them eventually demoting you from being an Elder because you refused to let Mum sleep on the street, I've written it all anyway and I'm entitled to because it's part of my story. You know Karl used to ask us for information he could use against you and Nana. And we used to tell him stuff too.' I feel triumphant, I feel like I can breathe.

Grandad shakes his beige head and murmurs softly, 'That's a terrible thing to do to children.'

'Nana used to do it too,' I crow. 'We used to visit you and Nana would spend the whole time prising information out of us.'

Grandad shakes his head as though to deny it.

'You were there!' I shout, 'you'd be sat in the corner and you used to tell her to stop if she made us cry.' I feel such love mixed with sadness. Love for the grandad who would eventually stick up for me, and sadness that it was so little – so late.

There is silence now on the outside of things at least, the cooking noises have died down entirely and I sense Mum, just inside the kitchen door, holding her breath. Have I gone too far? If this is killing him then it's bringing me to life. What a price, eh! Why can't we all be alive at once?

As penance I snap back to my old shape – curved spine, subservient, fussing small talk. Mum shouts, 'Dinner in five minutes!' so I lay the table and carry cold patio chairs in from

272

outside. The children noise their way into the house and they and their friend from down the road and our grandad fill the round dining table so that Mum and I, when we have finished fetching drinks, sit down and eat from our laps.

At the end of the meal I clear away the plates and the children run upstairs to play Spies. I pour myself a long glass of red wine and a smaller glass of white for Mum, as she will have to drive Grandad home in a little while. Grandad settles himself now, with his pudding and a cup of tea, into the armchair. I sit on the sofa and Mum makes herself comfortable on the floor, her feet curled underneath her. To her right, in the centre of the scene, a rectangle of glass glows orange in the black iron fire. I see that she is full of emotion and I don't feel angry like I used to. I used to feel that how dare she be upset when I have been through so much and it's all her fault. There are traces of that but mostly it's easy for me to soften to her; the whole of my heart is turned towards the fire and my mother – she feels this – loves it and grows in it.

'When times were worst,' she says, 'and I felt like dying, there was something tiny inside of me, no bigger than a match-head, that wanted to live. And I used to think, if only I could make that grow. And it has grown. Because I'm alive now and so he hasn't won. And you're alive, you and Katie. You know, the other day...I'm going to cry now.'

'It's okay to cry, Mum.'

'The other day when things were going well for you and Katie, you were both happy and I just had this feeling of being light. Light's not quite the right word but I don't know what the word is. I felt like I could breathe all the way in and all the way out. Does that make sense?'

'Yeah, so kind of the absence of holding, the absence of heaviness.'

'Yeah,' Mum cries profusely. 'And I love Isaac too, and he knows that. Karl can't get in the way of that.'

From his armchair Grandad makes glib and humourless jokes, trying to steer the room back to still waters. He laughs alone. We ignore him.

Mum rises and so do I and we hold each other. I can smell her salt tears and feel them against my cheek, mingling with my own. 'I love you Beth. And I loved you then. He couldn't break that because you're a part of me. The best part.'

Whether touched by this scene or by something else, Grandad, to my great surprise, says, 'I have some time to meet Friday if that would suit you. I don't know how much help I can be but I'll try to think about it in the meantime.'

'All right,' I say.

Friday comes round and Mum drives me to Grandad's apartment, one of about 30, in a low-rise block of sheltered accommodation – a fairly undescriptive term for a self-contained flat within a block where the residents live independently but staff are on hand just in case. Mum drops me just outside and I walk the sloped concrete to the ground floor flats, with their identical wide windows and tall glass doors. Pots of daffodils sit not quite at intervals along the tarmac walkway and I feel the meanness rise within me, fuck-ing daffodils, this fucking place. I think back to my home, why do I feel so superior? I live in a flat, essentially just one room, outside seagulls rip bin-bags open so there is always rubbish in the street. And yet it has something. It is not here – is that all? It is enough.

I've only been here once or twice before so I'm relying on memory to show me the way – I have no idea what number he is. But the window I thought it was has a different old man in it, white-haired, lithe with red-rimmed eyes, he stares at me. I wander along the row but all the other apartments are hung with thick white nets that block the interiors from view. I wander back to the first apartment. The strange man opens the door and steps outside. Grandad appears at his shoulder. In his best formal voice Grandad says, 'This is Simon.'

'Hello, Simon,' I say.

Simon says hello back and continues to stare at me. I can't decipher the meaning of his look and so I attribute it to loneliness and perhaps senility.

'Simon has had the same bug as me,' Grandad says in a loud stage voice.

'Must be going around,' I say and smile.

'Bye then,' Grandad says and Simon shuffles off carrying his weirdness away with him.

Inside the flat I ask Grandad about his eyes. 'Grandad why have you got orange around your eyes?'

He laughs, 'Have I, love? That must have been what your mum meant when she said she liked my eye make-up. I went to the opticians this morning, must have been what he used for his tests. Cataracts,' he says and he shrugs. 'But it's not a serious problem yet and might not be for years.'

'That's good.'

'Cup of tea?'

'Yes, please, half a sugar.'

'Half did you say?'

'Yeah, I'm trying to cut it out.'

'Very good,' he says and he shuffles the few steps into the tiny kitchen on unbending legs. I settle into a little space on the sofa. The rest of it is filled with laundry. It's hard to say whether the room is small or overfull, or both. Letters sit in sagging piles. Every year since Nana died Grandad is conned of a little more money by those companies who promise a cash-prize of fifty grand if the winner will just send the administration fee of £25. The single bed is made up with mismatched linen, a bright pink sheet clashes painfully with an orange and yellow duvet cover. Relics from my childhood – relics of flats past – a gold and black Arabesque clock shaped as a flower, photographs of us children, a photo of me aged 11, I can see the blue strap of my first bra riding down my arm, Katie, Isaac and me, bunched together, smiling cheekily.

Grandad hands me a cup of tea, I can tell, without tasting it that it is a perfect cup of tea, a small compensation for old age, this ability to produce the perfect cuppa every time. He shuffles back into the kitchen and returns with two plates. On one is a triangle of quiche. 'Mum said you'd gone vegetarian,' and he offers it to me and says apologetically, 'it doesn't look like much.'

'That's fine, thanks.'

He settles into the armchair opposite and balances his own plate on his poor knees, a wholemeal bread-roll, cut in half, topped with thick ham and yellow mustard.

'Do you remember Simon?'

'No, I don't think I've met him before.'

'Him and his wife have both had the same flu as I've had. In fact, I think I caught it from her,' he says and shakes his head disapprovingly, as though it could possibly have been her fault. I roll my eyes at the banality.

'And do they both live here?' I ask.

'Oh no, Simon, Simon Griffiths, from the Kingdom Hall.'

The name hits me like an electric shock.

'What?'

'Simon. Do you remember him?'

'He was there the night Mum came back, wasn't he? I'm not sure, I can't remember exactly but he was there, wasn't he?'

'He was on the judicial committee of Elders when your mother was disfellowshipped,' he says.

I'm breathless with shock but I have to talk anyway, I have to know. 'No, the night she came back from being away. Karl called a bunch of Elders to the house then you came later and picked her up. Alan Blake was there I know because I remember him picking me up and holding me away from Mum.' Grandad winces, I carry on, 'I think Arthur Thomas was there too and Simon. Was he?'

Grandad's voice thin, reedy, 'I believe he was, yes.'

A flash of red anger. I want to go back to the doorstep and knock that fucker out.

Grandad picks up half a roll and takes a big bite. He chews at the front of his mouth, because that's where the good teeth are, it makes him look like a turtle. He talks through the mouthful, 'In fact, I was taking Simon's advice about your book.'

Every hair stands on end; he has my full attention.

'I've told him, in confidence, about the progress of your case. I think it's best if the Elders aren't surprised by events. Best to let them know gradually. Simon says that you're entitled to write about your experiences. And of course he has the greatest sympathy with you. But he's advised me not to discuss this with you for the time being. He wants to think things over.'

I sit stunned, unable to respond. Why didn't I know? Why didn't I anticipate this?

'I hope you're not going to put Simon or any of those men on the spot,' he says sternly, wounding me horribly.

'What do you mean?' I jut out my chin defiantly.

'You're not targeting these Elders, I hope. I know they overreacted with your mother but I feel in hindsight that it was largely due to Karl's persuasion.'

My heart aches, I am in so much pain. 'I'm really hurt that out of everything that you know this is what you have to say to me, you're worried about protecting them from the truth of what they did. What about me? Why don't you want to protect me?'

I feel exhausted and very alive at the same time. The air between us is hyper-charged and Grandad tries to regain control. 'Eat your quiche,' he says in the stern voice he used to use when we were naughty children.

I look away from him, his orange-rimmed eyes and slow chewing mouth. I feel my own heart, my heart's pain, I want it gone from my chest, I want to cut it out. I look down to the arm of the red velveteen sofa, the plate of quiche balanced upon it. I wonder how he thinks I can eat.

'You must appreciate the fact that from day one my hands have been tied. In the first place I had no knowledge that anything improper had taken place and if I had I would have obviously taken action.'

I stare at him, fucking man.

'The other situation in which my hands were tied was the fact that a judicial committee was called because of the fact that your mother had been immoral and I couldn't go against that decision.'

'Well, you could have,' I say forcefully.

'No. I couldn't. As a Jehovah's Witness moral conduct is highly important and your mother had acted immorally.'

'But there are Jehovah's Witnesses who rape children and that's immoral as well.' I'm trying not to cry. Grandad chews his ham and mustard sandwich, his lips slapping one against the other. I can't believe he's a double agent. I can't believe he's been keeping them informed.

'You told them, secretly, without my permission. How dare you tell people without my permission.' You can tell, by the set of his lips, that he's not used to being spoken to like this.

'I don't see why it would be against your interests for me to let the Elders know. Like I say, it's best not to surprise them with this.'

I won't let it go, I level my gaze at his absurd orange eyes and hold steady. 'You do know that a person's rape is a deeply private thing. You do understand that. I don't believe that you don't know that.'

He looks uncomfortable but defiant.

'Besides I asked you not to tell anyone.'

'I don't remember you saying that.'

'I think you do remember. And what if Simon tells Karl? What if he's warning him all along?' I am breathless as I think back along all the opportunities this fool might have given Karl to prepare himself.

Grandad shakes his head, 'Simon wouldn't do that, I trust him.'

I think to myself, well I don't fucking trust him. I don't know what to do next, minutes pass in silence then, 'Your mother tells me the DPP has ordered that the case be reinvestigated. Have you been given a timeframe?'

I wonder on whose behalf he is asking. 'I don't trust you,' I say, loudly, unmistakably. 'I'm never telling you anything again.' And I cross my arms.

'Well, there's not much left to tell,' he says spitefully.

In my best voice for the deaf I say, 'I'm leaving now because I am so angry and upset. You have betrayed my confidence and you have no interest in protecting me.'

'Well, I'm sorry,' he says, his mouth a tight line. He shrugs, 'But I can't be anything other than what I am.'

'That's not good enough for me,' I say and I rise and walk out the door.

This is the last night of my trip. Today is my twenty-ninth birthday. We spent the day at the seaside, Mum, me, Jasmine and Tim. The sun was warm enough that we rolled up our trousers and paddled our feet. Now it is evening and the children, exhausted, loll on the sofa with cats in their laps, watching a DVD. Mum and I are in their bedroom. I am sitting under the cabin bed, in a wide red armchair. Mum kneels on the brightly striped rug at my feet. We talk about Grandad.

'Why though?' she asks. 'Why would he protect Karl?'

'He doesn't think he is protecting Karl. He thinks Karl is an anomaly within the religion. He doesn't see that Karl is supported by and protected by the male dominance and silence.'

She shakes her head, tears well in her eyes. 'When I left you all, while I was away from you, I wrote you letters,' she says almost at a whisper. 'I knew that Karl would never let you see them so I sent them to my parents asking them to pass them on or read them to you. After I returned, when I was staying at their flat, I found them, tied in a bundle. They'd never given them to you.'

'Oh God,' I cry, 'I didn't know. I thought you were dead. No one told me. I got ill – I got really ill from not knowing.' I remember the long, long nights. In the darkness I wanted one of two things to happen. I wanted my mother back. Or I wanted to not wake up.

She goes on, 'I was furious with them. But I forgave that. I forgave a lot of things. Maybe I shouldn't have.'

'They never told me,' I sob. 'They never even told me that they'd heard from you.'

We both sigh.

I long for those letters, I long to read them, kept from me, snatched from my hands. Letters from a mother to her two girls and her little boy. My mother did love me. She was trying to reach me in the dark.

My Letters

2 April 2008

Last night, in a dream, my letters arrived. In the dream I was back in the little box bedroom on one of the long, long nights. The letters come to me, tied in a bundle with red ribbon, blown to me on magic smoky-grey puffs of air. Floating on the magic air the letters glow mellow-gold and they undo themselves one by one. I see my mother's handwriting on ragged, uneven pieces of parchment...

Dear Beth,

I love you and am trying to get back to you. It might take me a little while my darling. Never forget that I love you and I always will, no matter what.

> *Mum*

Next to the writing, drawn in soft pastel blue, is a picture of a hand. Mum knows that this is what I miss of her most. Hands to love me, wash me, feed me.

In the dream my little body relaxes. I turn over, pull the blankets high under my chin and fall asleep.

Two Cars

I'm getting ready to travel to London and have lunch with David. Cherry has suggested I meet with him and ask him how he felt when he travelled to Wales to confront Karl – as it was such an emotionally pivotal moment she thinks it will be interesting for the book. As I'm about to leave the house the phone rings. It is Cherry telling me that I am in the newspaper today. On the way to the station I buy a copy of the *Guardian* and sit on the train, sipping tea from a corrugated cardboard cup and reading about myself and the DPP's criticism of the investigation.

I wait for David in the lobby of *Guardian* HQ; it feels really cool to be there the same day as I am in the paper – it makes me feel important. Couriers come and go and my eyes travel along the long leather sofa and up the wall, on which is painted the slogan, 'Owned by no one. Free to challenge anything.' The lift doors ping open and David rushes towards me, apologising for his lateness. I tell him I don't mind at all. We shuffle out of the building and along the Farringdon Road to where it softens from being office blocks into a little alcove of bars and restaurants. We sit opposite each other in a light wood and windowed Italian restaurant and I tell David about my trip to Wales and about the letters that were kept from me. 'I don't know how people can treat children that way,' I say.

David winces and shrugs, 'I don't know either.'

'But in a weird way it's like I did get my letters after all, knowing that they existed was like getting them.' I smile, 'There's no longer this gap in Mum loving me. There's no longer this time when I didn't have a mum.'

The waiter arrives with our lunches balanced on his arm.

Between mouthfuls of pizza David explains to me how he felt, all those months ago, as he sat outside Karl's house in a hire car. I rest my notebook on my lap and make scrawling notes as he talks. 'I knew it was Karl's address,' he says, 'because I'd confirmed it on the landowner's register and I sat outside for a long time.'

I can picture the house – semi-detached, ex-council, painted grey – because I got Mum to point it out to me when I was home. The strangest thing about it was how normal it looked, how much it looked like all the other houses, no dark cloud above it, no clues as to the demon that lived within. He's doing just fine. Two cars he had parked in the drive – two cars.

'I thought to myself,' says David, pouring dressing on to his salad, 'his wife will be there and she will answer and I don't know how to say, "I want to talk to your husband about how he abused his step-daughter." I thought, maybe she doesn't know. You know usually when you doorstop someone on TV or whatever, the trick is to get them when they're coming out of the house. I brooded about it and decided, I don't need to put myself in this position. All I need to do legally is put the letter through his door putting forward the allegations and giving him the right to reply,' he sighs and shows me his palms. 'So I did, I put the letter through his door and I shuffled off to spend the night in a Travel Lodge.'

I shovel in a forkful of rocket and tuna steak and stay silent, wary of interrupting David's flow.

'I was reluctant to confront the guy,' he says, 'because I thought there'd be a horrible scene. I really didn't know how to say, "You are a child-abuser". I've never challenged anybody about doing that thing. It's so hot,' he says sharply, 'it's so emotionally hot. I could really see how people avert their eyes – you don't want to deal with this man. You can see all those strategies of avoidance – blaming the victim – that people get into. I'm just thinking out loud now – I'm not sure all these thoughts were going through my head at the time.'

I keep my eyes on my notebook, trying to play reporter, not wanting a look from me to influence David's thoughts. He tears at his pizza with a knife and fork. 'I was very affected by this case,' he says, 'because I usually deal with bribery or corruption cases that are money-based, people giving bribes, that sort of thing. It's kind of a game to catch them. You never feel very angry with the people you're after – it's quite cool. But this case is probably more like what the police get when they're faced with people doing horrible things and I had an emotional reaction to everyone.' He lays down his knife and fork and looks directly at me. 'I really liked your mum, I thought she was really open. I thought Karl was horrible slime, and that you were really gifted and something had to be done to get your writing out there. And I got very angry with Nuala for blocking me.'

'And it still affects your relationship with her now?'

'Yes, yes. It was a horrible time for me professionally and I don't like thinking about it.'

I take the hint and leave the difficult things to rest and we talk about the books we are reading and more neutral subjects. As David pays the bill and rushes from the restaurant to a meeting he should have been at ten minutes ago, I slump back into my seat and realise that I'd forgotten to be nervous today and had just got on with being myself, as David had gotten on with being *himself*. David Leigh is a human being but for me he is also a totem – an example of what is possible – to find something difficult, to do what you can anyway, to acknowledge the difficulty, to be so completely oneself, to have that integrity. It is possible, look!

Echoes

I make my way to Laurence Kind's office for what will be our fifth session. I wish I had the courage to ask him to swap chairs, he has a view of the beautiful church, my view is a plain magnolia wall.

'How are you?' he asks, smiling.

'Okay,' I say. 'I keep thinking about my grandad. The way he betrayed me.' Cold air runs up my spine.

'We talked about that a lot last week,' Laurence says. 'I think we should move on. By the way, I should tell you, I'm going back to Australia in June.'

'June!' I shout, horrified, 'When in June?'

'I'm not sure yet,' he shrugs his big, soft shoulders.

I'm confused by his calmness and even though I don't feel right I keep talking and answering questions about my life. But after 20 minutes I realise that I'm actually feeling really angry. I try to push the anger down, and then realise that it's ridiculous to be covering up my feelings here of all places. To Laurence's next question I reply, 'Is there any point in me telling you?'

'What do you mean?' he asks.

'I mean if you're leaving at the beginning of June that means that altogether, after waiting for seven years, the NHS will have palmed me off with less than three months of therapy.'

Laurence looks perplexed, 'Three months would be enough for some people.'

His words and the ignorance they belie propel me back through time, back to my orange-eyed grandfather; further back to the dark box bedroom where I lie awake, straining to hear what decision the calm-voiced men will make about my life. I could go a very long time without another blank-faced, incredulous man making a decision on my behalf.

I cover my eyes with my hands, 'You're playing with people's lives. What are you doing flying around the world being a therapist for a few months? I've been getting really sick, I've been getting sick from coming here and for what? For nothing,' I exclaim, sobbing.

'This is how it is with the NHS,' he says but he sounds worried and out of his depth. 'It's a very similar situation for us in Australia.'

I get up from my seat, 'I am leaving now because I am so angry and upset and I see no point in continuing.'

'Can I call you tomorrow and see how you are?' Laurence asks.

'No!'

I walk out of the room – but the echoes follow me, they haunt me, take up all the space around me and I heave tears up the street and all the way home.

I call Cherry and tell her that for the first time in my life I have just walked out of a counselling session. She's shocked that he told me about the ending so abruptly. 'Endings should be worked through properly,' she says, her voice crisp and reassuring. 'I understand why you walked out but I do think you should go back next week, even if it's just to have a proper ending. Otherwise you're left with another aborted relationship.'

I'm really angry with Laurence and don't want to go back but on the other hand I'm inclined to trust Cherry's advice so I decide that I will go back the following week – until that is, I get a call from Laurence's secretary the next day saying that he's away next week but can see me the week after. One week less! He said at the beginning that he'd be here for 'a number of months'. I guess two and a half is technically a number. I refuse to emotionally drag this mess over a fortnight and so I opt to cut the tie. I leave an answer message at his practice saying that I won't be coming back.

I cry the whole weekend. For the first time in months I call the Samaritans. I spend days alone, crying into the phone. I don't know how to make it stop so I phone Cherry again. I go to her house and sit in a fug of grief and despair. Cherry thinks that my suicidal feelings are an emotional flashback, which is a symptom of post-traumatic stress disorder. She says, 'Most people think flashbacks are visual events like in films when a character suddenly remembers a past trauma so vividly it is as if it is happening to them all over again in the present. But it is the same thing with an emotional flashback, it is the past emotional trauma that is experienced all over again so it feels like it is happening to you the present. There is usually an event that triggers the flashback, like Lawrence Kind abandoning you.' I look at my hands. 'Most people would get upset or angry,' Cherry

289

says. 'But for you the emotional reaction is far worse because you are re-experiencing the terror you felt when you were abandoned and abused as a child, when you felt utterly worthless, ashamed and alone in such a terrible world you just wanted to die. This is what your step-father made you feel as a child. This is why it is so important that you try to hold on to your grown-up self and remember that what you are experiencing is PTSD and just like a physical illness it will pass.'

Easier said than done but it is good to see her – to not be so alone.

I dream of Grandad. In the dream I have hold of his shoulders and I'm shaking him violently. 'You sided with them over me!' I scream at him. 'He raped me anally, vaginally and orally and you sided with them.' Grandad starts to cry and I leave him be. That is what I want from him. I want him to cry for me.

Into this darkness the police arrive.

'Historical'

Detective Suzanne Hughes phones and introduces herself. It seems there is to be a reinvestigation after all and she will be heading it. She is extremely nice and friendly and eager to please. She apologises throughout the phone call for the poor service I have received from the police so far and assures me that everything will be different this time round. Suzanne wants to travel to Brighton to meet me and can do so any day, any time that would be convenient to me. I double-take – this is a bit different from Wayne and his if-when-maybe approach. I say to her, 'I suppose you'll want to meet in the afternoon, to give you time to drive down here.'

'Any time that works best for you,' she says in a sing-song Welsh accent. 'We can stay in a hotel overnight if needs be.'

In the end they do stay in a hotel because – determined not to be so alone this time, and determined not to invite them into my home – I arrange for Angela from Survivors' Network to be with me, and the only time she can make is early in the morning.

So I find myself, at an ungodly hour, in the cramped and over-heated Survivors' Network office, clutching a card-board cup of tea, nervous and groggy, staring at two Welsh police officers who stare right back, one of them kindly, one of them penetratingly. The huge, bull-like officer shakes my hand and introduces himself, 'I'm Detective Chief Inspector Paul Hurley of the Major Crime Department'. The muscles of his neck strain at his shirt collar. He is impeccably dressed, shirt, tie and highly shined shoes. He barely fits in the room – he barely fits in his clothes – and he doesn't yawn, scratch, flinch or lose concentration for a second. Suzanne doesn't look police at all, she is soft-bodied, maternal; she looks like a pretty farmer's wife, with curly, brown hair and teeth that protrude just slightly, through her smile. She looks at me with the same concerned eyes that Cherry turns on me every now and then. Angela sits at my side, her hands folded on her lap.

Paul Hurley fixes me in his gaze (Does he ever blink?) and explains that his department has reviewed the original investigation and come to the conclusion that an entirely new investigation is called for.

'So,' I say, 'does that mean you condemn the original investigation?'

He doesn't take the bait. 'I can't possibly comment on the original investigation. We've studied the file and come to the conclusion that it will be easier to start from scratch.'

'It might be easier for you,' I say, 'this is your first week, but for me, it's the third year.'

Suzanne interjects, 'To be honest with you Beth, we can never understand what you've been through. I'd just like to apologise for the service you've received from the police so far and assure you that we'll do our best to answer any concerns you have.'

'What I'm worried about,' I say, 'is that this reinvestigation has come about as a result of media pressure and it's just going to be a political box-ticking exercise until that pressure goes away.'

DCI Paul Hurley levels his gaze at me, 'I can't comment on whether the decision to investigate is a political one or not. The fact is that your file has landed in my department and I'm going to do everything I can to ensure that your case is investigated to the highest possible standard.' I feel my hair blown back by the force of his reply. 'I have a daughter, and if she had suffered like you had and then received the kind of service that you claim to have received I would...' he shakes his head as though looking for an answer. 'Well, I'm not quite sure what I would do. But, by the time this investigation is finished what we want you to think is, thank God Paul Hurley and Suzanne Hughes were assigned to my case.'

I look from him to Suzanne who sits, nodding, at his side. They are both very much present, bristling with energy, very much alive and in this room and eager to allay all my fears. Look at these people being what I need them to be.

For an hour they explain the actions they are planning to take, the witnesses they are planning to speak to. They explain that they will be working closely with the CPS to look for further avenues of enquiry. Suzanne says, 'If there's enough evidence to re-arrest Karl then be assured we will do that.'

Outside the window the sun wrestles with the clouds. 'Wait, so Karl might not be re-arrested,' I say, distressed.

Suzanne folds her hands in her lap and leans forward, 'I'm afraid Beth we're excluded from re-arresting Karl by the Police and Criminal Evidence Act, unless we can find some new evidence.'

I breathe a long, noisy sigh. One of the comforts of having all this dredged up again was at least that it was being dredged up for him as well. I feel like crying. 'So, it's not really a reinvestigation then, is it,' I say, petulantly. 'The reinvestigation is all on our side.'

The officers look at each other and Suzanne elects herself to speak. 'To be honest with you Beth, it's too early to say yet and it's for the CPS to decide whether there's enough evidence to re-arrest him or not. We're going to try our very best with this case and that's all we can say for now.'

Susanne explains that, unlike last time, I am to be assigned a Sexual Offences Liaison Officer, Paul Pritchard, and he will be my main point of contact.

'That's good,' I say, 'because last time Wayne expected me to pass messages back and forth to Mum and my sister and I won't do that this time. It was too stressful.'

'No one will expect you to do that,' Suzanne says and offers me a toothy smile.

Paul Hurley asks, 'What support do you have Beth, while all this is going on?'

I'm surprised by the question, 'Well, I see my therapist once a week or once a fortnight depending on what I can afford and I phone the Samaritans when I need to.'

'Do me a favour Beth, will you?' he says as he stands to leave. 'Programme the Samaritans number into your phone.'

'I don't need to,' I say. 'I know it off by heart.'

I shake hands with each of them and they leave.

A week later I am back in the Survivors' Network office with Angela who, bless her, is paid not a penny for supporting me in this way. This time we are meeting my Sexual Offences Liaison Officer, Paul Pritchard. He's awfully nice, tall and sleek. Paul ingratiates himself to me, 'What really struck me when I read your complaint letter to the DPP,' he says, 'was where you say that the complaint was always talked about as historical, and of course it's not historical to you.'

I shake my head, 'I wish it was, it affects me every day.'

'I've worked with lots of abuse victims and that's something that's never occurred to me before. If there's one thing I'll learn from working this case it's never to use the word "historical" again.'

When I leave I feel like I'm walking on air. I'm living in my very own power-ballad – Paul Pritchard will never use the word 'historical' again to describe past sexual abuse. See, it's not been for nothing – I do matter – I can make a difference.

Crying and Typing

It's all a bit much really, what with Grandad's betrayal, the horrible experience with Laurence Kind and the police being back in my life and inevitably I start to go under. On top of everything else I'm also trying to finish this book. This morning passed without me noticing the madness. I put in a good morning's writing and it's only now, when I'm trying to leave the flat and realise that I can't, that I see it – uh-oh, here we go. I move from my desk to the sofa, back to the desk, to the kitchen, to the armchair, to the window, back to the sofa. I do this for an hour. I have an unlucky day, Samaritans-wise, and can't find a person who seems to understand what I'm saying. Then I remember that I know *real* people and I call one of them.

Paula answers on the second ring. 'Hello,' she says. 'What have you been up to?'

'Crying,' I say.

'Have you been writing about your miserable childhood and crying again?' she asks in a nursey voice.

'Hah…hah…hah…oh my God, I haven't laughed in ages. Hah…yes, that's exactly what I've been doing, crying and typing, you know me, I can't help myself.'

'Is there anything I can do to help?' she says, serious now.

'No, I don't think so. I just need to get to the market. I haven't got any food but I can't get outside, I'm stuck.'

'What do you think you'd need to be able to get outside?'

'I don't know, maybe a crane to lift me out of the flat.'

'You can get one if you're obese enough.'

'I was abused. I hope I was abused *enough*, it seemed like a lot.'

'No, *obese*, you can get a crane to lift you out of the flat if you're obese enough.'

'Well that's a Catch-22 because I need to go out first and buy some food before I can get obese.'

'That's true.'

'Anyway, enough about my miserable life, what have you been up to?' I ask.

'Cutting myself.'

'Oh no, oh God, Paula, what happened?'

'I had a mental health assessment yesterday, it was awful,' she says and then takes a deep breath. 'Why don't you meet me for a coffee somewhere near the market? That way you can do your shopping and I can tell you all about it.'

'Are you sure? Are you okay to go out?' I ask.

'Yeah, I'm okay now. I'm okay.'

I'm at the market choosing apples when Paula shows up carrying her girlfriend's dog. 'I won't be a minute,' I say.

We sit at a flimsy metal table, outside a café on the busy main road. I drink a fruit tea. Paula opts for a chocolate milkshake. 'Tell me about the assessment,' I say.

'Basically, I went for this Mental Health Team assessment and they told me there was nothing they could do for me. I mean the guy seemed nice; it's not his fault. He said I was too self-aware to benefit from CBT, he said it wouldn't do anything for me and that with the state of the mental health services that was all that was on offer to anyone except those at highest risk. Then at the end he said, "You should try to focus on the future". It reminded me of all the times my mum told me to stop thinking about it – to just get over it. I went home and cut myself.'

'Oh Paula, it's been ages,' I feel like crying for her.

She nods her head, 'I haven't done it for months. And I haven't done it this bad for years.'

'Jesus, it's one thing not to offer any help at all but they actually make things worse – it's astounding.'

'I don't know, it wasn't the guy's fault, he seemed like a nice guy.'

'He should have been trained to know better than to say that to you. Laurence Kind is a nice guy – it doesn't make it okay.'

'I know,' Paula says and she brightens. 'So anyway, how are you getting on with your book?'

'It's fine; I just need to finish it now. Cherry says I only have a little bit more to do but even that seems like too much right now.'

I am suddenly deafened as a street-sweeping machine pushes by.

'What?' I say, having seen Paula's lips move but caught not a word.

'I said can't you just make the writing bigger?'

'Ha! It's not like a school exam, I think Cherry would notice. The other problem is I don't know how to end it – there isn't a nice, neat ending, it's just my life.' I make a sweeping gesture with my hand, 'It just goes on.'

'What's happening with the case?'

'The new super-efficient police have been investigating – no stone unturned and all that – but they haven't uncovered any major new evidence so it looks like it's just going to fizzle out.' I look up and see a young mother, late teens, walking lop-sided, helping a brightly smiling little girl cross the road.

Paula pulls a face like she's going to be sick, 'Yuck! Did you see that guy grabbing himself? Urghh.'

I look around but the guy has passed by and I just see his back disappearing into the bookies.

'Oh no,' Paula says, 'all I can think about now is penises.' And then she adds, 'Sorry, I know you like them.'

'It's not that I like them as such,' I reply, looking around to check that no one is listening. 'But yes, I am orientated that way.'

'Do circumcised penises look different when they're erect?' she asks.

I find the question distasteful but I think back anyway and remember a particularly unromantic one-night stand. 'Yes, yes they do,' I tell her, my eyes darting up and down the street. I finish the sentence in a whisper, 'Because the top is exposed.'

'The helmet?' Paula says loudly.

'Jesus Christ! Yes, the helmet,' I say and hope that she'll drop the subject.

'I've seen lots of penises!' she exclaims, enjoying my discomfort. 'When I worked in care I washed lots of them, seen them in all states. Sometimes they're like this small,' she demonstrates by holding her thumb and forefinger half an inch apart. 'But then, when they're erect they get really big and red.'

'Jesus, Paula!' I look around the street and can't help now imagining all the men I see naked, their grey flaccid cocks drooped against their thighs.

'You know,' I say, 'I only became friends with a lesbian because I thought I'd avoid these kinds of conversations. Jesus! I was starting to feel like I might fancy a shag but you know what, I think you've put me off for life. Thanks!' I cross my arms in outrage. Paula, not sorry at all, just laughs at me.

Paula has to leave, she has an appointment. I watch her disappear into the crowd and I wonder about our lives and whether recovery is really possible for people like us. Sometimes I believe it is. Sometimes I feel my life's journey as a thick, tangible thing, and I can pull myself along by it. Other times it is more elusive, like the shadow of smoke.

Faith and Hope

30 May 2008

I wake in pain, heartache pain and physical tension. Last night I cried and cried and still it is here. This is the end for me – as far as I can go. I can't carry this anymore and I don't want to. I can't drag this fractured life any further. It is so sad that it will end like this. I lie in bed, crying in an agony of miseries and I look up and around this home I have made, this cave. The white gauze curtains that drape the four-poster bed allow a muted version of the room: walls of books, just colours and shapes; the buttonfly fuzzy and friendly – it is beautiful here, in its way. So sad that I got myself this far but no further. I shall have to go out of course, to collect the implements of death, painkillers and razors – I shall use both – more than this life I fear a worse one, one where a botched suicide attempt leaves me paralysed or disabled, with brutal scars to explain and regret. I will leave a note. I wonder who will find me. Mum will be the first to worry but she is so far away; I wonder who will find me. I will leave the door on the latch so that it won't have to be knocked down. I envisage it so clearly – lying here – warm blood pumping from slit wrists, seeping into the cabbage-white sheets, deep, deep stains, never to be recovered. My heart runs cold, slows and stops, and my eyes and heart drift from here to someplace – anyplace – else. Rest.

*

I lean out of bed and grab the phone. I dial the Samaritans. A man answers – he has a kind voice. I tell him of my plan. I tell him that I cannot go any further in this life – with this life, battered and broken, that was handed down to me. I tell him of the pain of my past and the pain of my future and the pain of being here, right now. He doesn't try to talk me out of it, he just listens and when I cry he tells me to take my time. The tears come in great heaves, in between them words – 'abuse', 'police', 'failure', 'pain', 'no more' – the words of my life. The chest of my pyjama jacket is completely soaked with tears and they also run down the receiver of the phone and into the mouthpiece.

In the midst of the words and the crying I hear a tap at my door. Shit, I can't pretend not to be in, they probably heard me speaking – I hold my breath – perhaps they'll just go away. Three more sharp taps – fuck. I whisper to the Samaritan, 'There's someone at my door, I'll be back in a moment,' I put death on hold.

'Hello!' I call out.

'I want to talk to you about your note,' says a hard female voice.

'Urr,' I look down at my sodden pyjamas and can picture, without a mirror, the state of my face. The absurdity – that this should be happening now! Two days ago, in a fit of self-confidence and assertion, after a year of the downstairs neighbours leaving unnecessarily horrible notes about the correct use of the rubbish bins, I finally left a note of my own, in which I questioned the need for such hostility. What awkward timing, there's no way I can let her see me like this.

'I'm just in the middle of a phone call!' I shout. 'Could we do this later?'

'Fine, I'll be back at three o'clock,' comes the reply and I hear her walking back downstairs.

I return to my bed and the phone and try to pick up where I left off but I find that the weight has shifted. Something about the banality of the encounter with my neighbour has brought me down from the ceiling and I no longer feel suicidal. 'It's really weird,' I say to the Samaritan, 'I feel okay.'

'What do you think you'll do now?' he asks.

I look at the clock. 'I'm going to go to my yoga class, like usual.'

I wash my face in cold water to reduce the puffiness and I strip off and put on clean knickers, jogging trousers, a bra and a T-shirt. Dressing – the feel of cloth against the grain of my skin – it's as though I am putting on clothes for the first time. I leave the house and walk into town on shaky legs (I would be dead by now). At my class I'm aware that I'm living in extra space. I follow the teacher's instructions and for the first time in the two years that I've been coming to this class I get up into a shoulder-stand. As I rest upside-down, my feet where my head should be, I marvel at this turn of events. I thought I was going to die today but instead I am here doing this posture that I've never been able to do before.

Life has another twist in store for me. At roughly the same time that I'd been plotting my death and slowly drowning

303

the phone, Mum had been falling backwards down the stairs. She had put out her hand to grab hold of the radiator and the edge of it had snagged on a ring, dislocated her finger and taken most of the skin off it. I arrive home to find a tearful voice mail from her, 'Beth, I'm in hospital…'

Katie and I confer on the phone. Despite Mum's protestations that she will 'manage somehow', Katie and I both agree that while single parenthood is difficult enough, single-handed single-parenthood is not even to be contemplated. We discuss our options and conclude that, as my life is more easily moveable than hers, in that it doesn't include a husband and a child, I shall be the one to go. When I call Mum to tell her, 'I am coming. I am getting the next train,' she bursts into tears.

The rest of the day passes with an incredulous soundtrack attaching to every action. 'I might be dead now', the internal monologue goes, 'but instead I am making a packed lunch.' 'I might be dead now but instead I am sitting on a train.' 'I might be dead now but instead a guard is checking my ticket.' And best of all: 'I might be dead now but instead Jasmine and Tim are jumping all over me.'

Mum is bandaged, morphined up and tearful, curled up on the sofa. The children brim over, like star bursts, with excitement at my arrival. They recount their heroism that morning, staying calm and asking a neighbour to call an ambulance as Mum passed in and out of consciousness. 'Were you scared?' I ask Tim and give him a squeeze. 'No!' he shakes his head and wriggles out of my arms.

'Look, look,' I follow Jasmine's finger to where she is pointing at a black and white cat, one of the four feral and un-house-trained cats that live here. 'I bet you can't believe how big Tigi has got since you last saw her,' Jasmine says.

Mum, drugged, her mouth moving slackly, mumbles, 'Thanks for coming home,' and she wanders upstairs to bed, exhausted.

In the coming days Mum's friends troop through the front door, many of them without knocking – it's that kind of house. They bring boxes of chocolates and bottles of wine. After the weekend passes away I help to get the children ready for school and I walk them there and back. Jasmine clings to me, reluctant to let go until she is sure that everyone has seen us together – apparently there is some cool cache in having such a big sister. After school everyday Jasmine and I walk the tree-lined (and in some places tree-tunnelled) footpath, which starts at the end of our street and meanders gently up-up the mountain. I tell her about how plants make oxygen and she looks for twigs in the shape of letters of the alphabet. The wood that borders the meadows here is un-managed and all the more magical for it – for while the trees would not be worth a damn as timber, there's an enchanted beauty in their knotted shapes – as they twist and fight for light. There are pink foxgloves everywhere and fat bees hang out of the bell-shaped flowers. Dotted here and there, delicate red campion, orange dandelions and tall daisies.

Grandad knows I am home and wants to see me. Our only contact since our last explosive encounter has been a greeting card from him, containing £20 and a book of stamps and half a page about the weather. I never replied to it. I am in agonies about whether to go – I change my mind five times and then do go with Mum and have the saddest lunch of my life. I struggle to join in with his banal conversation and inwardly will him – *see me, please see me*. When Mum stops the car outside his sheltered accommodation I get out with him and walk (slowly, at his pace) and deposit him, and his shopping, on a bench outside his flat. 'You should sit out for a while Grandad, enjoy the sunshine.' He hands me a £20 note and a book of stamps. I would like to be loved more than this – but this is what I have. I put my arm on his shoulder (but don't kiss him) and turn to walk away, allowing the tears held in during the sandwich, during the conversation, during the walk to the flat, to roll down my cheeks.

The next day the police arrive, Detective Chief Inspector Paul Hurley and Detective Inspector Suzanne Hughes. Suzanne wears a long-jacketed trouser suit and a professional distance that is different from our last encounter. Paul Hurley is uber-himself, uber-boundaried – walls within walls. I try to picture him relaxing, shirt-collar unbuttoned, perhaps by a pool, but it's too great a leap for the imagination.

I've spent the whole morning cleaning for their arrival – I didn't want the house to smell of cat piss – I didn't want them to judge Mum badly – or me, for that matter. I wear a bright blue dress that reaches all the way up to my neck and all the way down to my calves, a serious dress. It's disconcerting, seeing these police officers against this background – I'd rather be on my own turf, where I feel more in control.

Mum sits down in a chair miles away from us all so I say to her, 'Mum, why don't you sit over here so we can all see each other.' She moves but looks jumpy and tearful.

'It's bad news I'm afraid,' Suzanne says. 'As you know, we were hoping that Katie would expand on her earlier statement but she's told us that she doesn't feel able to do that at this time. And that's perfectly understandable; you all have to live your lives,' she says, looking up at the wall of family photos. 'We've also spoken to a number of other possible witnesses hoping to uncover some evidence that supports your statement but as yet I'm afraid that hasn't happened.' She pauses and I realise that I am holding my breath. She continues, 'We met with the CPS this morning, as you know we are working closely with them on your case, and I'm afraid they have decided that as yet we have no fresh evidence upon which to re-arrest Karl.' She shoots us a pained smile. 'We're not giving up, not at all. But at the moment the prospects don't look good, I have to be honest with you both about that.'

Mum starts crying and rushes out of the room and I feel utterly helpless and somehow responsible for her misery. She returns with a wad of tissue and fire in her temper. 'Wayne's really cocked things up for us, hasn't he? He should have known that Karl could only be arrested once. He should have known that, shouldn't he?'

Paul Hurley swats her anger away, 'I've said it before and I have to say it again now, I can in no way comment on the earlier investigation.'

'This is our lives,' Mum says, her voice venomous.

Paul replies slowly, with careful rhetoric, 'We are searching for the evidence to get the justice that you both deserve.'

Mum heaves a great lungful of breath; she looks utterly defeated.

Suzanne tells us that their next line of enquiry will be to look into any records the Jehovah's Witness institution might hold. 'They claim to keep their own records of complaints of abuse,' she explains. She asks us whether we know where such records for an individual Kingdom Hall might be kept, a mystery that my mother and I, as mere woman and child, would never have been let in on.

Paul asks, 'How difficult do you think it might be for us to approach them?'

I consider it for a moment. 'Very,' I say. 'They believe the end of the world is coming and although members are expected to look presentable and live law-abiding lives, they believe in a higher power than the laws of men. I think most witnesses would put their duty to their religion before the law, as I found out with my grandfather,' my sentence trails off to a whisper.

Mum moves from her hard-back chair and curls up on the floor, at our feet. She tells them of one woman she remembers from years ago who was a Jehovah's Witness and tried to protect her teenage daughter from the father who was abusing her. 'A lot of pressure was put on her to try and stop her from pursuing an injunction. The Elders told her that the father had a right to contact with the girl. Poor woman, she was just trying to protect her child,' Mum shakes her head sadly and looks at the floor.

'That ties in with some of the things that I've been finding out,' Suzanne says. 'I've been checking our databases to see if there are any Jehovah's Witnesses who've been convicted of sexual offences in this area and there are two, though they're not from here, they've been moved to the area, both are living in halfway houses. As I was looking into their cases I was shocked to see that Jehovah's Witnesses from this area have been visiting them and inviting them to join their congregation, which would include, as you both know, small children. It's something that we're going to keep an eye on.'

'Well,' I shrug, 'that might be the one good thing that comes out of this.'

Paul tells us that he's waiting to hear from a police officer in Scotland who dealt with similar allegations in a Jehovah's Witness congregation up there, to ask him how he approached it. I appreciate this level of effort. I sense Mum softening as she feels she is being listened to. And I, somehow – I don't know how – am able to look beyond all this and to the future.

'Are you both clear about what's going to happen next, in terms of the investigation?' Suzanne asks.

'I think so,' I say 'you're going to try to get access to any records held by the Jehovah's Witness organisation, that's pretty much it, all that's left to do. Then you'll submit the file to the CPS and they'll have a look at everything and then most likely reject our case for a second time, and we'll appeal again, if we can.' My voice is edged with tears.

'I'm sorry', Suzanne says. 'I'm sorry I couldn't have come here with better news for you. You know we work on these historical cases and nine times out of ten we just can't get the evidence we need.'

'It's not your fault,' I say. 'The law doesn't work.'

'No Beth, it doesn't.' Suzanne looks at her hands, 'We always hope that we'll find that one piece of the puzzle. And we won't stop looking for it but we don't want to raise your expectations.'

I shake my head, 'I have no faith or hope.'

Paul Hurley fixes me in his laser vision, 'You can have faith that your case will be investigated professionally and with the utmost care. You can have faith in that.'

After they are gone I am haunted by my own words. Why did I say I had no faith or hope? Was I pretending I could no longer be hurt; letting them off the hook; or was I trying to jinx fate? Why am I pretending I don't care?

I go outside and choose the mountain path; my legs work with a fury – biting into the mountain. I come to a beautiful field I have been longing to break into all week. I shimmy under the barbed-wire fence; after all what am I today if not lawless? I wade through waist-high buttercups and meadow grass, my shoes soaking up the dew. I push my way through to the elevated ground where stands a jubilant oak tree and I sit on its gnarled roots, stare through the yellow buttercups and wonder.

The next day is hot and we spend it picnicking and exploring the countryside. Just after sundown, the four of us, my little family, trundle into the house, sleepy and glowing with sunburn. I put the kettle on for tea. Mum points out that the cat, Tigi, is a lot thinner than she was when we left the house this morning. 'Did anyone see where Tigi just came from?' she asks. 'Did she follow us in? I think she might have had kittens.'

Jasmine can't believe she could ever be that lucky, 'No, Mum,' she says. 'Probably she was just sick.'

Mum picks up Tigi, turns her around and eyes her suspiciously flat belly. 'Tig?' she says enquiringly. 'Tig where have you been?'

Jasmine, Tim and I follow Mum upstairs and we help her search. 'Shhhhh!' We all hold our breaths and hear a faint mewing. The three bedrooms are almost impossible to search – boxes, open drawers, piles of blankets – baby cats could be hidden anywhere. After 20 minutes we don't find anything and the mewing sound has stopped – maybe we were wrong.

The others give up the search but I stay where I am and, when I am alone, turn off the bedroom light and stay very quiet. The mewing sound again. I tiptoe from one end of the room to the other but the pitch of the mewing stays constant – it doesn't get any louder or quieter no matter where I stand. Then I understand; they're not inside the house! I rush down the stairs and, shoe-less, I walk down the garden path and onto the black tarmac road, which holds the heat of the day like a memory. The mewing is louder now, high-pitched and desperate. I follow the chorus of cries. In the moonlight I trespass on to the unkempt front lawn of the council house next door. There, in a flattened patch of grass, I see a mass of blind, squeaking kittens crawling over and over each other. I'm afraid that predators will pick them off if I leave them alone so I shout back to the house, 'Bring a blanket, quick!'

Within seconds Mum is stood at my side holding a soft fleece cat-basket. I bend and pick up the squeaking kittens one at a time and drop them into her arms. 'One...two... three...four. There's four of them,' I say proudly, as though I were the mother herself.

Inside the house the children are wide-eyed with disbelief. 'Aww...aww...Can I touch them? Can I pick them up?'

Mum carries the kittens upstairs and clears piles of books and papers from the bed in the spare room and gently lays them down on it. Tigi follows us up the stairs and counts her babies, while they bat at each other with tiny, useless claws and nose their way towards a nipple.

'Look Beth,' Jasmine says, 'that one's trying to get in Tigi's ear. That's not where the milk is,' she says and she plucks up the wriggling, patch-eyed creature and directs it to a more likely spot. We stare at them for ages, until our eyes start to droop.

Before giving in to sleep Jasmine kisses each cat on its head, 'I love you Tigi for being such a clever mummy. I love you Patchy. I love you black one. I love you greedy one drinking all the milk. I love you wriggly one.'

That's how I was. I loved all things before I learned it was safer to not to. I want to go back in time and take back what I said. I do have love. And faith and hope.